The
Curious
New Yorker

The Curious New Yorker

329 Fascinating Questions and Surprising Answers About New York City

* * *

By the writers of the popular "F.Y.I." column in
The New York Times

Andrea Kannapell, Jesse McKinley, Daniel B. Schneider,
Kathryn Shattuck, Jennifer Steinhauer

Drawings by Rupert Howard

TIMES 𝕋 BOOKS

RANDOM HOUSE

Curious New Yorkers can find additional "F.Y.I." columns from *The New York Times,* along with hundreds of other questions and answers about life in New York, on New York Today (www.nytoday.com).

All rights reserved under International and Pan-American Copyright Conventions. Published in the United States by Times Books, a division of Random House, Inc., New York, and simultaneously in Canada by Random House of Canada Limited, Toronto.

Library of Congress Cataloging-in-Publication Data

The curious New Yorker: 329 fascinating questions and surprising answers about New York City / the New York Times.—1st ed.
       p.   cm.
   Includes index.
   ISBN 0-8129-3002-9 (alk. paper)
    1. New York (N.Y.)—Miscellanea.   I. New York times.
  F128.3.E94   1999
  974.7'1—DC21   98-27399

Random House website address: www.randomhouse.com
Printed in the United States of America

98765432

First Edition

Book design by H. Roberts Design

Contents

Foreword

A New Yorker who is *not* curious? Rare, indeed.

If any trait binds more than seven million New Yorkers together, it is a desire to know what is knowable about our metropolis, a city unlike any other. Its buildings are taller, its traffic more jammed, its people more various (and maybe more contentious), its history more textured. And its critics as well as its admirers tend to be more numerous and more vociferous. "Love it or leave it," has been a commonly defiant refrain—though at the moment the lovers seem in the majority. But New Yorkers are realists, too, and they know that reputations can be fickle and that history is in the eye of the beholder.

It's odd, somehow, to think of New York as one of the oldest cities in the country, but it is—older than Philadelphia, older than Boston. The New York of history is a source of curiosity for visitors and residents, natives and newcomers, as are the city's geography, architecture, mythology, and language, to name but a few categories of local urban lore.

Often, New York seems to exist mainly for the delight of pedestrian explorers, and in few other places do so many shards of the past exist side by side with the signs of the present, which themselves stand a pretty good chance of becoming the ruins of tomorrow. Unlike the capitals of Europe, which tend to preserve their centers, New York enjoys cannibalizing itself. Reading the city is like following an endless mystery story whose chapters are the layers of stone and steel and glass that have been carved into, painted over, and built on top of one another. A sign advertising a theater long since closed is etched into the side of another building, which lies in the shadow of a monstrous praying mantis, a giant construction crane on the site of a postmillennium skyscraper. New York builds on itself, demolishes itself, then builds and builds again—a relentless dynamic that captures the visitor and keeps the longtime resident puzzled, even enthralled.

Does New York work? Usually. How does New York work? Who knows?

Why is the top of the Empire State Building, usually brilliantly illuminated, sometimes left dark on foggy nights? Does the numbering of the public schools follow any pattern? Is the Roosevelt Island tram ever taken out of service because of weather conditions? New Yorkers want to know and fervently believe there *is* an answer. So go find it. When *The New York Times* began publishing a section called "The City" five years ago, we wanted to tap into the insatiable inquisitiveness and renowned self-assurance of the average New Yorker. Thus was born the "F.Y.I." column. The concept was simple. Readers ask questions. The *Times* digs up the answers.

Readers certainly have held up their end of the bargain, to the tune of more than a thousand letters, phone calls, faxes, and e-mail messages a year. And being New Yorkers, they're not content to just fire off questions. They want to show what *they* know. Everyone's an expert about something. Often, about the same thing as someone else. No sooner has an elusive answer been tracked to the point of printing it than the deluge of reader comment begins: related facts, figures, theories, reminiscences, and, occasionally, a revision or correction. Think of a salon or chat room with New York as the nexus.

It's fascinating work but very often rather tricky. One reader was curious about the line "the daffydils that entertain/at Angelo's and Maxie's," from the old song "Lullaby of Broadway." What were the daffydils and where were Angelo's and Maxie's? Jesse McKinley, the "F.Y.I." supersleuth at the time, interviewed historians and experts in jazz and Broadway show tunes. He paged through old copies of the Yellow Pages to try to find listings for restaurants named Angelo's and Maxie's. Alas, he came up dry. Finally he called Joe Franklin, the former television host and a walking encyclopedia of show-business trivia, who explained that "daffydils" was "a pet word for chorus girls." Angelo's and Maxie's, on the other hand, may have been stretches of the imaginations of Al Dubin and Harry Warren, who wrote the song for the 1935 movie musical *Gold Diggers of 1935,* about a party girl's fall from grace. The song was resurrected for the 1980 musical *42nd Street.*

And a question about the phone company's use of exchange letters as telephone number prefixes (as in BUtterfield 8) sent us on a search of microfiche copies of the city's telephone books from the turn of the century through World War II.

Besides Mr. McKinley, Jennifer Steinhauer and Andrea Kannapell have researched and written "F.Y.I." Each

brought a distinct wit and style to researching and
writing the column. Daniel Schneider, another virtuoso,
has the gig now. All are—or have become—consummately
curious New Yorkers. This book is the result. We hope you
enjoy it.

Joan Nassivera
Editor, "The City"
June 21, 1998

The
Curious
New Yorker

1 What's in a Name?

Wrong Side of the Sun

Q. *It seems ironic that Morningside Heights and Morningside Drive are on the West Side, when the sun rises and mornings begin on the East Side. How did the area earn its name and what exactly are its boundaries?*

A. An 1867 report described the area's steep ridge as "inconvenient for use" and difficult to fit into the city's gridiron plan, and in 1870 city officials overseeing the construction of parks authorized a study for "Morning Side Park" at the site. They rejected one proposal in 1871 before approving a design by Frederick Law Olmsted and Calvert Vaux in 1873. It was revised in 1877.

The sheer cliffs at the park's western edge "face" the east, explains Jonathan Kuhn, director of art and antiquities for the New York City Department of Parks and Recreation. Mr. Kuhn said that many parks, including Central Park, acquired their descriptive name when an informal reference became the official designation.

The Morningside name stuck, or at least Olmsted continued to use it even as he argued against the park's construction. The hilly land was "difficult, unsafe, and in parts, unpractical to travel over," he said, and the recreation space was not needed, with Central Park and Riverside Park not far away. Construction was completed in 1887, and a promenade along the ridge above the park was added later.

In the seventeenth century the area had been known as Vandewater's Heights, after a landowner, Harmon Vandewater. Through most of the nineteenth century, it was known as Bloomingdale Heights, for Bloomingdale Road (now Broadway).

In the decade after the park's completion, a building boom transformed the neighborhood: construction began on the Cathedral of St. John the Divine in 1892 and Columbia University moved its campus uptown in 1897; luxury apartment buildings followed, as did subway service in 1904. Morningside Heights today encompasses the area between 110th and 125th Streets and between Morningside Avenue (the park's eastern border) and the Hudson River.

Which Lincoln Was It?

Q. *Is Lincoln Center for the Performing Arts named after the revered sixteenth president of the United States?*

A. Despite the center's stature in the roster of New York City attractions, the origin of its name remains maddeningly obscure. In 1956, Lincoln Center took its name from Lincoln Square, so designated in 1906 by the Board of Aldermen and Mayor George B. McClellan Jr. The board approved a resolution defining Lincoln Square as West Sixty-third to Sixty-sixth Streets, between Columbus and Amsterdam Avenues. The resolution gave no explanation of the namesake.

The Municipal Reference and Research Center has a typewritten note card, for use as an "in-house tool," stating that the square "may have been named for Abraham Lincoln."

The note continues: "Others claim there was a Lincoln family or farm in the neighborhood. This has never been proved." An employee emphasized the speculative nature of this note. The source, probably a librarian, is unknown, as is the date, which is between 1918 and the early 1950s.

In 1990, researchers for Lincoln Center's information resources department made exhaustive searches for evidence of any local landowner named Lincoln and found none. Nor did they find evidence that the square was named for Abraham.

St. Tammany's Acolytes

Q. *I know that the full name of the infamous Tammany Hall political machine was the Society of St. Tammany or Columbian Order of New York City. Was that organization, today synonymous with corruption, actually named for a saint?*

A. No. The name was actually derived from that of Tamanend, a legendary Delaware chief famed for his wisdom and devotion to freedom.

The "fraternity of patriots," formed as a spirited protest against aristocracy, was organized in New York City about 1788 after the establishment of Tammany Societies in Pennsylvania, New Jersey, and Virginia. The founders elevated "Tammany" to the stature of a saint to thumb their noses at royalist organizations that grew up during the American Revolution in support of the English cause and took names like St. George and St. David.

Though deeply colored by politics, Tammany ostensibly began as a social organization. Although it was plagued by scandal from its early days, almost a century passed before Tammany Hall was seen as a corrupt and powerful political machine.

Street of Easy Virtue

Q. *How did Featherbed Lane, the street that curves steeply down from University Avenue to Jerome Avenue in the High Bridge section of the Bronx, come by its unusual name?*

A. No small amount of folklore surrounds the name Featherbed Lane, but Lloyd Ultan, Bronx borough historian, says he believes that the most plausible of the many explanations dates from the 1840s, when the street was lined with brothels.

There are no official documents to tell us who named the street or why, Mr. Ultan said. One theory has it that residents padded the road with featherbeds during the Revolutionary War to muffle the sound of passing Continental troops. But Mr. Ultan pointed out that the area was sparsely populated at the time and no formal battles occurred there.

Another theory is that the muddy road once had the spongy softness of a featherbed. But the road actually climbs a hill of solid metamorphic bedrock, "as hard as hard can be," Mr. Ultan said.

A third theory is that local farmers found the road so rough that they used featherbeds to cushion their wagon seats. But, Mr. Ultan asked, why would people carry featherbeds in their wagons to travel a road only a few blocks long?

In the early 1840s a section of the Old Croton Aqueduct was built in the area by recent immigrants, many from Ireland. "They were straight off the boat, far from their families, all alone under near frontier conditions," Mr. Ultan said. According to some Bronx sages, Featherbed Lane began as a mischievous nickname for the red-light district that sprang up nearby. "Of all the explanations, this one comes closest to having the ring of truth," Mr. Ultan said.

The name appears on maps as early as 1868.

Call It Avenida Sexta

Q. When was Sixth Avenue renamed Avenue of the Americas, and why?

A. Mayor Fiorello H. La Guardia signed Local Law 43, renaming the avenue, on October 2, 1945. A protester at the hearing described the new name as "an awful mouthful."

The street was originally known as West Road, but the city renamed it Sixth Avenue in 1811 when the street grid was established. The avenue was paved between 1900 and 1910, in the shadow of the Sixth Avenue elevated railway, then rebuilt when the el was dismantled in the 1930s.

Many Sixth Avenue business owners, as well as Leon Spear, the developer, were dismayed at the time by the street's honky-tonk image. Spear later claimed that he tried to persuade some South American countries doing business in New York at the time to locate their business headquarters and consular offices on the avenue. Several countries agreed, Spear said, but insisted on the new street name. The change, however, was not approved by the City Council until after World War II. Medallions with the names and flags of Latin American countries were posted on lampposts along the avenue in the 1960s.

Some argue that New Yorkers have never accepted the new name; supplementary signs identifying the street as Sixth Avenue were posted in 1984.

The Dish on Soap

Q. *Does Port Ivory, on Staten Island, take its name from roaming elephants, or is there another explanation?*

A. Yes. Ivory soap. When Procter & Gamble built a sprawling 77-acre factory in 1907 on the island's northwest corner, where the Kill van Kull meets the Arthur Kill, the area took the name of the company's most popular soap bar—Ivory—which

was manufactured there. Initially about four hundred employees produced soap bars, chips, and granules in the eleven-building complex, but at its zenith in the 1920s, the plant employed fifteen hundred. When it stopped production in 1991, the plant was producing such sudsy favorites as Coast soap, Bold and Solo detergents, and Mr. Clean and Top Job liquid cleaners, as well as the famous floating bar.

Simple Plugs

Q. *In the Bronx neighborhood flanking the old Isaac L. Rice Stadium in Pelham Bay Park, I noticed with a jolt the names of four streets: Ohm, Watt, Ampere, and Radio. What is behind this electrical theme?*

A. Nothing terribly shocking.

Born in 1850, Isaac L. Rice was a man of exceptionally wide-ranging abilities; after graduating from Columbia Law School in 1870, he became a chess master, lawyer, musician, publisher, editor, inventor, and industrialist. He amassed a fortune serving as a counsel to railroad and mining companies, was president of the Forum Publishing Companies, and founded four chess clubs—even devising a chess opening now known as the Rice gambit. (Please don't ask.)

Perhaps more significant, Rice was a pioneer in the design and development of the electrical storage batteries used in cars and submarines, and was president of the Electric Storage Battery Company. After his death, Isaac L. Rice Stadium—known since 1989 as Aileen B. Ryan Recreation Field and used for Parks Department events—was designed (by Herts & Tallant) and built in his honor in 1916 with a $1 million gift from his widow, Julia Rice. In their gratitude, Bronx officials in 1922 gave the streets south of the park names that reflect Rice's avid interest in electricity.

A Utopia in Queens

Q. *Why is Utopia Parkway so named? It seems like "Queens Parkway" would be more appropriate.*

A. In 1905, the Utopia Land Company announced plans to build a new, cooperative town for Jews from the Lower East Side of Manhattan. The community was planned for 50 acres in north-central Queens, between what is now 164th Street and Fresh Meadow Lane, from the Long Island Expressway to Jewel Avenue. The north-south streets of Utopia were even to be given Lower East Side names like Division and Hester. But before lots could be staked out for the perfect neighborhood, funds ran dry in the real world, and the land was sold in 1911. Utopia Parkway takes its name from the unrealized plan.

Hoo Knows?

Q. *How did Owl's Head Park in Bay Ridge, Brooklyn, get its peculiar name?*

A. There are two traditional explanations.

The first says that the shoreline in that area once followed the contours of an owl's head, a geographical detail disputed by many and difficult to discern today.

The second rests on the fact that the 27-acre park was originally part of the estate of Henry C. Murphy, a notable Brooklyn editor and politician who founded *The Brooklyn Eagle* (then *The Brooklyn Daily Eagle)* in 1841, drafted the bill in the New York State Senate authorizing construction of the Brooklyn Bridge, and framed the entrance to his estate with a pair of stone owls. Both theories could be true, of course, or neither. Our research continues.

White or Red?

Q. *Why is Manhattan clam chowder so named?*

A. Philosophers disagree, but Nach Waxman, owner of Kitchen Arts and Letters, who is an expert on food history, theorizes that the Manhattan chowder was simply an Italian clam soup renamed for reasons of style. "Clam chowder," in its cream-based New England version, has been around since the mid-1700s, he said, adding that no mention of any "Manhattan" chowder has been found that predates the 1930s.

Mr. Waxman pointed to this passage in *Down East Chowder,* by John Thorne (published in 1982 and now out of print): "The combination of clams and tomatoes is part of a long Italian tradition. In fact, I suspect that the so-called Manhattan clam chowder is just a version of the Neapolitan clam soup 'zuppa di vongole,' whose composition is suspiciously similar. Many New York fish houses are owned and run by Italians, and it is quite probable that an enterprising chef or menu writer renamed the house clam soup as 'Manhattan clam chowder' to make it more appealing to the clientele."

Many New Englanders argued that the soup was not a true chowder. But according to Mr. Waxman, "A chowder can be defined as any fish-based, long-cooking soup." Manhattan clam chowder, he said, "is not a transformed New England chowder. It doesn't have salt pork. It doesn't have cream. It doesn't get its substance from potatoes. What it has in common with New England clam chowder is . . . clams."

The Other Edward Albee

Q. *I heard that Albee Square at Fulton Street and DeKalb Avenue in downtown Brooklyn was named after a relative of Edward Albee, the playwright. True?*

A. THE SCENE: Albee Square, Brooklyn. George and Martha sitting in the mall.

Perhaps with a cocktail . . .

GEORGE. Do you want to talk about him, Martha, or shall I?

MARTHA *(braying)*. Just get on with it!

GEORGE. All righty. According to the Blue Guide to New York—

MARTHA. The what?

GEORGE *(ignoring her)*. —Albee Square was named after the playwright Edward Albee's grandfather Edward F. Albee, who owned and operated, I believe, a movie house in the square.

MARTHA. What a cluck you are, George. Old Albee didn't start in movies—he started in vaudeville.

GEORGE. Do you want to take over, lovey? *(grumbling)*. I did run the history department.

MARTHA. Awwwwww! Georgie-porgie!

GEORGE. Please, lovey.

MARTHA *(ignoring him)*. Anyhow, the Albee RKO theater was the last remnant of an era when glamorous picture houses were all over Brooklyn. It was ripped down in 1977, but the square kept his name. Then they put up this mall.

GEORGE *(pouting)*. Are you done?

MARTHA. Yes. I swear, if you existed I'd divorce you.

THE END. With apologies.

Dakota in New York

Q. *Is it true that the Dakota apartment building is named after the state? If so, North or South?*

A. Not the state, the territory.

One West Seventy-second Street is one of New York's most esteemed addresses, having housed, over the years, luminaries like Boris Karloff, Roberta Flack, and Leonard Bernstein (can you imagine the cocktail party?). But it wasn't always such a fine locale, according to *Living It Up: A Guide to the Named Apartment Houses of New York* (Atheneum, 1984), by Thomas Norton and Jerry Patterson.

When the sewing machine magnate Edward C. Clark decided in 1884 to build at Seventy-second Street, the area was at the city's barren northern fringe. Derision was rampant. The Dakota was labeled Clark's Folly and was said to be so far uptown as to be in the Dakota Territory. (Ding!)

Clark seized upon that insult and had his building adorned with all manner of Dakotan emblems in relief: cornstalks, arrowheads, etc. By the way, the Dakota Territory became the states of North and South Dakota in 1889.

The Mott Squad

Q. *Mott Street (Manhattan). Mott Haven (Bronx). Related? Discuss.*

A. Well, they're not named after the same fella, but it's all in the family.

First a little history. The Motts were an influential family descended from one Adam Mott, who landed on these pristine shores in the 1630s and spawned a line of successful scions. Mott Street, a main drag through Little Italy and Chinatown, was named after Adam Mott's grandson, Joseph Mott, "a prosperous butcher" who also ran a tavern at what is now 143rd Street and Frederick Douglass Boulevard, according to *The Street Book* (Hagstrom, 1979), by Henry Moscow.

The tavern was apparently a prewar hangout for none other than Mr. Cherry Tree himself, George Washington, who used it as his headquarters in 1775 before moving into the classier environs of Morris-Jumel Mansion. Why a street so far south of Mr. Mott's establishment was given his name is uncertain, but it first appeared on a city map in 1776. (There are two other streets—East 148th Street and East 176th Street—that were once called Mott Street.)

Fast-forward some seventy years and the Motts were still doing fine in the northern parts of the city, according to *History in Asphalt: The Origin of Bronx Street and Place Names* (Harbor Hill, 1978), by John McNamara. In 1853, Jordan L. Mott, Joseph Mott's great-great-grandson, founded an ironworks on the Bronx side of the Harlem River in an area that came to be known, not coincidentally, as Mott Haven.

Sheep-Shaped?

Q. *Why is Sheepshead Bay so named? For the life of me, I can't see the resemblance to a woolly little noggin.*

A. There are a couple of theories floating about. The first, suggested by the Blue Guide to New York (Carol von Pressentin Wright, *New York,* 2nd rev. ed., W. W. Norton, 1991), is that the bay, which is now shaped like a Cubist leg of lamb, was sheep-shaped before it was dredged, cemented, and reshaped with landfill.

The neighborhood's name dates to the 1850s, says John Manbeck, Brooklyn's official historian, so it's possible that the bay's outline may have been more sheep-y at one point. Still, Mr. Manbeck doubts it. He suspects that the bay takes its name from a once-prevalent inhabitant of its waters, the sheepshead.

A greenish-yellow, black-striped relative of the bass, the sheepshead once flourished in the coastal waters around the city before pollution dwindled its numbers. And since Sheepshead Bay was, and still is, considered one of the city's best angling locales, it makes sense that early locals would named their bay after their prey.

Patriot Lanes

Q. *I was born and grew up in Williamsburg (Brooklyn, that is, not Virginia). I was told by my teachers that the streets in my neighborhood (Clymer, Taylor, etc.) were all named after signers of the Declaration of Independence. Is this true? And if so, when were they named?*

A. It's as true as a patriot's heart. The triangular portion of Williamsburg bounded by the East River, Broadway, and Park Avenue may in fact have the city's most revolutionary-minded streetscape. Most every street in the neighborhood, from Wythe Avenue near the river to Ellery Street just north of Park Avenue, is taken from the list of fifty-six rebels who scrawled their names on the famous document.

The streets probably were formally named during the early 1850s, when most streets in that area were gridded, says Brooklyn historian John Manbeck. (Williamsburg, by the by, isn't named after the colonial Virginian hot spot, but after Jonathan Williams, the area's surveyor.)

There are a few exceptions to the patriotic patronyms: Marcy Avenue, which may have been named for the 1830s governor, William L. Marcy; Wallabout Street, which comes from the early Dutch name for the neighborhood and nearby bay; and Lorimer and Keap Streets, whose origins are uncertain.

Oddly enough, none of the Williamsburg streets were named for New Yorkers; most of those honored were from Pennsylvania.

Major Who?

Q. *George Washington Bridge, okay. John F. Kennedy Airport, fine. But the Major Deegan Expressway? Did I miss something in civics class?*

A. Only if you went to the School of Political Connections.

William F. Deegan was an architect by profession and a political leader at heart. He served as a major in World War I under General George W. Goethals—though he supposedly never came within 3,000 miles of an enemy bullet. His military career was with the Army Corps of Engineers in New York. (Goethals built the Panama Canal and was the first consulting engineer of the Port Authority. Ever heard of the Goethals Bridge?)

Deegan served as the president of the Bronx Chamber of Commerce and eventually, in the late 1920s, as Mayor James J. Walker's commissioner of tenement housing and New York's official greeter of distinguished persons. He died suddenly in 1932 at the age of forty-nine after an attack of appendicitis.

Deegan received a send-off worthy of a war hero, featuring two bands, sixty mounted policemen, and three thousand marchers from the Army and the Marines, as well as the Police and Fire Departments. During the service at St. Patrick's Cathedral, twenty-five Army Air Corps planes circled in tribute overhead. His political allies affixed his name to the Bronx expressway, which was completed in 1956.

Asher or Asser?

Q. *The school I tutor at in Manhattan is the Asher Levy School, and the community center I swim at is the Asser Levy Center. Who was he, and why the discrepancy in spelling?*

A. No, you're not seeing double. The discrepancy is probably due simply to the Anglicization of the Hebrew name. But the man is one and the same: Asser Levy fled the Inquisition in Brazil in 1654 with a group of twenty-three Jews headed for what was then New Amsterdam, where the colony's governor, Peter Stuyvesant, immediately fought to send the impoverished immigrants back. Their cause was supported by Jewish stockholders of the Dutch West India Company, Stuyvesant was rebuffed, and the "Jewish pilgrim fathers," as they were known, planted roots and formed Congregation Shearith-Israel, the first in America. Levy won the rights of Jewish citizenship in colonial times, and was the first American Jew to join in the armed defense of his land, during an Indian uprising.

He was also the colony's first kosher butcher. Levy (pronounced LEE-vee) is a popular figure in New York lore—so much so that several city sites have been named for him, including the former Seaside Park on Coney Island, the Asher Levy School (P.S. 19) on First Avenue near Twelfth Street, and the Asser Levy Community Center at Twenty-third Street and Avenue A, which was renamed in 1954 on the three hundredth anniversary of his arrival.

The Great Skating Benefactor

Q. *Who was the Wollman Rink in Central Park named for? My guess is it's the Kate Wollman who the rink in Prospect Park was named after.*

A. Well, not exactly.

The rink in Central Park was actually dedicated in honor of Kate Wollman's parents, Jonas and Bettie, who lived in Kansas, and her brothers: William, Benjamin, Morton, who were bankers, and Henry, a lawyer.

Ms. Wollman, a philanthropist who lived in New York for forty years and who was the last family survivor, donated $600,000 for the completion of the rink.

After her death in 1955, the William J. Wollman Foundation (founded by Ms. Wollman's brother) donated money for construction of a rink in her honor. The Kate Wollman Memorial Rink, in Prospect Park, was the result. It opened in 1961.

Yellow Hook, Until...

Q. *I was reading a historical biography and saw a reference to Yellow Hook, Brooklyn. This surprised me. I know Red Hook, but Yellow?*

A. More than a century ago, the area now known as Bay Ridge was called Yellow Hook, according to documents from the Bay Ridge Historical Society. The name referred to the yellow sand and clay in the soil.

But yellow fever swept through the area in 1848–1849, and the name Yellow Hook suddenly lost its charm. "Yellow anything didn't sound so good," according to Rita Unz, secretary for the historical society. So in December 1853, many of

the large landowners from the area met to change the name. A florist named James Weir put forth the name Bay Ridge as one that suggested "the geographic nature" of the land.

The name, unlike the fever, stuck around.

Eponymous Bruckner

Q. *For years, I have been passing the Bruckner Boulevard exit sign and wondering, Who was Bruckner? And when was this boulevard named?*

A. Henry Bruckner was the popular, if unexceptional, Bronx borough president from 1918 to 1933, according to Lloyd Ultan, a Bronx historian. "He made no ripples," Mr. Ultan said. "The job, at that point, just kind of asked you to sit on your hands and do nothing. And that's what he did."

Bruckner was a state legislator and U.S. congressman before being handpicked in 1918 to run for borough president by the Bronx Democratic leader, Edward J. Flynn. He won reelection four times before failing health and a changing political climate forced him out of office in 1933. His most memorable act besides his clockwork reelections, Mr. Ultan said, may have been founding Bruckner Beverages, whose big seller during Prohibition (1920–1933) was a fizzy concoction called U-No-Us Soda.

The boulevard, originally called Eastern Boulevard, was renamed in 1942, shortly after Bruckner's death.

A Pilot and His Field

Q. *I have a question about Floyd Bennett Field on Jamaica Bay in Brooklyn: Who is Floyd Bennett?*

A. The area, now part of the Gateway National Recreation Area, was once dominated by an airfield named in honor of Floyd Bennett, who piloted Admiral Richard E. Byrd's celebrated (and since challenged) flight over the North Pole in 1926. (A 1990 biography of Byrd, *Beyond the Barrier,* by Eugene Rodgers, suggested that Bennett admitted after Byrd's death that they never actually reached the pole.)

The airport, New York City's first, was built in 1931 on reclaimed marshland and was the starting site of several famous early flights, according to *The Encyclopedia of New York City* (Yale University Press and New-York Historical Society, 1995), edited by Kenneth T. Jackson. In 1933, Wiley Post started and ended his trip around the globe (which set a speed record) at Floyd's field, and Howard Hughes used it in 1938 to break Post's record. After La Guardia Airport opened in 1939, Floyd Bennett Field was sold to the Navy. It has been under the authority of the National Park Service since 1972.

The Flushing Flip-Flop

Q. *Where does Flushing, Queens, get its name? (P.S.: I hope it has nothing to do with the verb.)*

A. Follow closely. This is confusing.

Flushing's early settlers were mainly English families who came via Vlissingen, a port city in the Netherlands. In 1645, these folks named their community Vlissingen.

The area remained known as Vlissingen until about 1663, when the name was changed to New-Warke or Newark, according to documents from the Queens Historical Society. In 1665, however, the name Flushing, an English version of Vlissingen, was adopted, and it stuck.

Why the flip-flop?

One theory: In 1661, John Bowne, a converted Quaker, built a house that was used by other Quakers as a meeting place. (The house still stands at 37–01 Bowne Street; it is the oldest structure in Queens.) This greatly displeased Governor Peter Stuyvesant, a Calvinist who had outlawed Quakers in 1657, and Bowne was banished to the Netherlands in 1662. One theory has it that the change to New-Warke was meant to further divorce the town from its Quaker roots.

But in 1664, the English took control of the city from the Dutch. William Asadorian, a researcher at the Queens Borough Public Library, thinks that lobbying efforts may have gotten the name Vlissingen reinstated, in a more English-sounding way.

Why "Times" Square?

Q. *I'm four years old, and I want to know where the name Times Square came from.*

It does not tell the time.

A. This is a surprisingly oft-asked question, even from older New Yorkers. Times Square's name dates back to 1904, when *The New York Times* moved its headquarters to the building now known as 1 Times Square. As the handy Blue Guide to New York tells it, the *Times* managed to have its name affixed to the newly built IRT stop. The area was formerly known as Longacre Square, but the name Times Square, even without a clock, has stuck.

Checkitout

Q. *I'm aware that Times Square is named after your paper. But prior to that assignation, the location was known as Longacre Square. Whence that name?*

A. Like most of the place names in America, it was stolen.

Longacre Square's name was taken from that of a commercial street in central London called the Long Acre, according to *On Broadway: A Journey Uptown over Time* (Rizzoli, 1990), by David W. Dunlap, a reporter for *The New York Times*. The reason was this: Back in the second half of the nineteenth century, the principal businesses in the area were horse dealerships, carriage factories, and stables.

The location made horse sense because Broadway was

the city's major thoroughfare. Long Acre in London had the same type of businesses. So, the area came to be known as Longacre Square (us 'Mericans had to crunch it all together, of course).

The Ear of the Beholder

Q. Where did Aqueduct Racetrack get its name? Belmont is named for August Belmont, who founded that track, and Saratoga is named after Saratoga Springs, the upstate town where the track is located. But isn't Aqueduct a strange name?

A. Actually, Aqueduct got its name the same way Saratoga did. When it opened, on September 27, 1894, it was in an area known as Aqueduct. And that was so named because there was an aqueduct there.

Almost 54 million gallons of water a day were pumped through a 48-inch-wide iron conduit from the Millburn Pumping Station in Freeport, Long Island, to a distribution reservoir in Ridgewood, Queens, according to historians and newspaper accounts. This provided the water for much of Queens and Brooklyn until the turn of the century, when the Croton aqueduct system went into use.

Cathy Schenck, a librarian at Keeneland Racetrack in Lexington, Kentucky, found an article in the September 15, 1894, issue of *Livestock Record* that sheds a little light on this. "Some months ago, several gentlemen went to that part of Long Island called Aqueduct and bought a large tract of land. They conducted their business quietly, but it soon had been noised that the ground had been secured for racing purposes." The article went on to say that the land was bought by members of the Queens County Jockey Club for $50,000.

TriBeCa Family Tree

Q. *I heard that Leonard, Worth, and Thomas Streets in TriBeCa are named for three brothers from France. Any truth to this?*

A. The streets were, in fact, named after three brothers of French descent: Leonard, Anthony, and Thomas Lispenard, who lived in the area in the early 1800s. Anthony, though, later lost his street name to a hero of the Mexican War, General William Jenkins Worth, according to the Blue Guide to New York. The Lispenard boys were the proud sons of Anthony Lispenard, a French immigrant to New York City during the mid-1700s. The elder Lispenard built a swampy land empire in Lower Manhattan, called Lispenard Meadows, which stretched over portions of what is now TriBeCa, SoHo, and Greenwich Village. As a result, he got to name the streets, including another street four blocks north of Leonard Street, Lispenard Street.

After New York State's own General Worth made his name in the Mexican War (1846–1848) and shortly thereafter died, Anthony Street was renamed Worth Street.

Sheridan in the Park

Q. *I assume that the statue to the back of Sheridan Square (at Seventh Avenue and Christopher Street in Greenwich Village) is of General Sheridan, and I assume that the square is named after the general. But why is this so and when was the square so named? What is the history of Sheridan Square park?*

A. You know what happens when you assume. . . .

First off, the patch of ground where the statue sits is not actually Sheridan Square. It is Christopher Park, which has been around since 1837, making it one of the city's oldest parks. Sheridan Square is the garden-centered triangle right around the corner, bordered by West Fourth Street, Washington Place, and Barrow Street. Sheridan Square was pretty much a concrete crossroads until 1981, when a partnership of local residents and the Parks and

Transportation Departments created the garden.

You are right about the Christopher Park statue being of General Philip H. Sheridan, who was a Union general during the Civil War and later an infamous Indian hunter, according to the Blue Guide to New York. (It was Sheridan who uttered the twisted, and oft-misquoted, aphorism "The only good Indians I saw were dead.") Sheridan's surly, and oddly placed, likeness was installed in 1936.

Batters Up, Parades Out

Q. *Why are the Parade Grounds south of Prospect Park called that? It's almost all tennis courts and baseball fields. I've never heard of a parade going on there.*

A. Well, if it wasn't for the popularity of those newfangled ball games, parades might still be all the rage at the Parade Grounds. According to Brooklyn historian John Manbeck, the 40-acre Parade Grounds was created in 1867, when Brooklynites still thought a good military parade beat just about anything. (It was set apart from Prospect Park to protect the park's lawns from

the crush of parade spectators, Mr. Manbeck said.) However, as sports, particularly baseball, became more popular
in the 1890s, the Parade Grounds was gradually converted
to cater to more casual civilian pastimes.

Four Mystery Letters

Q. *How did the PATH system get its name? I assume it's
an acronym involving the Port Authority, but I can't figure the
last two letters.*

A. The PATH system was named in 1962 after
the Port Authority of New York and New Jersey took over
the ailing Manhattan-Hudson Railroad (once nicknamed
"the haul and maul").

According to Lloyd D. Schwalb, a spokesman for the
Port Authority, planners mulled over several names ("Port
Authority Railroad," or "PARR," definitely would not do)
before one moved them: Port Authority Trans Hudson.

Quoth the Raven...

Q. *How did the community of Ravenswood, Queens, get
its name? Was that sinister bird responsible?*

A. The little neighborhood to the north of the
Queensborough Bridge owes its name to the Reverend
Francis Hawks, who around 1840 changed the name of
the settlement from Matona to Ravenscroft in honor of his
buddy, the Right Reverend John Stark Ravenscroft, according to documents from the Queens Historical Society. As
the story goes, when John Ravenscroft became Bishop of

North Carolina, Mr. Hawks apparently felt his chum might be offended at having such a small place as his namesake and changed the name to Ravenswood.

Aye, Comrade-Matey!

Q. *Red Hook seems to me to have the most grisly name of any of the city's neighborhoods. What's the story? Some Communist pirate?*

A. No such luck. Red Hook, according to the Blue Guide to New York, gets its name from Dutch settlers. They called the area Roode Hoek—"Roode" deriving from either the redness of the area's soil or its once-luxuriant cranberry bogs, and "Hoek" simply meaning a jutting point of land.

On the map, at least, the area has become significantly more hookish since the early 1980s, when the Port Authority built a sharply curved set of piers off the coast. With those cement additions, Red Hook's crook would make any pirate proud.

Better than Rego Park

Q. *How did Rego Park, Queens, get its name? Who was Rego?*

A. The infamous Rego the Destroyer, of course. Or was it Rego the Invulnerable?

Actually, Rego Park got its name from a truncation of the developer's expression of pride in his work. When Henry Schloh, a German entrepreneur, bought the land south of Queens Boulevard in 1923, he began building what he felt were "real good" houses and apartment buildings that became the neighborhood.

In an attempt to give his development a catchier name than the town-idiotesque Real Good Park, Schloh coined the hybrid Rego Park, according to documents at the Queens Historical Society. The name caught on, and by 1925, most residents had embraced Rego and abandoned stuffier neighborhood designations like Hastings. The Post

Office lent the name permanence when it opened the Rego Park branch in 1946. And the Rego Park Construction Company, while out of the naming business, still pounds nails.

It Once Was Rustdorp

Q. How did Jamaica, Queens, get named that? Is there some connection to the island?

A. Possibly, though a survey of historical references suggests that a more likely explanation has to do with a large water-loving rodent. (Stay with me, now.)

The land that the village of Jamaica was built on was once the domain of the Jameco Indians, a small Algonquian tribe that took their name from the Algonquian word for, you guessed it, beaver. (The Dutch, meanwhile, were calling the area Rustdorp, or "quiet village.") When English farmers settled in the area they called their village Jamaica, presumably a twisting of the Indian name, though some histories suggest that the En-glish, traders with the West Indies, may have gotten the idea for the name from the island.

Regardless, the name Jamaica seems a great improvement on Rustdorp.

Drawing the Line

Q. Why does Park Avenue become Park Avenue South at Thirty-second Street? Why isn't the whole thing just Park Avenue? And wouldn't it make more sense to change the name at a major crossing like Forty-second at Grand Central?

A. Park Avenue wasn't always Park Avenue, and neither was its southern half.

Frank Vardy, an urban historian working with the Department of City Planning, says that the avenue was originally laid out on city planning grids as Fourth Avenue and was the route, starting in the 1830s, of some very loud, very dirty steam trains that ran from their terminal at Twenty-sixth Street to Ninety-sixth Street.

Because northbound trains were not powerful enough to steam up the incline that begins at Thirty-second Street, a tunnel was dug from there to about Forty-second Street, where trains emerged and continued traveling north in a rut cut down the middle of the avenue.

Above the tunnel, a park was built and extended along the tracks of the train, all the way to Ninety-sixth Street. As steam trains were replaced by cleaner electrical models and the park and its neighborhood began to flourish, locals decided they wanted a snazzier name for their tree-lined promenade. Park Avenue leapt to mind.

Beginning in 1861, the avenue's name and addresses were gradually changed. By 1924, the entire length, from Thirty-second Street north to Ninety-sixth Street, was officially Park Avenue, according to James Trager, author of *Park Avenue: Street of Dreams* (Atheneum, 1990).

But the change extended only as far south as the park, so the avenue below Thirty-second remained drab old Fourth Avenue until the spring of 1959. The City Council then voted to extend the cachet of the name down to Seventeenth Street and renamed the stretch of pavement from Thirty-second Street to Seventeenth Street Park Avenue South. All that remains of old Fourth Avenue is a stretch from East Fourteenth to East Fourth.

About Mother Gaston

Q. *My name is Mark Gaston. There is a street in the Brownsville section of Brooklyn called Mother Gaston Boulevard. I am curious about who Mother Gaston was and why the street is named for her.*

A. Rosetta Gaston was a black historian and community advocate in Brownsville, known for helping take black history out of academic circles and into communities, especially to children.

Born in a tenement in 1885, Gaston was forced to leave school and go to work at age fourteen. For forty years, she was an elevator operator at Bergdorf Goodman, but she also attended seminars at the Association for the Study of Negro Life and History (now known as the Association for Study of Afro-American Life and History, the sponsor of Black History Month). She described the seminars as informative, but seemingly "only for teachers and learned folk."

Gaston began organizing small groups of children and young adults to study black history. In 1943, she met Carter G. Woodson, the noted black historian and founder of the A.S.N.L.H., who encouraged Ms. Gaston to open a chapter devoted to teaching black history in Brownsville. She eventually did found the Brownsville chapter of the A.S.N.L.H., helped in part by donations from Bergdorf's.

Known as Mother Gaston for the maternal care she took with her students, she continued to work to teach local children about their ethnic histories, the arts, and the humanities until her death, in February 1981, at age ninety-five. Shortly after she died, a bronze statue of Mother Gaston was placed along Dumont Avenue (the first such memorial in Brownsville), and Stone Avenue was renamed Mother Gaston Boulevard.

East Village History

Q. *When did the East Village become the East Village and stop being part of the Lower East Side?*

A. The answer "depends on who you talk to," said Seth Kamil, an urban historian and East Village tour guide.

The East Village is roughly defined as the neighborhood east of the Bowery from Fourteenth Street down to East First Street. The name was never formally bestowed on the area, but it appears to have cropped up in the early 1960s. It owes its origins to a migration of artists fleeing the rising rents of Greenwich Village, say Mr. Kamil and John Manbeck, another city historian.

This assertion is echoed by the *Guide to New York City* (3rd ed., Harcourt Brace Jovanovich, 1988), which says: "In the 60's, the area assumed the name East Village as a result of the incursion of hippies and flower children."

A 1958 *New York City Guide and Almanac* makes no mention of an East Village and includes the neighborhood in its section on the Lower East Side. But a 1964 guide, *Earl Wilson's New York* (Simon & Schuster), reports that in the "melting pot" of the Lower East Side, "artists, poets and promoters of coffeehouses from Greenwich Village are trying to remelt the neighborhood under the high-sounding name of 'East Village.' "

The *East Village Other,* a weekly newspaper chronicling the comings and goings of the psychedelic set, appeared in 1966. And on June 5, 1967, *The New York Times* reported that the area "had come to be known" as the East Village.

William Gottlieb, a realtor in the Greenwich Village area for more than thirty years, says he recalls the neighborhood's first being called the East Village in his business "in the early sixties, when Timothy Leary was prevalent."

Kevin Davitt, a spokesman for the Department of City Planning, says that while the East Village is not listed as such in city zoning maps, the term has been recognized by department officials for "about twenty-five, thirty years."

Geographobia

Q. *Why is the Brooklyn area of Gravesend called that? (Or do I not want to know?)*

A. As with much of early New York history, no one is certain. But there are two theories, according to urban historian John Manbeck. Neither is particularly creepy.

Gravesend was one of the five original Dutch towns established in Brooklyn, Mr. Manbeck said. The most logical source for its name is a town in Holland called 's Gravenzande (it means "the count's beach" in Dutch, he said).

But of those five towns, he noted, Gravesend was the only one settled by the English, who may have taken the name from a town in England 20 miles east of London. The name of the English town means "place at the end of the grove," according to a dictionary of British place names, because the Old English word for "grove" is "graf."

Vale of Brooklyn

Q. *How did the Vale of Cashmere in Prospect Park get its name?*

A. First, be aware that it had nothing to do with Frederick Law Olmsted. (He detested the name.)

It was first officially used in the park's annual report for 1893, according to M. M. Graff, in *Central Park, Prospect Park: A New Perspective* (Greensward Foundation, 1985). She cites the theory of the historian James Hurley: the name was taken from an 1817 poem, *Lalla Rookh,* by Thomas Moore. It's a kind of East Indian *Canterbury Tales,* with travelers entertaining one another with stories.

One of the stories is set in Kashmir. "The Vale, with its winding shores, deep coves and hinted islands, may have suggested a likeness to the Dal Lake in the mountain-rimmed Kashmir Valley, especially to one who had never been there, but knew it only through Moore's highly colored verse," Graff writes.

Monoxide Gardens?

Q. *Does any neighborhood bear a more untrendy name than Ozone Park in Queens? How did the name come about?*

A. Obviously you've never had to live in Hell, Michigan, or Boring, Maryland. In 1880, the music publisher Benjamin Hitchcock built a development in an area of Queens that was largely farmland, and named it Ozone Park for the invigorating breezes that came off Jamaica Bay and the ocean.

"It didn't mean what it means today," according to James Driscoll at the Queens Historial Society. "It had a nice connotation."

Honoring Horace...

Q. *I have been living in Queens for thirty years but have never been able to find out who Horace Harding (of Horace Harding Boulevard) was.*

A. Horace Harding was a broker with as much interest in golf as in stocks. In the years after World War I he frequently traveled from Manhattan to Long Island to play golf—a trip that sometimes took as long as four hours over rough roads.

Hoping to get Queens officials to build a thoroughfare, he personally commissioned engineering studies, and the road was finally built in the administration of Mayor James J. Walker, who opened it in 1928 as Nassau Boulevard. Harding died in 1929 (when golf, at least, still looked promising).

Though construction of the Long Island Expressway in the 1950s largely obliterated the old road, Harding has kept his small, but concrete, place in city history.

...and Throg?

Q. *What is a Throg and why is there a New York bridge named after its neck?*

A. This question suggests more levity than curiosity. Nonetheless: Throg is what's left of the name Throckmorton, says Frank Pascual, director of public information for MTA Bridges and Tunnels, which operates the Throgs Neck Bridge.

John Throckmorton, he said, settled on the piece of land in the Bronx that juts out into the river—a neck of land—in 1643. The area retained the vestige of his name that was given to the bridge, which opened in 1962.

A Misnomer Revealed

Q. *I heard that the Washington Irving house is erroneously named. True fact?*

A. The house at 40 Irving Place on the corner of Seventeenth Street was built in 1845, but its residents were Elsie de Wolfe and Elisabeth Marbury, two ladies of "taste and social ability," and not Irving, according to the Blue Book.

Exactly how it got its current name is not clear, but it sits across the street from a bronze bust of the early American author, which stands in front of a high school that was also named after him.

The Blue Book recalls a different name for the house in de Wolfe and Marbury's day. The two, an interior decorator and a literary agent, ran a Sunday salon that attracted a lot of foreign guests and became known as the "immigrants' home," the Blue Book says.

Watery Spring Street

Q. *What is the origin of the name for Spring Street in SoHo? Is it as obvious as one thinks?*

A. The Street was named for a spring that was tapped by Aaron Burr's Manhattan Water Company, which was set up as a sort of late-eighteenth-century utility but became a banking company instead, according to the intrepid Blue Guide to New York.

But here is a creepy twist of death and supernaturalism: Local legend has it that in 1800, Juliana Elmore Sands was found floating in a well on the corner of Broadway and Spring Street, minus her shoes, hat, and shawl. Her fiancé was acquitted of murder charges, the Blue Guide maintains, but Miss Sands returned as a ghost.

The latest sighting was in 1974, when a local resident said a gray-haired apparition wearing mossy garments rose from his water bed.

Whence Mosholu?

Q. *What is the origin of the name Mosholu, as in Mosholu Parkway and the Mosholu neighborhood in the Bronx?*

A. Historians believe that Mosholu was the name the Wechguasgeeck Indians gave Tibbets Brook, and that the word means "smooth stones" or "small stones." Also, John McNamara, in the book *History in Asphalt: The Origin of Bronx Street and Place Names,* cites an 1887 map that said Mosholu was the name of a small village on the Albany Post Road near what is now Broadway and West 242nd Street.

The Dairy Ferries

Q. *How did the body of water known as the Buttermilk Channel, between Red Hook, Brooklyn, and Governors Island, get its name?*

A. According to legend (which seems to be the standard reference when it comes to the history of local bodies of water), in the seventeeth century, when Governors Island was governed as part of Long Island, the channel was so narrow and shallow that only cattle and flat-bottomed boats could make it across. These boats were known as buttermilk boats for their regular trips to carry the preferred beverage of the Dutch from the dairies of Long Island proper to Governors Island and New Amsterdam. The channel, which deepened over time, reportedly took its name from the boats.

The Mark of Ansonia

Q. *On the Upper West Side, we have the Ansonia Hotel and the Ansonia Station Post Office, and various businesses that use the name Ansonia. What is its origin?*

A. The precedent was set by the hotel, built in 1904 on Broadway between Seventy-third and Seventy-fourth Streets. The lovely Beaux Arts building offered suites and full domestic staffs at the end of the nineteenth century.

It was developed by William Earl Dodge Stokes, who, according to the Blue Guide to New York, the ever-accurate if grimly prosed bible of New York history, kept ducks, chickens, and a pet bear on the roof.

Stokes named the hotel for his grandfather Anson G. Phelps.

Streets of Citrus

Q. *Why are so many streets in the northern part of Brooklyn Heights named after fruit? There's Pineapple, Cranberry, and Orange. What's the origin?*

A. There are two stories that explain this, and no one knows for sure which is true, according to Brooklyn historian John Manbeck.

One tale is that the Hicks brothers, who originally owned the land, sold exotic fruits in the area, and named the streets to honor this occupation. But the story Mr. Manbeck prefers is the one about old Mrs. Middagh, a Brooklyn Heights resident at the beginning of the century who didn't care for the tradition of naming streets after rich residents. As the story goes, she pulled the signs down and put up botanic ones in their place. (Oddly enough, the street named after her is almost the only one left in that part of the neighborhood put up in accordance with the practice she so loathed. Go figure. The Hicks brothers got one, too.)

Moore or Less

Q. *Is N. Moore Street North Moore? Or is it N. Moore as in Nathaniel Moore, as I have often heard?*

A. Even city agency folks have been tricked into believing that Nathaniel Moore story. The Manhattan borough president's office says North Moore Street, in TriBeCa, was named after Benjamin Moore, the Episcopal bishop of New York in the early 1800s and the president of what was then Columbia College, now Columbia University. What's more, he was the father of Clement Clarke Moore, who wrote "A Visit from St. Nicholas."

East Side or West Side?

Q. *Please explain why Fourth Street is called West Fourth Street at the point where it intersects University Place, and not East Fourth Street. It confuses both locals and tourists.*

A. South of Washington Square Park, there is no longer a Fifth Avenue, which, as you know, divides Manhattan into East and West. The dividing avenue becomes Broadway, and Fourth and Third Streets happen to be the only numbered streets that are both south of the park and west of Broadway (West Fourth becomes East Fourth on the other side, West Third turns into Great Jones).

"Astor" as in "Castor"?

Q. *While trying to explain to some Parisian friends why there are reliefs of beavers in the Astor Place IRT station, it* *occurred to me that there was a suspicious similarity between the trapper John Jacob's family name and the French word for beaver: castor. Have I stumbled across something? Did old J. J. purloin his name from his favorite fur?*

A. No, but you get points for imagination. Though the Astors' connection (and debt) to the beaver is unquestionable, the Astor family name is an Anglicized version of the family's ancestral German name, Ashdoer, according to the 1898 *National Cyclopedia of American Biography.* The fur trader and his brothers were using the name Astor in Britain, well before they began their American adventures.

One footnote: John Jacob Astor did have a ship called the *Beaver,* which was famous for a trip to China in 1808 in which Astor disguised a Chinese dockworker as a diplomat to circumvent an American embargo on trade with China.

Astor took a load of furs, returned with a shipload of tea, and turned a cool $200,000 profit.

2 Myths and Mysteries

Cries and Whispers

Q. *A friend told me about a "whispering gallery" outside the Oyster Bar in Grand Central Terminal, where people can stand at opposite ends of the hallway and hear each other's whispers. How does it work, and are there others in the city?*

A. This effect occurs when walls are shaped and curved in such a way that the sound follows the contour of the wall around a gallery, bouncing across the arcs of the surface and reaching a distant listener's ears at almost the same volume, explained Professor Daniel R. Raichel, a mechanical engineer and acoustics specialist at Cooper Union. "The surface has to be extremely hard, so that it does not absorb the sound, but lets it continue on its way," he said.

The phenomenon is commonly associated with larger domed or vaulted spaces, particularly those of St. Peter's Basilica in Rome and St. Paul's Cathedral in London, or the rotundas of state capitols and university buildings. But it can occur across other types of curved surfaces, including those found in canyons and caves. "The principal thing is, the surface must be smooth and hard, without any projections that could interfere with the sound," Professor Raichel added. Semicircular stone benches often meet these acoustical requirements.

A number of churches in New York have the right conditions for a whispering gallery, especially those with a dome or a vaulted crossing, the professor said.

The spot by the Oyster Bar is where three passages meet beneath a vaulted ceiling. Another local whispering gallery is a small one at the base of the main staircase in

Butler Library at Columbia University, beneath the shallow
dome in front of a mosaic of the goddess Athena.

Dylan's Village Days

Q. *The cover photo for Bob Dylan's second album,* The
Freewheelin' Bob Dylan, *captures him in the middle of a New
York City street, walking arm in arm with a smiling young
woman. What street were they on, and who is the woman?*

A. The answer, my friend, is Jones Street in Green-
wich Village, between Bleecker Street and West Fourth
Street. The woman is nineteen-year-old Susan Rotolo, an
artist who was Dylan's girlfriend during his folkie days in
New York and the reputed subject of such compositions as
"Boots of Spanish Leather" and "Don't Think Twice, It's
All Right." The two shared an apartment at 161 West
Fourth Street while Dylan recorded the album in late 1962
and early 1963. Late one afternoon that February, Don
Hunstein, a staff photographer for Columbia Records,
arrived and brought the couple outside to the snowy street
for a photo session. "I can't tell you why I did it," Hunstein later recalled, "but I said, 'Just walk up and down
the street.' There wasn't very much thought to it." In the
photo, taken on Jones Street, the sun is low in the sky, and
the two look a little chilly standing in the dirty slush. It
was, in fact, a last glimpse of Bob Dylan leading the life of
a relatively ordinary young man. The album, which included "Blowin' in the Wind" and "A Hard Rain's a-Gonna
Fall," was released three months later, and Bob Dylan became Bob Dylan. As of this summer, Susan Rotolo was
reported to be living in the Village.

Heliopolis to Metropolis

Q. *I know that Cleopatra's Needle, the thirty-five-hundred-year-old Egyptian obelisk in Central Park, came from Alexandria on a steamship, but how was it moved from the waterfront to its site behind the Metropolitan Museum?*

A. Very slowly. The last leg of the obelisk's 6,000-mile journey—from a Ninety-sixth Street landing on the Hudson to the present site—took almost four months as the 200-ton shaft was inched overland atop wooden rails laid for that purpose.

The Needle arrived in the Egyptian steamer *Dessoug* in July 1880. A gift to the city from Egypt, the obelisk was one of a pair raised before the Temple of the Sun in Heliopolis around 1475 B.C. to mark the third jubilee of Pharaoh Thutmose III. The obelisk was towed on pontoons to the foot of Ninety-sixth Street, where the 69-foot shaft was placed lengthwise on a cradle made of two parallel beams joined by struts, attached to a pile-driver engine with a winch.

The cradle, set on rollers, rested on tracks made with wooden beams. An anchor chain borrowed from the *Dessoug* connected a drum in the engine to a block anchored in the street ahead; the engine pulled itself and the monolith forward by winding the chain around the drum. Extra beams were used to extend the track forward, length by length, as work gangs cleared the way and periodically moved the block forward.

As autumn turned to winter and the city watched, enthralled, the Needle was inched forward, day and night. Setting out on September 30, the obelisk climbed Ninety-sixth Street and reached the West Boulevard (Broadway) on October 27. It was laboriously turned south, then rolled down to Eighty-sixth Street and turned east. It entered the park on November 25. On December 16, the obelisk reached Fifth Avenue, where it was turned south. It reentered the park at Eighty-second Street, and reached its destination in the Graywacke Knoll on January 5, 1881—112 days after it touched ground in Manhattan.

A Remnant of Royalty

Q. *The elaborately carved pulpit at St. Paul's Chapel, on Broadway at Fulton Street, is topped by a crown and an array of feathers. What is the meaning of this odd symbol?*

A. It is believed by many to be the only surviving symbol of British rule in New York. The carved, gilded crown and plumes above St. Paul's two-tiered pulpit depict an insignia of British nobility, according to "One Peppercorne: A Popular History of the Parish of Trinity

Church," a 1982 essay by John C. Goodbody, a historian associated with Trinity Church and its parish, which includes St. Paul's.

Often called "the Prince of Wales's feathers," though more correctly known as the badge of the heir apparent, the symbol generally comprises a group of ostrich feathers that rise through a gold coronet of crosses and fleurs-de-lis, and dates from the fourteenth century. The feathers and crown caught the eye of others before you, according to David Jette, a lay official at St. Paul's. "Many in the city wanted to remove them when America declared its independence," he said. "They do stand out a bit."

St. Paul's Chapel, Manhattan's oldest surviving church and one of the city's few extant pre-Revolutionary buildings, was built from 1764 to 1766, early in the reign of George III of England. It was, in fact, a small yet sophisticated copy of the Church of St. Martin-in-the-Fields in Trafalgar Square in London, which was designed by James Gibbs, a protégé of Sir Christopher Wren. The chapel tower, added in 1794, was based on designs from a Gibbs pattern book. The chapel, sometimes attributed to Thomas McBean, the American architect, survived the fire of 1776, which claimed the old Trinity Church. George Washington, no royalist, worshiped in a pew in the north aisle of St. Paul's after his inauguration at Federal Hall in 1789.

Protection from What?

Q. *I've seen listings in classified real estate advertisements for "Broker Protected." What does this mean?*

A. "Broker Protected" is a compensation guarantee from property owners to brokers, said Faith Hope Consolo, senior managing director of the brokerage firm Garrick-Aug Associates. "What that means," she said, "is if they bring a tenant to the place, they will be paid for their service." It applies mainly to commercial real estate. The industry is so unscrupulous that many agencies see a need to tout this feature in their classified ads, Ms. Consolo said. As anyone who has timidly ventured into the real estate market knows, there is no protection from brokers.

Lenin and a Crazy Clock

Q. *On Houston Street between Avenues A and B is an apartment house called Red Square. On the roof is a large statue of Lenin. There is also a large clock on the side of the water towers. The clock numbers are arranged: 12, 1, 9, 6, 4, 10, 5, 11, 7, 2, 3, and 8. What's the story?*

A. Red Square, a 130-unit rental apartment house at 250 East Houston Street, was built in 1989, the year of the fall of the Soviet Union. The clock's purpose was simple: to cover the water tower and elevator roof, according to Michael Shaoul, a co-owner with Michael Rosen, the original developer. Mr. Rosen chose M & Company's "Askew" design with random, out-of-sequence numbers, from a watch featured in the Museum of Modern Art collection.

"It fit the building's image as being a little off-center," Mr. Shaoul said. "Subsequently, we've had terrible problems with it."

Winds took the clock out of commission several

times, until the solid faces were redesigned with a honey-comb web. The clock's two faces, south and west, can be seen from the Brooklyn Bridge, the World Trade Center, and Broadway, Mr. Shaoul said. Red Square's name "related to changes in Eastern Europe," Mr. Shaoul explained, and it suited a red, squarish building. (Mr. Rosen has described himself as a radical socialist turned real estate developer.)

The 18-foot Lenin statue, by Yuri Gerasimov, was originally a state-commissioned work, but the Soviet Union's implosion prevented it from going on public display. The statue was found by an associate of Mr. Shaoul's in the backyard of a dacha outside Moscow. The developers have made a postcard that reads "Greetings from Red Square"; it depicts Lenin with his right arm raised victoriously over the downtown skyline. Mr. Shaoul noted that Lenin faces Wall Street, capitalism's emblem, and the Lower East Side, "the home of the socialist movement."

Was Toynbee an Alien?

Q. *While crossing various streets in midtown Manhattan, I have often noticed a message stenciled near the crosswalk: "Toynbee Ideas in Kubrick Movie 2001: Resurrect Dead on Planet Jupiter." Where do these messages come from, and what do they mean?*

A. An informal poll of graffiti and stencil artists, urban folklorists, curators, academics, and boulevardiers has yet to uncover the author or artist. The cryptic messages started showing up in a number of Northeastern cities, including Washington, Baltimore, and Philadelphia, in the late 1980s, and have since been the source of no small amount of speculation and inquiry.

There is even a Web site on the subject. Each message appears in a stencil-like shoebox-sized patch made of a whitish adhesive material similar to the thick paint used for crosswalks, and the letters appear as black cutouts. More than twenty have been sighted in New York alone, most of them in the Forties and Fifties on Broadway and Fifth and Seventh Avenues. They crack and yellow with age and fragment with the pounding of traffic.

A few include colored borders and dark, paranoid ramblings about the news media, but the vast majority hew to the basic formula. A tentative decoding of the message is possible. Arnold J. Toynbee, the English historian (1889–1975), is best known as the author of the ambitious twelve-volume *A Study of History,* published between 1934 and 1954—a comparative examination of the development and decline of civilizations.

Scholars have written that Toynbee felt humanity was propelled toward a more perfect knowledge of God by the recurring development and breakdown of its civilizations. Stanley Kubrick's mind-bending 1968 film *2001: A Space Odyssey,* explores the episodic advancement of human civilization, leading to a rendezvous with a cosmic force that occurs on a mission to Jupiter. Toynbee, however, never said anything about Jupiter, and Kubrick's trippy film doesn't explore the idea of resurrection.

The Russ Daughters

Q. *I often pass an old-fashioned smoked fish emporium on East Houston Street called Russ & Daughters. Why did Mr.*

Russ take the unusual step of sharing top billing with his daughters?

A. It was business. Joel Russ, a Galician Jew from a village in what is now eastern Poland, began his career on the Lower East Side in 1911, peddling Polish mushrooms from a horse-drawn wagon. He established his "Cut-Rate Appetizing Store" on Orchard Street in 1914. But the gruff, hard-working Mr. Russ had little patience with his finicky customers, and business suffered until he put his three pretty, smiling young daughters, Ida, Anne, and Hattie, behind the counters. (He had no sons.)

Renamed Russ & Daughters, the store moved to its present location at 179 East Houston Street, between Orchard and Allen Streets, in the 1940s, according to Maria Federman, wife of Mark Russ Federman, present owner of the store and son of Joel Russ's daughter Anne. It still sells fresh Malossol caviar and fifty varieties of smoked and salted fish prepared on premises from recipes unchanged in this century: like lox, smoked

salmon (including sweet-smoked Gaspé), smoked white-fish and lake sturgeon, *matjes* herring, and the rather sweet chopped herring salad.

Ms. Federman said each of the three daughters met her husband while working at Russ & Daughters. Today a portrait of the Russ daughters, all now retired and living in Florida, still adorns a wall of the store, and hanging in the window are long necklaces of dried Polish mushrooms, the kind that Joel Russ sold on these same streets years ago.

Fire and Water

Q. *Between Sixty-sixth and Sixty-ninth Streets on the west side of Manhattan, twisted, blackened structures jut diagonally into the Hudson, apparently the remains of some long-ago conflagration. What burned, and when?*

A. Old railroad sheds, which were seared and re-shaped, spectacularly, by a tremendous unexplained fire on the piers on June 8, 1971, that sent flames shooting 30 feet into the air. The 400-foot-long piers were part of the 76-acre Penn Central Railroad yard that once went from Fifty-ninth Street to Seventy-second.

Years before the blaze, the two northern piers served as a freight link between Manhattan and New Jersey, according to Wilbur Woods, director of waterfront planning for the city's Planning Department. Freight cars traveled by rail into wooden sheds on the piers, Mr. Woods explained, then onto barges called float bridges, which crossed the Hudson. The piers were probably used until the 1950s, Mr. Woods said.

Mysterious Signs

Q. *I have noticed signs reading "Shaftway" in windows of old factory and commercial buildings in places like SoHo and the Garment District. What are the signs for?*

A. Shaftways are simply elevator or light shafts with windows, which are often found in old industrial buildings and lofts. The law requires that the signs be placed across the front of all such windows. Without them, a firefighter might see the smoke-filled window during a blaze and, unaware that there is no floor below, climb through and fall down the shaft. If they need to vent that window in a fire, firefighters simply smash the glass above the sign, leaving it intact as a warning to their fellows. Do firefighters actually look for the signs? Definitely, fire officials say.

Moondog's New Phase

Q. *What ever happened to Moondog, the blind, bearded eccentric who dressed as a Viking and played music on a midtown street corner?*

A. Though it strains credulity, at the age of eighty-one Moondog still has the beard, still spends much of his time writing and recording music, and is in many ways still . . . Moondog.

The son of an itinerant minister, Moondog was born Louis T. Hardin in Marysville, Kansas, in 1916. He was blinded in 1932, when a dynamite cap exploded in his hands, and began studying musical composition at the Iowa School for the Blind. Arriving in New York in 1943,

he studied music when he wasn't hanging around
Carnegie Hall listening to rehearsals.

By 1947, Mr. Hardin was a fixture at Sixth Avenue and
Fifty-fourth Street, near the entrance to the Warwick
Hotel. Dressed in a leather-and-fur Viking costume of his
own making, replete with helmet and spear, and calling
himself Moondog, he stayed there almost three decades.
He survived by selling sheet music and poetry on the
street and playing instruments of his own invention.

Moondog got attention, as street Vikings will, and his
skills as a composer did not go unnoticed. He recorded
his eclectic music for labels like Prestige
and Columbia. Charlie Parker and
Charles Mingus hailed him; Philip
Glass and Steve Reich cited him as an
influence. In 1974,
Moondog was
invited to tour
West Germany, and
he decided to stay.

Two years later he
met a young geology
student named Ilona
Goebel, who became
his assistant, publisher,
and companion. The
two live today in Oer-
Erkenschwick, in the
Ruhr Valley. In 1989, he
returned to New York to
perform a thirty-minute
suite of his works with

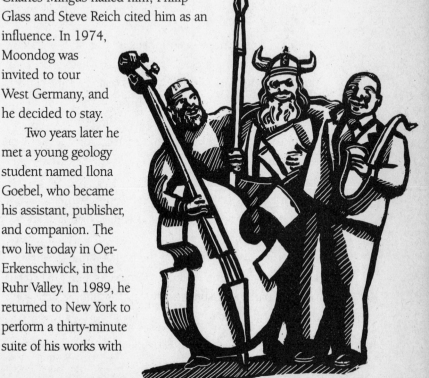

the Brooklyn Philharmonic Chamber Orchestra. A recording of his compositions for a big band was released in Europe in 1995, and many of his old recordings have been rereleased on CD. On the telephone recently, Moondog, or Mr. Hardin—whatever—was a polite, serene, and affable man.

"I miss New York," he said. "I still have a strong attachment to it." And what of his old Viking garb? "Ilona got rid of all that years ago," he said. "She even hid my spear."

Off the Rambling Path

Q. *I've heard about the Indian Cave in the Central Park Ramble, but I've never seen it, and I don't know anyone who has. Any ideas?*

A. You've never seen it because the cave—actually a naturally occurring rock cleft with a slab of stone set over the top by the park's builders—was sealed at both ends in the 1930s. It can still be found, hiding beneath a cliff south of the Bank Rock Bridge, according to Henry J. Stern, the parks commissioner. Created long after Indians left the area, the cave—also known as the Sea Cave—was a home only to tramps.

And it was never easy to find, even in winter. Frederick Law Olmsted and Calvert Vaux designed Central Park in the 1850s to offer an intriguing variety of pastoral experiences; the cave site is among the park's more secretive. Located north of the Lake, the Ramble is a tangled web of twisting paths that spin and swoop through 38 acres of dense woods, outcrops, hills, and lake coves, one of which conceals the Indian Cave.

Hollywood East

Q. *In front of the theater at 80 St. Marks Place in the East Village are squares of sidewalk that appear to bear hand-prints and autographs of old-time movie goddesses. They aren't real, are they?*

A. Many people have assumed that the old theater had indulged in playful fakery. But they're wrong. Howard Otway, owner of Theater 80, at 80 St. Marks Place, near First Avenue, gave a party on August 26, 1971, to celebrate the opening of a movie musical revival series at his two-hundred-seat theater. A former singer and stage actor, Mr. Otway invited friends from his salad days in the theater to drop by; they included Gloria Swanson, who acted as hostess.

Mr. Otway played the occasion to the hilt, recalled Florence Otway, his widow, who still owns the theater. As limos purred and klieg lights circled the sky, some of the stellar attendees pressed their hand- or shoe-prints into squares of wet concrete in front of the theater and scratched in their autographs with a chopstick. More of Mr. Otway's glamorous friends later dropped by to leave their prints.

By the end of that year, the sidewalk, though not exactly Grauman's Chinese, had the imprints of Gloria Swanson (shoes), Joan Crawford (both hands), Joan Blondell (shoes), Ruby Keeler (shoes), and Myrna Loy (right hand). The theater, which had been a speakeasy and a jazz club in previous lives, under Mr. Otway became the city's first year-round revival house, and showed Hollywood classics and foreign films until shortly after his death in 1994. Mrs.

Otway now rents the theater, which Mr. Otway designed and built himself, to the Pearl Theater Company.

Mystery Streets

Q. *On the No. 7 subway line, the stations at Thirty-third, Fortieth, Forty-sixth, Fifty-second, and Sixty-ninth Streets are also identified on maps and signs as Rawson, Lowery, and Bliss Streets and Lincoln and Fisk Avenues. Yet the streets are not to be found in these neighborhoods. What's going on?*

A. Queens—the borough that can't forget. The Flushing line of the IRT—or the Corona line, as it was initially known—was constructed between 1915 and 1917, when the streets of Queens were still known by the familiar names you mention. The five wards of Queens were consolidated into New York City in 1898, and despite its explosive growth after the opening of the Queensborough Bridge in 1909, the borough still clung to its identity as a constellation of distinct villages.

A new road system, with Queens Boulevard as the central artery, was built to accommodate increasing traffic, but a uniform code for naming and numbering streets met with local opposition. The old names were used until the 1920s, when the Queens Topographical Bureau finally employed a numerical system borrowed from Philadelphia to rename streets and renumber addresses. The old street names were retained on subway maps and platform signs—and called out by conductors—so passengers unaccustomed to the new designations would recognize their stops, says a spokesman for the Transit Authority, Termaine Garden.

Why keep using the old names? "We've retained the names pretty much for their historical significance," Mr. Garden said, a little tentatively. "It's one of those things no one really notices."

Flaw, or Modern Art?

Q. *Why is each pair of columns at the Fifth Avenue entrance to the Metropolitan Museum of Art crowned not with the sculpture that was obviously intended but with a pile of unfinished, uncarved stone blocks?*

A. This is one of those cases where an unintended condition takes on, over time, many of the felicitous qualities of something deliberate. As designed by the Beaux Arts–trained architect Richard Morris Hunt, the façade of the new east wing of the Metropolitan Museum was to be built of gleaming white marble, with an extensive program of inscriptions and thirty-one separate pieces of sculpture.

These were to culminate in four monumental figural groups, which the architect left unidentified, over the paired columns, according to Morrison Heckscher, curator of American decorative arts and building historian for the museum. The State Legislature approved only $1 million for the project in 1895, and after Hunt died suddenly in July of that year the project was turned over to his son, Richard Howland Hunt.

The east wing was completed under the direction of the younger Hunt in 1902, but severe financial constraints had by then forced the builders to substitute Indiana limestone for the white marble, and to leave much of the elder Hunt's extravagant sculptural scheme undone.

Since 1902, of course, the Metropolitan Museum has vastly expanded its collections, and the current square footage of the building suggests that more than enough capital is available for a few blocks of limestone to be sculpted at the main entrance. But Mr. Heckscher points out that the subject matter for the sculpture remains undetermined, and that after many years exposed to the elements, the blocks themselves are no longer in ready-to-carve condition. "I personally find it to be successful, almost as modern sculpture," he said. "There seems to be a tacit belief that this is a very attractive solution to modern eyes." Frankly, we agree.

From the Ex-Lax Files

Q. *There's a building on Atlantic Avenue in Brooklyn that has "Ex-Lax" above the door. Am I right to assume it was an Ex-Lax factory? What is it now?*

A. A factory it was. But the Ex-Lax building on Atlantic Avenue, between Bond and Nevins Streets in Boerum Hill, was converted to loft co-ops in 1979. Marsha Meyers, board president and a resident since the outset, says the stigma of living in one of those five units has mostly disappeared—within the neighborhood, that is. But elsewhere, she said, mention of the name-branded building draws "startled expressions."

Photos of the building from 1940 show a giant painted sign on the side touting Ex-Lax as "The Ideal Laxative." Ex-Lax has been manufactured since 1906 and was originally owned by many families, including that of State Senator Roy M. Goodman. Over the decades the product and factory were the property of various pharmaceutical companies. Many old-timers recall an odd piece of the factory's history: the monkeys kept atop the building used for product testing.

Bernard Wolfier, a retired employee of Culbro (the company that bought Ex-Lax in 1969) recalls: "My fondest recollections are that they had on the roof these monkeys, which were the vilest-tempered monkeys you've ever seen. Personally, I don't blame them." That glass-block roof structure that housed the primates is now part of loft 5-E.

Who's Waldo?

Q. *Just inside Central Park at Seventy-second Street and Fifth Avenue is a curved marble bench, dedicated to a Waldo Hutchins and inscribed "Alteri Vivas Oportet si Vis Tibi Vivere." What does this mean?*

A. The literal translation is, "One must live for another if he wishes to live for himself," according to Jonathan Kuhn, director of art and antiquities for the Department of Parks and Recreation. The bench is one of fifteen semicircular, or exedral, benches in city parks, and honors the efforts of Hutchins, a lawyer, Central Park founder, and Parks Department board member during the system's formative years in the last century, Mr. Kuhn said.

It was built of Concord white marble in 1932 for $15,000, with funds provided by Augustus S. Hutchins, his son. The bench, which was designed by Eric Gugler, the architect, is accompanied by a number of celestial timepieces. Three arcs inscribed in the semicircular area in front of the bench coincide with its shadow lines at ten A.M., noon, and two P.M. at the vernal and autumnal equinoxes. A small sundial, which sits at the back of the bench, was designed by Albert Stewart and includes a bronze female figure attributed to Paul Manship, sculptor of the *Prometheus* at Rockefeller Center, Mr. Kuhn said.

Another Latin inscription is on the sundial: *"Ne Diruatur Fuga Temporum,"* or "Let it not be destroyed by the passage of time."

Pan Am's Dead Letters

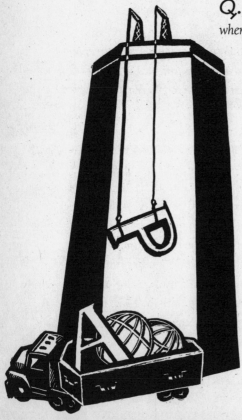

Q. *I recall that it was 1963 when the huge Pan Am letters were put atop what is now the Met Life building and that it was 1992 when they were taken down. But I never heard what happened to them after that.*

A. Most of the letters and the accompanying logos did not survive removal; exceptions are in warehouses. Pan American World Airways, a pioneer in international aviation, occupied fifteen floors of the fifty-eight-story building on Park Avenue just north of Grand Central Terminal, until it went bankrupt and left the building in 1991.

The letters, each about 15 feet tall, and the logos—25-foot-wide globes—had to be cut into sections and pulled up onto the roof by technicians from Universal Unlimited, who built and installed their replacements, the Met Life signs. Workers took pains to avoid a peregrine falcon's nest that remains on the south façade. Many letters were destroyed in the process; others were too corroded to salvage.

The Metropolitan Life Insurance Company, which has owned the building at 200 Park Avenue since 1981, donated the survivors—"P," "a," and the globe logos from the east and west façades—to the Pan Am Historical Foundation, an organization formed by former Pan Am employees. Jeff Kriendler, the director, said the foundation's goal was to create a museum filled with Pan Am archives and artifacts in Miami, where the airline was launched with a flight to Havana in 1927 and where a new, smaller Pan Am company now operates. Until a museum is built, the letters will sit in a New Jersey warehouse, while the two globes are stored in Miami.

Fair Times Preserved

Q. *At the 1939 and 1964 World's Fairs, the Westinghouse Electric Corporation buried two time capsules that were to be opened in five thousand years. Where are these capsules buried, and who maintains them?*

A. The capsules are buried at 40 degrees 44 minutes 34 seconds north latitude and 73 degrees 50 minutes 44 seconds west longitude, according to the copious *Book of Record,* published after the 1939 World's Fair and updated after the 1964 fair. But if you don't have a geographical survey map (or if you're unwilling to wait 4,943 years), you can find the site in a small grove of pine trees and bushes in Flushing Meadows–Corona Park, in front of the site where the Westinghouse Pavilion stood for both fairs.

The area is midway between the Unisphere and Meadow Lake, opposite the old New York State Pavilion. A small path from there leads to a round concrete marker, about the size of a tabletop, that indicates the spot where the two identical steel cylinders, each 7½ feet tall, sealed in pitch and encased in concrete, are entombed 50 feet underground. The 1939 capsule contains items like a slide rule, a woman's hat, and an alarm clock; the 1964 capsule includes birth control pills, bikinis, and contact lenses.

Harsh Reality

Q. *I've heard a tale of opulence: that an elevator descends deep beneath the Waldorf-Astoria Hotel and stops at a private train platform. Supposedly, the elevator and the train were used to transport President Franklin D. Roosevelt in and out of the hotel when he visited New York. Any truth to this?*

A. Yes, but the real story isn't all that plush. The elevator in question is a huge, electric, manually operated Otis freight elevator that opens onto Forty-ninth Street between Park and Lexington Avenues, just outside the door of the Waldorf-Astoria's parking garage. The elevator, which has a caged roof, is mammoth (over 20 feet long, almost 8 feet wide, and can carry up to 4 tons) and slow (about 50 feet per minute), according to Dan Brucker, a spokesman for Metro-North Commuter Railroad, which owns the elevator.

The elevator has been used by Metro-North machinists to transport tools and equipment from street level to the train yards and steam tunnels below since before the hotel was built over the tracks in 1931. Beneath the steel pillars that support the Waldorf, the elevator stops at a short, dimly lighted landing. It can accommodate up to three train cars switched over to that track from Grand Central Terminal, Mr. Brucker said.

So in reality, President Roosevelt, crippled by poliomyelitis, traveled in a Pullman car to the cavelike underground platform, then in a wheelchair to the dank, snail-slow freight elevator, up onto Forty-ninth Street, and through the Waldorf parking garage to get to the lobby of the hotel. Not exactly what you pictured, is it? Presidents no longer arrive this way, but to this day, the tracks, platform, and elevator are secured by the Secret Service during presidential visits to the hotel, Mr. Brucker said.

Urban Mini-tornadoes

Q. *I've noticed that those devilish little whirlwinds that pick up leaves or snow or paper and spin them in the air always seem to form in the same places. What are they?*

A. The answer is easier to illustrate than explain. First, think of the air as a fluid. "Go to any bridge and look at the water as it flows past a pier," said Ysrael Seinuk, a professor of architecture at Cooper Union. "When the water passes the pier a whirlpool is momentarily visible, then it disappears. This is essentially the same thing."

In terms of fluid dynamics (which includes the study of wind movements), these vortices, or eddies, are formed by the natural flow of a stream of air around the corner of a building at an intersection, according to Joel Hollenberg, a professor of mechanical engineering at Cooper Union who specializes in aerodynamics. When an air stream is channeled through a street, the air closest to the buildings is slowed by friction, while the air moves more quickly in the middle of the street, Mr. Hollenberg said. The divergent currents contribute to the creation of an eddy.

"The air doesn't turn the corner and follow the contour of the building. It starts to turn and often separates from the corner of the building. One can think of the flow as beginning to rotate there."

Depending on the shape of the corner, the velocity of the wind, and other factors, very small, very weak whirlwinds can form, he said. This is why umbrellas tend to turn inside out on street corners.

Mr. Hollenberg said it takes more than pencil and paper to calculate precisely why vorticular eddies spin off the wind on some corners and not others. "But certain corners on the Avenue of the Americas seem particularly susceptible to this. Wide avenues, narrow cross streets, tall buildings—you have a whole system there."

Legendary Treasure

Q. *Rumor has it that there's a treasure ship sunk near Hell Gate. Is there any truth in this?*

A. Hell Gate, the aptly named strait between Wards Island and the northwest corner of Queens, has claimed hundreds of ships over the years, including HMS *Hussar,* a twenty-six-gun British frigate that sank there in September 1780. The *Hussar* was bound for London with a cargo of eighty American prisoners and a payroll of gold when it struck a rock and sank.

The crew escaped, the story goes, while the prisoners drowned. But the *Hussar*'s legend lived on. In 1985, a salvage expert by the name of Barry L. Clifford claimed he'd found the wreckage using the same equipment used to eye the *Titanic,* according to the Blue Guide to New York. Reports had suggested that the golden cargo, lying a mere 80 feet under, might be worth some $550 million.

A year later, Clifford hired a diver to try to reap the fortune. Problem was, though the expedition did find seven other wrecks, none matched the *Hussar*'s eighteenth-century design. Some china was recovered (valued at considerably less than $550 million), but even that couldn't be linked definitively to the *Hussar*. The ship's exact position remains uncertain.

Three-Way Street

Q. *West Sixtieth Street seems to have a mind of its own. It runs west from Broadway to Columbus Avenue, both ways from Columbus to Amsterdam Avenue, and east from Amsterdam to West End Avenue. Why?*

A. On Sixtieth Street, it seems, all roads lead to Lincoln Center, which has remade the neighborhood in many other ways as well. Sixtieth Street is crucial for westbound traffic leaving the complex; hence the two-way flow between Columbus and Amsterdam Avenues, which run on either side of the superblock. The routing also eases access to the Fordham University campus on its own smaller superblock from Sixtieth to Sixty-second, just south of the arts complex. So you can thank the city's traffic planners the next time you try to escape a late night at the opera.

Minuit Waltz

Q. *At the northern tip of Manhattan, in Inwood Park, there is a monument indicating the spot where, in 1626, Peter Minuit bought Manhattan from the Shorakkopoch Indians. Imagine my surprise when I found a similar monument in Peter Minuit Plaza at the Battery claiming that the deal was brokered there. So which is it?*

A. Most experts, says the Blue Guide to New York, agree that the actual purchase of Manhattan took place nearer the Battery than the Bronx. In 1626, the only portions of Manhattan that had been significantly settled by the Dutch were in the Battery. The Inwood section was primarily a wilderness. The Inwood plaque, which was laid in 1954 by the Peter Minuit American Legion post, does hedge its bets, saying that the location is "legendarily" where Minuit sealed the deal.

But where the American Legion got the legend is a mystery, says Jonathan Kuhn, director of art and antiquities for the Department of Parks and Recreation. Walter Cubita, aged sixty-nine, one of the last remaining members of the post, seems just as baffled. "I don't know why the hell we put it up in Inwood," says Mr. Cubita, who was a twenty-four-old veteran at the time the plaque was laid.

Marriage Vowels

Q. *Why is Houston Street pronounced as it is? In other words, who put the "House" in Houston?*

A. The "ou" in "Houston" is pronounced like an "ow," rather than the "oo" sound of the Texas city, because that was likely the way William Houstoun pronounced his name. And the street was named in his honor, according to *The Street Book* by Henry Moscow.

Houstoun was a Georgian delegate to the Continental Congress of 1784 who secured his place on New York City maps by marrying the daughter of Nicholas Bayard III, who owned part of the land on which Houston Street is built. Sometime in the early 1800s, the spelling of the street was shortened. Houston, Texas, on the other hand, was named after Samuel Houston, who was the fiery president of the Republic of Texas and pronounced his name with the "oo" sound.

The name is derived from either a truncation of "Hugh's Town," an area outside Glasgow named after an early-seventeenth-century landlord, or from the Mac Uistean clan, another Scottish family, according to *A Dictionary of Surnames* (Oxford University Press, 1988), by Patrick Hanks and Flavia Hodges. According to Michael Agnes, editorial director of *Webster's New World Dictionary,* the discrepancy in pronunciation probably comes down to a familial preference. Mr. Agnes also said the "ow" sound of New York's street makes sense.

"Pronouncing 'h-o-u-s' as 'house' is perfectly logical," said Mr. Agnes. "I mean, the name Houseman is pronounced 'houseman.' "

Seward: Man and Myth

Q. *Someone told me that the bronze statue of William Seward in Madison Square Park is actually Abraham Lincoln's body with Seward's head on it. Any truth to that?*

A. According to *The Art Commission and the Municipal Art Society Guide to Manhattan's Outdoor Sculpture* (Prentice Hall, 1988), by Michele Cohen and Margot Gayle, the story is false. But you're not the only one to think it might be true. "It's a very frequently repeated rumor," according to Jonathan Kuhn, director of art and antiquities for the Parks Department, who oversaw a restoration of the statue.

But he sees why the rumor persists: William Henry Seward was shorter and heavier than Lincoln, and the sculpture doesn't quite represent him that way. Mr. Kuhn said that if the Seward in the sculpture stood up, "he would be rather lanky."

The root of the myth lies in the fact that the sculptor, Randolph Rodgers, completed the 1876 sculpture shortly after finishing a similarly posed statue of Lincoln in Philadelphia. Seward's and Lincoln's lives were intricately linked. Seward, a New York governor and U.S. senator, was, like Lincoln, a fervent abolitionist, and he served as Lincoln's secretary of state from 1861 to 1865. (He continued in that role until 1869. His most memorable act, the purchase of Alaska from Russia in 1867, was known as Seward's Folly at the time.)

Both men were the targets of Confederate assassination attempts on April 14, 1865. Unlike Lincoln, Seward survived.

Monument to Obstinacy

Q. *In front of the Village Cigars shop at the corner of Seventh Avenue and Christopher Street, there's a bewildering triangular mosaic in the sidewalk that reads "Property of the Hess Estate which has never been dedicated for public purpose." What is the story behind this tessellated tease?*

A. The mosaic is the result of a bitter dispute between the former owner of the property, the estate of David Hess, of Philadelphia, and the City of New York. This is the story, according to *Greenwich Village and How It Got That Way* (Crown, 1990), by Terry Miller.

The Voorhis, a five-story apartment building at that corner owned by the Hess estate, was condemned when the city built the IRT subway lines during the late 1910s. The city wanted the Hess estate to donate the rest of that property, a triangle measuring about 500 square inches,

for part of the sidewalk. The Hess estate obstinately refused and took legal action to keep the tiny plot, leaving
the smallest piece of private property in the city. And they
covered it with the headstrong message that you saw. The
Hess estate got out of the miniature business in 1938
when they sold the plot to the owners of Village Cigars for
$1,000. Or about $2 a square inch.

The Sky, Upside Down

Q. *I was told years ago at home in Australia that the
mural depicting the constellations on the ceiling of Grand Central Terminal is incorrect. Rumor is that it is reversed. I'm no
astronomer so I am turning to you to dispel or confirm this tale.*

A. The stars, which at the terminal's opening were
professed to be accurate enough to teach schoolchildren
the firmament, are in fact reversed, north to south, with
the exception of the Orion constellation. How they got
that way is the subject of considerable speculation, according to a 1994 report by Deborah Rau on the ceiling's history.

First off, the very existence of the stars, writes Rau,
was more a result of lack of cash than esthetic insight.
Original plans for the terminal, which opened at midnight
on February 2, 1913, called for a skylight to provide natural light for commuters. When money and time began to
run out, the suspended ceiling was completed sans skylight while designers scrambled for a plan to decorate it.
The architect Whitney Warren came upon the idea of stars
and enlisted the help of a French artist, Paul Helleu, to
design the constellations and accompanying lights to emu-

late a night sky, while the undercoat of paint was sky blue to represent the daytime sky.

The starscape was based on a sketch by a Columbia University astronomy professor, Harold Jacoby, and was supposed to be accurate right down to the gold-leaf equatorial line. Indeed, when the doors opened, visitors were amazed. It was only after an anonymous commuter noticed a month later that the stars were twisted around that theories began to fly. An embarrassed Dr. Jacoby accused the artist who painted the stars, your fellow Australian Charles Basing, of placing the diagram at his feet while painting, rather than looking through the thin paper sketch. Other rumors suggested that the reversed design was derived from a medieval design, in which the perspective was God's, opposite to man's.

The clearest, if most flippant, response may have come from Charles Gulbrandsen, who worked as an assistant on the original job and was employed to repaint the stars, again incorrectly, in 1944. "The ceiling is decoration, not a map," said Mr. Gulbrandsen at that time. "The constellations are north. They should be south. So what?"

East Side, West Side

Q. *There's a "compass" laid into a mezzanine floor at Grand Central, near the Lexington line at the Pershing Square exit. But unless my sense of direction has completely failed me, the "N" arrow is pointing due west. Is this just there to confuse the tourists?*

A. Don't worry, not only the tourists are confused. The problem is that for most practical purposes in New

York, uptown equals north and downtown equals south, so people get into the habit of thinking that uptown actually is north. But "north in Manhattan happens to be seventeen degrees off the Avenue towards the west," said Peter Samton, who designed the 36-foot mosaic back in 1988. The "N" of his compass, he confirmed, "is pointing to the magnetic north"—i.e., skewed toward New Jersey. Compounding the underground confusion, the Lexington Avenue platform (along with the mezzanine above and Mr. Samton's compass) is set diagonally to Manhattan's "east-west" grid by approximately 40 degrees.

"See?" Mr. Samton said. "Everything is slightly cocked in New York." So maybe it would be easier just to carry a real compass to figure out what direction you're going in.

Trauma of City Trees

Q. *Is it true that trees near tall glass buildings grow faster because of the reflection off the buildings? Why then are there not more tall trees in our fair city?*

A. It is true that tall glass buildings do produce more light, and indeed heat and light both make trees grow faster, but they also cause them to lose water faster. Trees find water scarce in urban areas because their roots are limited by concrete and asphalt, and since they depend on water for fortification, their growth is actually stunted, according to Nina Bassuk, the director of the Urban Horticulture Institute at Cornell University. Trees, like New Yorkers, are stressed out by an urban environment, and the ones planted in highly reflective spaces actually do poorly, she said. Unless, of course, they are irrigated, in which case they would probably grow faster.

The Legend of Tess

Q. *Five or six years ago, there was a mysterious outburst of handposted signs that read, "DJ NO X-MEN TESS." Recently, they have reappeared. What are they all about? My best theory is that the ex-members of Menudo, forced into retirement when they passed the age of fifteen, formed a group called the X-Men and hired a vocalist named Tess, and are protesting because disk jockeys won't play their album. True?*

A. A fabulous tale, though totally apocryphal. Calls to record industry know-it-alls proved they didn't—but finally one Damien Nesbitt, who answered the phone at the New Music Seminar, said that DJ is the street name of a founder of the X-Men, a group of graffiti writers. Mr. Nesbitt, who is a graffiti guy himself, speculates that Tess is another partner, and said that he doesn't know why they have come back on the scene. Their heyday was in the 1980s, when they were spraying down subway cars. Mr. Nesbitt said the point is strictly artistic: the signs have no real message (just like those ubiquitous "COST REV" posters).

A Bronx Tale

Q. *Chiseled in stone on one side of P.S. 36 in the Castle Hill section of the Bronx is "Avenue D"; on the other side it says "Eighth Street." Was the building moved from Manhattan?*

A. No, though Manhattan does have a role in the story behind the mysterious inscription. The Bronx was

annexed to New York City before the modern City of New
York was consolidated in 1898. So even prior to consolida-
tion, letters to people in, say, Morrisania were addressed to
"New York, N.Y.," explained Lloyd Ultan, the historian at
the Bronx County Historical Society. The postal system,
however, could not tolerate duplication of street and avenue names within one postal district, so one of the two
areas—Manhattan or the Bronx—had to come up with
new names for its streets.

Guess which one saw a flurry of street sign changes?
What is now Zerega Avenue in the Union Port–Castle
Hill section of the Bronx used to be Avenue A. Have-
meyer Avenue was Avenue B. Castle Hill Avenue was
Avenue C, and so forth through Avenue E. First through
Fourteenth Streets in the Bronx also underwent name
changes: Eighth Street became Blackrock Avenue; Fourteenth Street became Newbold Avenue; First
Street became Turnbull Avenue. The rechris-
tenings honored landowners from the
area's olden days.

When the Music Stops

Q. As I'm walking along the north
side of Fourteenth Street just east of
First Avenue, and on parts of
Houston Street, the tape in my
Walkman comes to a dead
halt, and I hear buzzing in my
earphones. What is this, and
more important, what does it do
to my body?

A. What you are probably experiencing are electro-magnetic fields, the combination of electric and magnetic fields from sources like power substations. In fact, there is a Consolidated Edison generating station near the first location you mentioned, though a spokesman there said it was impossible to tell for sure if that is what is playing games with your tunes. As far as the possible health risks go: "There is a great deal of debate as to how much risk these pose to the public," said Richard Stapleton, a spokesman for the Federal Environmental Protection Agency. "It has been a question as to what level and how much."

It Comes Naturally

Q. *I live in Japan and publish a dictionary of New York lingo for Japanese visitors. Here is my question: What is the origin of the Bronx cheer?*

A. Like the nebulous origin of fruit streets in Brook-lyn, the genesis of the Bronx cheer seems to exist only in popular myth, perpetuated by those who love it, like Lloyd Ultan of the Bronx County Historical Society. As the story goes, Professor Ultan said, sometime in the early part of this century, in a vaudeville theater in the Hub section of the Bronx, there was a vaudeville act so abhorrently bad the audience booed it off the stage with this sound: *pfffffft*. A critic reportedly later described the audience reaction in a review: "The act was so bad, they gave it the Bronx cheer."

Giving Them the Hook

Q. *Did the practice of giving an unpopular stage performer "the hook" begin at the Apollo Theatre's famous amateur night?*

A. Actually, "the hook" first appeared at Miner's Bowery Theatre, where in the 1890s amateur night was held every other Friday.

Vaudeville was born on the Bowery and Miner's added a popular twist by offering a dollar to anyone willing to take the stage and perform, regardless of talent or ability, according to Luc Sante, whose book *Low Life* (Farrar, Straus & Geroux, 1991) includes a history of the early New York stage. Audience reaction became part of the spectacle, Mr. Sante said, and the less talented jugglers, blackface comedians, and newsboy quartets who took the stage endured a salvo of jeers, whistles, and catcalls.

To get the more excruciating acts off the stage as quickly as possible, an inspired stage manager apparently lashed a stage-prop shepherd's crook to a pole and started yanking the most scorned performers bodily from the stage in midperformance. The audience responded lustily, Mr. Sante said, and "Give 'im the hook" became a favorite taunt.

Vaudeville was already in decline when the Apollo was built at 253 West 125th Street in 1913. In 1935, Ralph Cooper introduced the Apollo's amateur night, which showcased some of the best—and worst—black entertainers of the era.

The best included Ella Fitzgerald and Sarah Vaughan, said Billy D. Mitchell, the Apollo's unofficial historian. The worst "got the hook" from "Porto Rico," a clownish figure in a bonnet who was actually Norman Miller, a stagehand. Several others later functioned as the "executioner," including the tap dancer Howard (Sandman) Sims, who fired a cap gun and chased the hapless from the stage.

Amateur night is still held every Wednesday at the Apollo, without a hook.

Three Choices, No Chance

Q. *How come they say you can never win at three-card monte? It seems that even if you guessed blindly, you'd still have a one-in-three chance of getting the right card. But of course that's naïve, right?*

A. Right. Because the three-card monte dealers cheat. What the dealer does is palm the card you are following with a quick sleight of hand. Thus he or she always wins, you always lose. (So much for the expression "Cheaters never prosper.") Another reason not to play, according to the Times Square Business Improvement District, which has tacked up warning signs around the area: Dealers are professionals who work discreetly in groups to either pick your pocket while you play or mug you after you leave, if by some fluke you should win.

Say Cheesecake

Q. *I've heard that the recipe for cheesecake, that classic New York dessert, came here from Italy. A friend insists that it* *was "invented" here at the turn of the century. Care to get mixed up in this?*

A. You're both at least partly correct. New York cheesecake, the kind made famous in this century in restaurants like Reuben's, Lindy's, and Junior's, is considered by some to be a dense, sweet, creamy adaptation of traditional Italian cakes made with curd or cottage cheese. Recipes for coarser, less sweet ricotta cakes like the Tuscan *crostata diricotta* and the Neapolitan *pastiera* have been around for centuries, according to Matt Sartwell, a resident scholar at the Kitchen Arts and Letters store in Manhattan.

In fact, the writings of Cato the Elder, the Roman statesman and moralist of the second century B.C., include a recipe for *savillum,* a relatively simple honeyed ricotta cheesecake. But it wasn't until about 1872 that cheesecake baking as we know it in New York became practical and popular, according to *Cheesecake Madness* (Biscuit Books, 1996), by John J. Segreto. That was when William Lawrence of Chester, New York, accidentally developed a method of producing cream cheese while trying to duplicate the French Neufchâtel. Soon after, a dairyman living in South Edmeston, New York, produced a particularly silky version for the Empire Cheese Company, which was later sold under the brand name Philadelphia Cream Cheese.

"The New York–style cheesecake that we know depended on the development of this cheese," Mr. Sartwell said. He added that the graham cracker crust, another American innovation, would have been impossible before the cracker was introduced early in this century.

Myths Shown the Door

Q. *We're debating "twenty-three skiddoo." Does it relate to the Flatiron Building at Twenty-third Street, or to the 1920s? Winner buys dinner.*

A. Go dutch. "Twenty-three skiddoo" was "certainly commonly associated with the era of the flapper," says Leonard Zwilling, an editor at the *Dictionary of American Regional English.* He said the phrase was then used mostly as an expression of delight but is best remembered now as a term of dismissal.

Though *The WPA Guide to New York City* says the slang is "supposed" to have originated at the windy intersection near the Flatiron Building where policemen used the phrase to chase off loafers waiting for lifted skirts, Mr. Zwilling calls that "specious." Both "twenty-three" and "skiddoo" were spread to New York from the West Coast via the newspapers, specifically their syndicated comics.

The term "twenty-three" (nix on that) appeared in 1902 in *The New York Evening Journal* and "skiddoo" (make tracks) in 1904 in *The San Francisco Bulletin.* S. J. Perelman and others attributed the combination of those words to Tad Dorgan, a Hearst cartoonist who was also the supposed father of "Yes, We Have No Bananas." But after Mr. Dorgan's death in 1929, a *New York Times* reader postulated in a letter that "twenty-three" as a dismissal goes back to Dicken's *A Tale of Two Cities.* (Sydney Carton was the twenty-third prisoner beheaded on the guillotine.) And "skiddoo," the reader said, was "added as an interpretation of the numerical expression, for the benefit of those to whom 'twenty-three' alone had no meaning."

The Anatomy of a Plaza

Q. *Everyone I know seems to have his own idea about the origin of the plaza at Lincoln Center. One friend says it is obviously a copy of the main square at Siena. Another says it is a copy of St. Mark's Square in Venice and, moreover, that it was the result of a collaboration of the three architects who designed the buildings facing the plaza. Now I have come across a book on Philip Johnson in which he says, "I did the plaza," and that the design was taken from Michelangelo's Capitoline Hill in Rome. Can you clear this up?*

A. More than likely, the collaborative theory holds true, said Judith Johnson, director of information resources at Lincoln Center. "No one architect can claim credit for designing the plaza," said Ms. Johnson, adding that one credit can be definitively assigned: Philip Johnson (no relation to Ms. Johnson) is responsible for the fountain.

As for the design of Lincoln Center Plaza as a whole, it almost certainly came out of meetings in late 1958 and early 1959, when all six architects charged with building pieces of the center—Mr. Johnson, Wallace K. Harrison, Max Abramovitz, Gordon Bunshaft, Eero Saarinen, and Pietro Belluschi—consulted on the layout and the open spaces. Debate ranged from height and number of structures to whether to make the center open to the street or walled off. The plaza's design, Ms. Johnson suspects, was a melding of their ideas.

But was there any direct influence? There is a clue that may declare a winner in your squabble. In photographs taken of the planning sessions, one photograph is seen tacked to the wall. Its subject? St. Mark's Square.

India *India?*

Q. I've been noticing that manhole covers say "Made in India." So is that India as in *India?* How is it that we're going all the way to India for manhole covers?

A. Because they're cheap!

Ian Michaels, a spokesman for the Department of Environmental Protection who had received calls from many New Yorkers wondering the same thing, said that the answer is simply economics.

"The Department of General Services puts out contracts for purchasing manhole covers to our specifications," he said, "and the company that had the lowest bid produces them in India. I'm not even sure there's a company in New York that makes them." He said the department has also purchased manhole covers—which run between $50 and $75 each—that were made in China. "We just look for the best value for the taxpayers," he added.

Mr. Michaels thought you might be interested in another bit of manhole-cover trivia: why they are round. "Square manhole covers could be lifted up, turned on their sides, and dropped down the shaft," he said. "As long as they're round, you can't do that."

3 The Natural City

The High Point

Q. *What is the highest point in the Manhattan landscape?*

A. It is Linden Terrace in Fort Tryon Park, built on the precipice above the Hudson at the northern tip of the island, said a Parks Department spokeswoman, Maia Miller. The terrace is 268 feet above sea level.

An outpost of Fort Washington to the south, the fort there fell on November 16, 1776, to Hessian mercenaries fighting for the British, who then renamed it for William Tryon, the last British governor of New York (1771–1778). John D. Rockefeller Jr. bought the land in 1909 and had it landscaped by Frederick Law Olmsted Jr., the son of Central Park's designer, before donating the 66 acres to the city in 1930.

A few blocks south is Manhattan's highest natural elevation—265 feet—in Bennett Park, between 183rd and 185th Streets and Fort Washington and Pinehurst Avenues.

Is Nature a Fake?

Q. *I heard that the entire topography of Central Park— the hills, the promontories, everything—is man-made. This shocked me. Is it true? Everything seems so natural.*

A. Actually, that's only partly true, and anyway, Frederick Law Olmsted's design has had a lot of time to mature. The land—craggy, overgrown, and squalid—was bought by the city in 1856, and after an extensive competition for the design commission, construction began in 1858. The Blue Guide to New York, a respected reference book on the city, says the park was pretty much created from scratch, with the exception of the northern part, which was left with its little-bit-wild look.

The southern regions (roughly below the Great Lawn at Eighty-fourth Street) were completely landscaped. Rocky glacial ridges were blasted out to create softer meadows, and rough hills were covered with tons of topsoil to improve the view and support vegetation. Marshy areas were drained to create glens. Four to five million trees were planted, sometimes on top of the garbage mounds that once dominated the area.

The Innermost City

Q. *Where is the exact geographical center of the five boroughs?*

A. If only it were that simple, says Klaus Jacob, a researcher at the Lamont-Doherty Earth Observatory in Palisades, New York. The problem is that you can find a couple of "centroids" (or centers, in lay terms), depending on whether you are considering just the city's land portions or its land and water boundaries.

But Frank Vardy, a demographer with the Department of City Planning, says the official answer, probably based on land boundaries alone, is that the city's heart beats loudest in Bedford-Stuyvesant, Brooklyn, on a block bounded by Malcolm X Boulevard and Lafayette, Greene, and Stuyvesant Avenues. That puts the center smack dab in the middle of the playground of P.S. 26.

The Biggest One of All

Q. *Which is the biggest park in the city? Central? Van Cortlandt? Prospect?*

A. Would you believe Jamaica Bay?

While Central Park (840 acres) is bigger than Prospect Park (526 acres), and Van Cortlandt (1,146 acres) is bigger than either, the real green monster is the Jamaica Bay National Recreation Area, with some 9,151 acres of territory, according to the *New York City Handbook*. (Well, make that the blue-green monster: the measurement includes the area's marshes, inlets, and coves.) The largest city park is the Bronx's Pelham Bay Park, with over 2,100 acres.

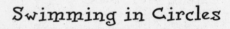

Swimming in Circles

Q. *Do people actually swim in the waters off Manhattan? I heard this and cannot believe it. Why would they do that? Isn't the water disgusting? Isn't it illegal?*

A. Last things first. It is not illegal to swim in Manhattan's waters, according to spokesmen at the Police Department and the Coast Guard, but it is no walk in the park: the Coast Guard says that swimmers venturing far from shore should obtain a permit and be accompanied by a boat to prevent interference with boat traffic.

Now, as far as water quality is concerned, urban swimmers in the Hudson, East, or Harlem Rivers might be safer than those taking a dip in a country pond, at least according to a man named Morty Berger.

"Water quality is not the issue," said Mr. Berger, who is the executive director of the Manhattan Marathon Swimming Foundation. That is the group that sponsors not just any swim, but a yearly race that goes all the way around the island, with the start (and finish) at the Battery.

"We've had swimmers get out and tell us that the water's better than Indiana, better than Australia," Mr. Berger said. However, race participants are urged to get two shots: a tetanus shot, to ward off infection from potential cuts from flotsam or jetsam, and a gamma globulin shot, to keep hepatitis at bay.

After a big rain, overloaded city drainpipes may carry some garbage into the water, Mr. Berger said, but generally the tidal pull on the rivers keeps them relatively clean.

It is the tidal action, which creates strong, shifting currents, that is the greatest danger, Mr. Berger said, not disease—though there is also the occasional oblivious boater.

Black Water

Q. *There's something odd about the water in the pond at the Central Park Zoo. The water is a strange, inky black that shimmers in an otherworldly fashion. Any explanation?*

A. Yes. A granular dyeing compound called nigrosine is added to the water. The harmless jet-black dye provides a natural shading that inhibits photosynthesis, preventing the pond from becoming choked with algae and vegetation, said Alison Power, a spokeswoman for the zoo, formally known as the Central Park Wildlife Center. The powder has been added to the pond sporadically since it opened in 1988, and does not otherwise affect the three black-necked swans and ten Japanese snow monkeys that swim in the water, she said.

By obscuring the concrete bottom of the shallow artificial pond, which is about 110 feet long and only 5 feet deep, the mirrorlike surface helps sustain the illusion of a more truly natural setting. It also discourages visitors from tossing in coins, Ms. Power said, because they can't watch them descend to the bottom.

She added that black-water ponds do occur in nature, in swamps and glacial kettle ponds where water cannot circulate and vegetation at the bottom turns black from decay.

Fill It Up

Q. *How much of Manhattan is built on landfill . . . and what, exactly, is it?*

A. About 14 percent, or about 2,027 acres, said Ann L. Buttenweiser, a professor at the Columbia University School of Architecture and Urban Planning. Landfill, she added, is just about anything: "It's debris."

Since the Dutch started filling Manhattan swamps in the seventeenth century, garbage, rubble from demolished buildings, ash, sand from dredgings, and earth from excavations have been used as fill, she said.

Until the Civil War, landfill was used primarily to expand the lower Manhattan port. Later, it was used under highways and parks. Randalls Island and Wards Island were connected by landfill from coal ashes; cheap fill from subway excavations extended Riverside Park into the Hudson River at the turn of the century. Landfill, Ms. Buttenweiser said, accounts for about one third of Manhattan south of Fourteenth Street and much of the island's shoreline.

Not all landfill is local. During World War II, when landfill materials were scarce, ships arriving from Bristol, England, to pick up goods in New York carried broken masonry in their holds as ballast, said Owen D. Gutfreund, a Columbia University historian. This rubble—blasted brick from buildings destroyed by the Luftwaffe—was used as fill for the construction of the Franklin D. Roosevelt Drive in the vicinity of Thirtieth Street.

The Local Climates

Q. *I've noticed that local television news broadcasts give weather readings from each of the five boroughs. I haven't paid much attention, but is the weather really that different across the city?*

A. The weather can, in fact, vary greatly from borough to borough. For instance, the most intense thunderstorms in the area tend to concentrate over Lower New York Bay and Jamaica Bay, said John Davitt, a staff meteorologist at New York 1 News, the all-news cable channel. Thus, he said, the southern sections of Brooklyn and

Queens, like Bensonhurst, Flatbush, Canarsie, and Howard Beach, are always hardest hit by rainfall.

"They get much more rain than midtown and the Bronx," he said, "as much as two inches in some storms." The same areas also tend to be foggier, he said.

Which borough is the coldest? "In the daytime it's Brooklyn, because they've got a real sea breeze coming in," Mr. Davitt said. "But in Staten Island and the Bronx, the overnight temperature tends to drop down well below the others."

The warmest, according to Mr. Davitt? "For some reason, Queens, by about five degrees."

The windiest? "Manhattan has the highest gusts," he said, "but in terms of steady wind I'd have to say Brooklyn."

The snowiest? "That would be a tie between the Bronx and central and northern Queens," Mr. Davitt said. "Snowstorms in areas nearer the water will turn over to rain or mix with sleet sometimes four or five hours before other areas further from the water, which cuts down a lot on their accumulated snowfall."

Getting to the Source

Q. *I was startled to hear from a friend in Queens that her water comes from a well. I thought all city water came from the upstate reservoir system. Are wells still in use?*

A. Yes. Some communities—St. Albans, Hollis, and Rosedale in Queens, among others—get the major portion of their water from wells.

The last remaining area of the city served by a system of freshwater wells is the southeastern section of Queens,

where water for more than five hundred thousand residents originates below ground. Starting in 1887, the area was served by the Jamaica Water Supply Company. The privately owned concern was bought by the city, which continues to operate sixty-nine of its wells, said Cathy DelliCarpini, a spokeswoman for the New York City Department of Environmental Protection.

"There are several hundred private wells in use for business, industrial, or commercial purposes," Ms. DelliCarpini added. "The vast majority of these are in Brooklyn or Queens." She pointed out that the bedrock beneath Manhattan makes it more difficult to reach water.

Water from the wells has a higher mineral content and a lower pH (meaning that it is slightly more acidic) than reservoir water, said Bob Swartz, a former project director for Jamaica Water Supply. Although some have detected a "metallic" taste in the water, Mr. Swartz said, he finds it tastes much the same as the reservoir variety.

The Central Park Lake

Q. *Is the Central Park lake, where you can row boats, a naturally occurring pond, or do they have to maintain the water level?*

A. Like almost every other landscape component of that great chunk of nature, the Lake is man-made. And since there's no natural spring to feed it, it relies heavily on "storm water" (meaning rain or snow) to maintain its capacity, says Bradley Tusk, a Parks Department spokesman. A heavy winter, a drought, or even a mere thunderstorm can quickly affect the water's level.

To keep the level stable, the Parks Department turns to a complex irrigation system that lurks underneath the park's surface. (The system, which feeds the park's water fountains, swimming pool, ice-skating rinks, ponds, and reservoir, is tied into the regular city water supply.)

When heavy rains swell the lake, partly submerging the boat dock, the department opens a sluice gate and a valve near the boathouse to drain some water off. (That water is pumped to the Newtown Creek Waste Water Treatment Plant in Brooklyn and discharged into Newtown Creek, says David Golub, Department of Environmental Protection spokesman.)

The department can pump water into the lake through the same pipes if the water level drops, or if the oxygen level of the water falls, as happens during dry summer months, when the water evaporates rapidly. That's to protect the lake's population of bass, carp, perch, and pumpkinseed fish, as well as recently added turtles.

Lids for Landfills

Q. *Is there a limit on the amount of garbage that will fit in the city's landfills, and when is this limit likely to be reached?*

A. Though it's not an official city tourist attraction, the world's largest garbage dump at 2,200 acres, Fresh Kills on Staten Island, turned fifty on April 16, 1998.

"From an engineering standpoint, it has about another fifteen years of life left in it," Lucian Chalfen, a spokesman for the Department of Sanitation, said of the city's only active landfill. But in 1996 Governor George E. Pataki signed legislation ordering it to close by December 31, 2001.

Approximately 10,300 tons of residential and institutional waste are produced in the city each day. (That is down from 16,000 tons before the city began recycling in 1993.) Of that, the 1,500 tons that Staten Island generates daily are shipped by truck to the landfill; the remainder, from Manhattan, Brooklyn, and Queens, is transported by barge. Commercial trash and trash from the Bronx are trucked out of the city.

And what happens when Fresh Kills is shut? "There is no answer," Mr. Chalfen said. Two options: transporting garbage out of state or incineration.

Nests for Squirrels

Q. *In Union Square Park, there are these strange little boxes in some of the trees that don't appear to be there for the birds. What are these boxes, where did they come from, and who put them there?*

A. The boxes are the result of one man's lasting love for that furry little nut-eater, the squirrel.

Alfonso Santos, a sixty-year-old retired handyman who lives on West Nineteenth Street, has been coming to feed the squirrels in Union Square since he arrived in the United States from Cuba thirty years ago. In 1985, he came upon the idea of building a shelter for pregnant squirrels in need of, in Mr. Santos's mind, a good place to bring up a brood.

So he put together eight boxes from scrap wood, bored squirrelways in them, stuffed the habitats with shredded newspaper and other creature comforts, and mounted them in the forks of trees around the park. The squirrels, used to the hardships of urban living, took to the shelters immediately.

For months, everything seemed rosy. But one August morning Mr. Santos discovered the shelters had been dismantled and taken away by an unknown rodent-hater, leaving the squirrels homeless, their only possessions stuffed in their cheeks.

Aghast, Mr. Santos wrote to once and future parks commissioner Henry J. Stern and pleaded his case. Mr. Stern re-calls their meeting. He said he recognized Mr. Santos as a "friend to all species" and accepted his offer to reconstruct and mount his squirrel nurseries.

"I guarantee it makes the Union Square squirrels the best-housed squirrels in the city," said Mr. Stern.

Ten years later, Mr. Santos is still the super for the Union Square Squirrel Homes, which he visits twice a day, every day, with his wife, Jacqueline.

"I no have a baby," said Mr. Santos. "This is my family."

The River That Isn't

Q. *I've been told that the East River is not really a river. Could this be true?*

A. It is true. A river, you see, is a stream of fresh water that empties into another body of water. The East River is basically an arm of the sea.

Captain James De Simone of the SUNY Maritime College described the East River as "a tidal estuary, fed by the Atlantic through Long Island Sound and by the Atlantic through New York Harbor."

In further proof that it is not a river, Captain De Simone said, the East River's current changes directions: when the tide is going out, it flows south, and when it's coming in, it flows northeast. Incoming tides also bring in water from Long Island Sound, creating treacherous whirlpools.

"Le Gran Bwa"

Q. *I'm told that at the southeastern edge of Prospect Park, along the pond, there are tree trunks carved into interesting sculptures, and that religious ceremonies are celebrated there. What's this all about?*

A. You have about half of a very interesting story. Five years ago, a Flatbush artist and community leader named Deemps Bazile stormed into the park's administrative offices demanding to be compensated for carving tools that had been stolen while he was in the park carving up tree stumps, without official permission.

After some consultation with the New York State Council for the Arts and the Brooklyn Arts Council, it was decided that what Mr. Bazile was doing was Haitian folk art, and he became an artist in residence, working on tree stumps near Prospect Lake. There are three pieces there now, the largest and most visible one of which is *Le Gran Bwa*. They depict symbols significant in African religion, like faces of animals and various facial features of people, said Barbara Caldwell, the park's director of cultural programs.

The site has different uses to different people. Mr. Bazile teaches neighborhood children about Haitian culture there; Haitian drummers play there frequently in the summer; others gather to meditate and pray.

The site is not officially sanctioned as an altar, Ms. Caldwell stressed, adding that any number of religious observances take place in the park, from Buddhists throwing goldfish in the pond ("We suggest that this is not a good thing to do," she said) to Muslims celebrating a-Id (ah-EED), the end of Ramadan.

"A lot of people," she said, "use the park as a place of central convergence."

Man on a Horse

Q. *On Fifty-ninth Street by Central Park is a statue of a golden man on a horse. Who is he and what is he pointing at?*

A. The statue is of General William Tecumseh Sherman with Victory, dedicated on May 30, 1903.

In fact, he isn't pointing, Victory is. But the way it was designed by the sculptor, Augustus Saint-Gaudens, their motions are meant to look as one, according to *The Art Commission and the Municipal Art Society Guide to Manhattan's Outdoor Sculpture,* by Michele Cohen and Margot Gayle.

The statue had lost its golden sheen over the years, but around 1990 the Victorian Society in America spiffed it up. As for whom or what Victory is pointing at, Abbey Lavine, a reference assistant at the New-York Historical Society, said, "Well, at whatever Victory would be pointing at."

The Truth about Pine Barrens

Q. *A friend of mine maintains that there is a small pine barrens in the city, in southwest Staten Island, near the Outer-bridge Crossing. Is this true?*

A. Sort of, but the tiny 80-acre patch might be better called a sandy oak barrens. A pine barrens is defined by its sandy, acidic soil and an abundance of pitch pine trees, which vastly outnumber hardwoods. The pitch pines of a pine barrens require the heat of periodic fires to open their cones, reseed their habitat, and maintain primacy over competing vegetation.

Unlike the pine barrens of New Jersey and Long Island, the barrens in Clay Pit Ponds State Park Preserve have dry soil that supports mostly post, scrub, and blackjack oaks, though scattered small pitch pines are also evident, according to Edward Johnson, science curator at the Staten Island Institute of Arts and Sciences. Blackjack oaks are otherwise rare in New York State, he said.

Besides the Fowler's toads, black racer snakes, and box turtles typical of the Clay Pit Ponds area, the barrens also provide a habitat for the northern fence lizard, otherwise found only in the New Jersey pine barrens and in Southern states, Mr. Johnson said.

The lizards, about five inches long, with dark, wavy bands, flourish in the abundant undergrowth of sheep laurel, catbrier, and blueberries. They were introduced to the sandy oak barrens area in the 1940s by the Staten Island Zoo.

Health Nut?

Q. *Do any plants that grow in the city lend themselves to medicinal uses?*

A. New York woods, fields, and parks abound in grasses, wildflowers, and woody trees and shrubs known or believed to have medicinal properties, said Thomas

Ching, director of horticulture for the Department of Parks and Recreation. Among the most common, he said, are tufted grasses like the bluestems, which grow along marshes and waterways, and were made into tea and used by American Indians for stomachaches.

In the late summer and fall, the roots of common wildflowers like chicory, New England aster, and milkweed can be used to make teas to treat fevers and diarrhea, Mr. Ching said. The flowers and fruits (or hips) of beach roses can be collected to make teas that are thought to ease rheumatic pain and dysentery. The twigs of the dogwood tree can be used as a quinine substitute and can be chewed to clean the teeth. Extracts from the barks of redbud, Eastern hemlock, and witch hazel can be used as astringents, Mr. Ching added.

American yew shrubs and willow trees, found in city parks, are used, or once were, to produce commercially available medicines, Mr. Ching said. Taxol, derived from yew bark, is used in cancer treatments. Salicylic acid, from willow bark, is the precursor to aspirin.

Dr. Seth D. Feltheimer, a general internist at Columbia-Presbyterian Medical Center, said modern doctors were well aware that many plants have "good, legitimate medical properties," but warned that when using brews and teas, it is difficult to control dosage intensities. "You may be delivering a therapeutic medication in a subtherapeutic dosage."

Turtle Power

Q. *A friend insists he saw a turtle the size of a manhole cover lumbering out of Newtown Creek, but I don't believe such a large reptile could inhabit those fetid industrial waters. Who is right?*

A. Your friend. The murky depths of the creeks, ponds, rivers, and marshes of all five boroughs teem with giant snapping turtles (*Chelydra serpentina serpentina*), which somehow flourish, largely unseen, in brackish and even polluted city waters, according to Bill Holmstrom, a herpetologist at the Wildlife Conservation Center of the Bronx Zoo. The turtles, which spend almost their entire lives underwater, are to be found in the salty tidal marshes of Jamaica Bay, the freshwater lakes of Central and Prospect Parks, in the Hudson, East, and Bronx Rivers, and yes, even the dank channels of Newtown Creek.

The turtles have yellowish or gray skin (sometimes covered with algae); pale underbellies; sharp claws; long, serrated tails; and hooked beaks. Feeding on dead fish, small animals, and aquatic vegetation, a mature New York snapper can grow to weigh 35 to 40 pounds and measure 20 inches down the length of its dark brown shell. Though the turtles are not aggressive, "they have strong crushing power in their jaws," Mr. Holmstrom said.

Though vulnerable while young, snapping turtles often live for fifty or sixty years. But females must leave the water once a year to dig a nest, seeking sandy loam or soil in which to lay their clutch of twenty to forty eggs, each about the size and shape of a Ping-Pong ball. During this perilous three- or four-week period in late May or early June, many are crushed by cars while crossing the roads that today fragment their watery habitat.

For a Small Turtle Soup?

Q. *Recently I have seen numerous street vendors selling small live turtles. The turtles are green and have shells perhaps two inches in diameter. Where are they coming from? What are they for? Are they safe? Are they legal?*

A. Those are baby red-eared sliders, raised in bulk in the southern United States and sent to port cities for export, only to be diverted for street sales, say local turtle experts. They're basically being sold as pets for children—a tradition long honored in America.

"Those of us who are my age—that's about midcentury—and whose parents took us to the circus, remember, if we were lucky enough, bringing home a little cardboard box with one of those turtles inside," Steve Matthews, a health department spokesman, said in 1994. And there's the rub. Children are the most likely to be presented with the little guys, and they are, as Mr. Matthews noted, the least likely to "observe hand-washing protocols." The danger is salmonella: turtles can carry the bacteria, and because the southern turtle farms often use chicken offal as feed, the baby red-eared sliders are teeming with them. So, finally: No, they are not legal to sell.

A federal restriction bans the sale of the turtles until they reach 4 inches long, explained Barbara Daddario, the public education chairwoman for the New York Turtle and Tortoise Society, but not because salmonella bacteria are not present in adults. "Health officials figured that a turtle above that would be less appealing to a child," she said, "and wouldn't fit in a child's mouth." They do make nice pets, she said, but a person needs to be prepared for a serious commitment: they grow to about 10 inches long and have a forty-year lifespan.

Seals Show Approval

Q. *Though I've read that harbor seals reappeared along the city's shoreline, I've yet to spot one. What's the best time of year to look?*

A. Wait until winter. Harbor seals head north when the water gets warm. "We get numerous sightings every winter and early spring," said Paul Sieswerda, a curator at the Aquarium for Wildlife Conservation at Coney Island. "As they become accustomed to humans, we are starting to see more and more of them drift south every year."

After a long absence, harbor seals began to appear again in the last decade and are the only marine mammal to visit the city's coastline regularly. The grayish-brown seals, which can grow up to 6 feet long and weigh 300 pounds, spend almost all their time in the water, Mr. Sieswerda said, but they can be spotted on the sandy, more secluded beaches of Brooklyn and Queens when they lie in the sun. Harbor seals swim into the city's rivers in pursuit of fish from time to time and some have even been seen sunning themselves on rocks in the East River.

Roots

Q. *Why are there so many weeping willows growing in the East Village?*

A. Because of a sequence of events in the early 1970s, according to Phil Tietz, associate director of the Green Guerrillas, a nonprofit gardening group. When vacant lots began to appear in their neighborhood in the early 1970s, East Village residents began to plant gardens. They sought advice and supplies at the Houston Street garden where the Green Guerrillas formed in 1973 (the garden is now named after the founder, Liz Christy).

Most of the weeping willows were planted then, from the leftover nursery stock donated to the group each fall, Mr. Tietz said. Some East Village streets have three or four gardens to a block, many with a stately *Salix babylonica* or *Salix tomentosa*.

Mr. Tietz has a couple of theories as to why the mournful willows, which have a tremendous thirst for water, thrive in tenement gardens built atop vacant lots. "Beneath the garden topsoil," he explained, "the loose sand and masonry rubble that fill the basement level of a demolished building could allow a great deal of moisture to collect lower down in the soil—almost like an aquifer—and a willow's roots could easily tap below that loose rubble."

Or, since the Lower East Side was originally built on landfill over streams and wetlands, the willows could be tapping into water sources buried long ago. "There's a lot of water in the ground in some of these neighborhoods," Mr. Tietz said.

Snakes and the Big Apple

Q. *I read that the Dutch called the Mount Morris Park area of Harlem Snake Hill because it had so many rattlesnakes. Are there still rattlesnakes in the city?*

A. "There are currently no venomous snakes in New York City," said the parks commissioner, Henry J. Stern. Rattlesnakes haven't been seen in New York City since the turn of the century, when the Bronx's plentiful population dwindled into extinction, he said.

"Certainly the habitat was suitable," said William Holmstrom, a herpetologist at the Bronx Zoo. "Human encroachment, urban development, and outright killing account for their absence." He added that rattlesnakes, though rare, still inhabit the Palisades of New Jersey.

About 98 percent of the snakes in the city today are harmless Eastern garters, which can be found in almost any park. They have yellow stripes going the length of their bodies, tend to be olive or tan, and can grow to over 2 feet long.

New York snakes are usually found in the larger parks. The city is also home to Eastern ribbons, Eastern hognoses, and northern brown, or DeKay, snakes. Black racers, common until the 1950s, are now rare. Northern water snakes—which bite but carry no venom—also live in the area, especially in High Rock Park on Staten Island, where they are often seen sunning, Commissioner Stern said. Some species are more metropolitan than others.

"DeKay snakes are typically found in empty lots, trash piles, even building foundations or basements," Mr. Holmstrom said. "They are a small, secretive snake."

But There's a Catch

Q. *What kinds of fish are most common now in New York Harbor, and are they safe to eat?*

A. The city's waters are home to an abundant fish population, and you don't need a license to catch them. Among the local species are summer flounder (fluke), winter flounder, bluefish, striped bass, and porgy, along with blue crabs.

But if you're hankering for a fish fry, it might be best to try a seafood restaurant. Bill Hewitt, a spokesman for the State Department of Environmental Conservation, warns that there are plenty of hazardous chemicals— PCBs, dioxins, mercury—lurking out there to turn even the most innocuous-looking guppy into a health hazard.

To educate fishermen about these dangers, the department issues regular advisories and began the Fish Advisory Compliance Project, which travels to libraries and housing projects to get the word out. Of New York's indigenous seafoods, bluefish, striped bass, and blue crabs are potentially dangerous consumed in large quantities.

Otherwise, follow these guidelines: If you are under fifteen or are a woman of childbearing age, it's best to abstain from eating these seafoods. After that, the toxin levels depend on exactly where in the New York area they are caught, and how they are cooked. So, when in doubt, you can check out your local fishing advisory by calling the State Department of Health. You can also limit exposure to contaminants by choosing smaller fish, which are generally younger. Or better yet, follow the DEC's guidelines for "catch and release"—swallow your pride and throw back your prize.

Pigeons, but Not Fools

Q. *Whenever I am in Times Square, I see pigeons swooping back and forth, seldom alighting and seemingly never going anywhere. What are they doing? Are they feeding? Practicing up for migration? Stretching their legs? Or just confused?*

A. According to Irene Brown, retired coordinator of Project Pigeon Watch and self-declared Pigeon Lady of Ithaca, New York, pigeons fly around in circles for the same reason many of us run around a track: exercise.

Both the city pigeon and its simpler country cousins fly to keep their flight muscles in shape in case they need to escape threats. Country pigeons are often the target of predatory birds, like hawks and eagles.

Likewise, city pigeons have to escape mechanized foes like buses and taxis. Pigeons are a communal species, and fly in flocks, which explains why groups sitting on a ledge all suddenly leap into the air. They fly in circles for the same reason pigeons have been used as carriers of mail, messages, and anything else they can lift. Equipped with very accurate eyes and ears, pigeons have an uncanny instinct for finding their way home to their roost.

"Humans have long exploited pigeons' natural habit of coming home," said Ms. Brown, adding that pigeons have recently been used in London for transporting blood samples above traffic. While pigeons may circle for hours, they will almost always return to where they began the day.

This instinct is repeated on a small scale when they lift off to avoid danger or to exercise in the air above Times Square. "Pigeons are, altogether, much too successful a species," she said. "Their problem is that they like to get together and brag about it."

Shy Fliers

Q. *I've heard that several species of bat make their home in New York. Why have I never spotted one?*

A. Though bats are not often seen or heard here, the city is home to several species, most of them very small and dark in color. Like all bats, they are nocturnal.

"The best time to see them is at dusk, when they can be seen in silhouette against the little bit of blue left in the sky," according to Patrick Thomas, the curator of mammals at the Bronx Zoo. "Bats tend to fly up high in the sky, so there is very little to draw your attention to them. But they are all around."

He added, "They are gentle, shy creatures that don't want to have anything to do with people."

Little brown and big brown bats are by far the most common species in New York, Mr. Thomas said, though the more solitary red, silver-haired, and hoary bats are also seen. Some species live in the woods, among the trees, while others, like the big brown bat, can be found in attics, storm sewers, and, of course, belfries. All prefer quiet areas. All these bats are insectivores, some consuming as many as six hundred bugs an hour, Mr. Thomas said.

"Anywhere insects gather, you tend to find bats," he said. "A good place to look is near small ponds or lakes, where mosquitoes gather, or in a clear area at the edge of a woods. They can even be seen in well-lit parking lots, where bugs fly beneath the artificial lights."

Whither the Bugs?

Q. *What accounts for the relatively small population of airborne insects in New York City (one of the great, unsung pleasures of living here)?*

A. For insects to reproduce, said Louis Sorkin, an entomologist at the American Museum of Natural History, "you need the proper conditions." Many of those are in short supply here. For instance: quick-moving streams for horsefly larvae and flowers for mosquitoes to dig pollen out of (yes, pollen—blood is only for the females, and they only need it for egg-laying). In addition, the plethora of lights in the city may function almost like insect crack, igniting an irresistible desire that drags the varmints away from their life-cycle responsibilities, Mr. Sorkin said.

Bringing Up Pigeons

Q. *It seems to me I never see baby pigeons in New York. How could this be?*

A. Marc Matsil, the director of the Natural Resources group at the Department of Parks and Recreation, explained that baby pigeons tend to stay in the nest and are usually spotted only by people who live in buildings with perennial pigeon problems.

Because the pigeons grow quickly on hearty diets of scavenged peanuts and leftover Chinese food, they look just like their parents within a year. And the baby birds are not without predators.

Mr. Matsil said that New York City has the largest breeding population of urban peregrine falcons in the country. These endangered birds, which rest on top of Riverside Church, the Met Life Building, and other buildings, and on bridges, sometimes swoop down to prey on the baby pigeons.

No More Duck Intrigue

Q. *I am reading* The Catcher in the Rye, *which poses an intriguing question that no one really answers: Where do the ducks in Central Park go during the winter, or does someone take care of them there?*

A. About fifteen types of waterfowl pass through Central Park during the year. Most migrate south, but many Canada geese and mallards stay all year, fending for themselves or relying on the kindness of strangers.

Urban Inbreeding?

Q. *Is it not true that when animals are confined to a small area, such as a block-long city park, they will inbreed and mutate their future offspring? Why then are New York City squirrels not inbred and odd-looking?*

A. Though you may not see New York City squirrels zipping across town to visit other sites, in fact city parks are not closed systems, said Dr. Dan Wharton, curator of animal management at the Wildlife Conservation Society in the Bronx.

"There are a lot of risks but there is migration, both human assisted and not," he said. "The Bronx River, for example, serves as a gateway to other wildlife coming in and out of the Bronx."

There is still plenty of inbreeding, of course, but the result is not a two-headed, one-pawed animal. "Inbreeding does not cause mutation," Dr. Wharton said. "It only increases the possibility that recessive genes will express themselves in things like decreased fertility and survivability, and someone like a park visitor would not normally notice this."

4 Cityscape

Tall, Taller, Tallest

Q. *How many buildings in New York City were at one time or another the tallest in the world? What are they, and which ones still stand?*

A. The title of "world's tallest building" began to bounce around in the 1880s with the development of skyscraper technology.

Until then, the tallest buildings in the world were generally churches, according to *The Sky-scraper* (Knopf, 1981), by Paul Goldberger of *The New York Times*. In New York, the tallest structure was the 284-foot-tall Trinity Church, built in 1846.

All that changed when architects, inspired by the tall designs of trendsetters like Louis Sullivan in Chicago, started imagining buildings that soared higher than church spires. By the 1920s, most major American cities had remarkably tall buildings, like the 708-foot-tall Terminal Tower in Cleveland and the 500-foot-tall Smith Tower in Seattle. (Other countries followed suit. The current biggies include the Central Plaza, in Hong Kong, which is 1,028 feet tall, and the Land-mark Tower, in Yokohama, Japan, which is 971 feet tall.)

But New York buildings led the way. Perhaps the first office building recognized as the world's tallest was the 1892 Pulitzer Building, a 309-foot structure on Park Row. (It was demolished in the mid-1960s.) In 1899, the thirty-three-story, 386-foot Park Row Building, at 19 Park Row, surpassed it, and this record stood until 1908, when the forty-seven-floor Singer Tower, at Broadway and Liberty, took over. (It was demolished in 1967 amid widespread protest.)

A year after the Singer, the fifty-story, 700-foot Metropolitan Life Building opened on Madison Square. Next came the 1913 Woolworth Building, all 792 feet of it, at 233 Broadway.

The greatest battle for tallest was fought in 1929: 40 Wall Street (927 feet) lost out to the Chrysler Building (1,046 feet) when a 175-foot spire, built secretly, was hoisted on top of the Chrysler after 40 Wall was too far along to be changed. It became a Pyrrhic victory, however, when the Empire State Building (1,250 feet) opened in 1931. And the Empire State held the record until the World Trade Center opened in 1973 (1,368 feet times two towers). Call it Sullivan's redemption, but a year later the Sears Tower in Chicago, at 1,454 feet, became the world's tallest building and maintained that status until the Petronas Towers were built in Kuala Lumpur, Malaysia, in 1996, surpassing it by roughly 30 feet.

The "God Box"

Q. *What is the story of the imposing nineteen-story building on Riverside Drive between 119th and 120th Streets, named the Interchurch Center but popularly called "the God box"?*

A. Built to provide offices for Protestant and Orthodox religious organizations and nonprofit agencies, the
Interchurch Center was intended to be a national symbol
of Christian unity when it was dedicated in 1960. Among
the largest tenants are the United Methodist Church and
the National Council of Churches, according to Mary
McNamara, president and executive director of the nonprofit center; others include the Presbyterian Church, the
American Baptist Churches, and the World Council of
Churches.

Designed by two firms—Voorhees, Walker, Smith,
Smith & Haines and Collens, Willis & Beckonert—and
built on land provided by John D. Rockefeller Jr., the center includes over 500,000 feet of office space, a library,
two art galleries, a chapel, and underground parking.

About eighteen hundred people work there, Ms.
McNamara said. Housed in a more graceful building, the

Interchurch Center would probably have a different nickname, but "the God box" seems to fit these quarters.

Occupying the full block between Riverside Drive and Claremont Avenue, the building is a squat cube, sheathed in grayish-white Alabama limestone and pierced by row upon row of 1,289 identical 4-by-6-foot windows. Described as "Stalinist" by one critic and "clumsily articulated" by another, the center looks like the box that a more beautiful building might arrive in.

The center was never particularly popular with conservative and evangelical churches, and several denominations moved out in the 1980s. Today, one third of the office space is rented by Columbia University or by nonprofit or social service agencies, including Alcoholics Anonymous and the American Guild of Organists.

Seeing Double

Q. *Aside from the drama they provide as an architectural backdrop to the park, is there a reason why so many apartment buildings on Central Park West have twin towers?*

A. The buildings in question were built nearly seventy years ago, when block-long sites along the park were ripe for development and a new housing law allowed construction of striking, skyscraper-height apartment houses.

Before 1929, housing laws had allowed apartment construction only up to a height proportional to the width of the street, according to Andrew S. Dolkart, an architectural historian at Columbia University. The Multiple Dwelling Law, passed that year, permitted taller buildings on large plots of land if setback rules to allow enough light into the apartments were followed.

"It essentially did away with height limitations," Mr. Dolkart said. "If you had a large enough plot of land, you could build towers."

The first of the new buildings to seize the opportunity was the classically detailed San Remo, designed by Emery Roth and built between Seventy-fourth and Seventy-fifth Streets in 1930. It was followed the same year by the sleek, thirty-story Majestic, between Seventy-first and Seventy-second Streets, designed by Irwin Chanin with Jacques Delamarre.

The twenty-eight-story Eldorado, by Margon & Holder with Emery Roth, was built in 1931, between Ninetieth and Ninety-first Streets, and the thirty-story Century, between Sixty-second and Sixty-third Streets, was designed by Chanin and Delamarre, and built in 1931 and 1932. Each featured a number of shallow setbacks and a pair of towers, and they stand like a row of chess pieces over the avenue.

"A single tower would have been much bulkier, which meant you had a lot of space that was really far from the windows," Mr. Dolkart said. "You could get more apartments—with beautiful views—by dividing the building into two separate towers. On Central Park West, with an entire block, there was enough space in between towers to meet the light requirements. And of course, the builders and the designers were not unaware that these would create striking silhouettes."

Not for the Birds

Q. *I've noticed that the top of the Empire State Building, usually brilliantly illuminated, is occasionally left dark on foggy nights. Why?*

A. The colored lights that usually illuminate the Empire State's top thirty stories are turned off on foggy nights during the spring and fall so birds will not fly into the building, said Lydia A. Ruth, a spokeswoman for the building.

Surprisingly, it's not the soaring height of the building that makes it hazardous to migrating birds, but the gaudy illumination—the 255,000 watts poured into 1,326 lights that bathe the spire in a variety of colors from the 72nd to the 102nd floor.

When skies over the city are foggy or rainy, migrating birds are forced to navigate at a much lower altitude, said Norman Stotz of the New York chapter of the National Audubon Society, and for reasons not fully understood, many become disoriented by bright light and rush toward it.

Many birds smash into the buildings and perish; others fly around the light source until they fall from exhaustion. Most of the birds—including various warblers, vireos, blackbirds, tanagers, grosbeaks, flycatchers, and orioles—are already tired and vulnerable by the time they reach the city.

Lights that shine upward into the sky—like the Empire State's—are the most perilous, Mr. Stotz said. He added that thousands of birds pass by the building every day during peak migratory periods in April and May, and from August to October. Ms. Ruth said the lights during these periods might be darkened several times a month.

Wind Breaker

Q. *I've heard that the Citicorp building at Fifty-third Street and Lexington Avenue has some sort of giant concrete block on the roof to keep it from swaying too much in strong winds. How does it work?*

A. By sitting still. When the building sways in one direction, the 400-ton block of reinforced concrete doesn't. All very tall buildings sway in high winds. But the 914-foot Citicorp Center, completed in 1978, was the first to employ a "tuned mass damper" to minimize this sway, said a Citicorp spokesman, John M. Morris.

The idea was to place a large mass atop the building, allow it to remain stationary while the building moves, and to convey this tendency to remain still, or inertia, to the swaying building through connections to the structure. The damper, which measures 30 feet by 30 feet by 8½ feet, is housed with the mechanical equipment in the building's angled crown, and is connected to the building's walls by a system of pistons and spring mounts, Mr. Morris said.

But the damper itself is free to slide on a thin layer of oil. About eighty days a year, when gusts are strong enough to sway the building, sensors feed the wind speed and direction into a computer that controls the pistons. The damper floats on the oil, essentially remaining still as the building moves under it. The mechanism then pulls the building back toward its original position. Then the pistons move the damper in the direction opposite the sway, further stabilizing the building.

The damping effect reduces the sway about 40 percent, Mr. Morris said. The mechanism is "tuned" so the time required for the mass to complete its movement is the same as that required for the building to go through a complete swing. The mechanical engineers for Citicorp Center were Joseph R. Loring & Associates, and the structural engineers were LeMessurier Associates / SCI and James Ruderman. Mr. Morris said he knew of no other tuned mass dampers operating in New York City.

An Old Old Folks' Home

Q. *At 320 Washington Avenue in Fort Greene, Brooklyn, there's a boarded-up building with a plaque inscribed "Graham Home for Old Ladies." Can you tell me anything about the place, and its oh-so-blunt name?*

A. If you think that name is notable, wait till you hear the building's other monikers. The institution was founded in 1851 as the Brooklyn Society for the Relief of Respectable, Aged, Indigent Females. The name was changed in 1899 to the more insouciant Graham Home for Old Ladies, according to documents furnished by the Brooklyn Historical Society and the Brooklyn Public Library.

The home was built on land donated by John B. Graham, a paint manufacturer, who also contributed to the $22,000 cost of the imposing neo-Georgian brick building, which housed ninety women over the age of sixty from Brooklyn. They paid a $60 admission fee. By 1958, the fee was $2,000. A brochure that year described a tenor of life that had endured for a century: "Here every week . . . meets the Thimble Bee. So violently do the machines whirl, the needles ply, it is a problem to keep them in work."

When the Graham Home closed, the hulking building became a cheap hotel for prostitutes, and by 1985 the building was one of the most notorious welfare hotels in the city. Up to twenty-seven families were temporarily housed in such Gothic squalor that newspaper articles were written about it. Bob Herbert, the *New York Times* columnist who was then with the New York *Daily News*, described the former home as an "ancient, soot-black, five-story building that sits back from the avenue and looks dismal enough to have been designed by Edgar Allan Poe."

No Sign of Fallout

Q. *I see old black-and-yellow "Fallout Shelter" signs on buildings all over the city, but I've never heard of a functioning shelter. Why are all those signs still up?*

A. "The signs were just left up," said Bradford Billet, deputy director of the Mayor's Office of Emergency Management; he added that there are no longer records of where the signs were or how many are left.

Records from the mid-1960s show that more than thirteen thousand New York City buildings were designated fallout shelters and identified with the distinctive—and decidedly ominous—black-and-yellow signs. Some even bore numbers at the bottom indicating capacity. Shelters were located in concrete basements

and supplied by the Federal Government with dehydrated food, medicine, water, and other survival aids.

The shelters were decommissioned in the early 1970s, when the strategy of underground protection from radioactive particles after a nuclear attack was deemed unrealistic, Mr. Billet said. The signs, once posted in metropolitan areas throughout the country, turn up in junk stores and flea markets from time to time. In SoHo they sell for as much as $45.

Wright's Work

Q. *Besides the Solomon R. Guggenheim Museum, are there any Frank Lloyd Wright buildings in the city?*

A. The architect who once sniffed that "New York has reproduced much and produced nothing" felt nonetheless inclined to leave his imprint here. The Guggenheim's spiral is familiar to many who have never set foot in New York, but Wright's two other creations are much less celebrated.

The city's only Frank Lloyd Wright residence—the prefabricated 1959 William Cass house, or "Crimson Beech"—is on Manor Court on Staten Island's Lighthouse Hill. And how many urbanites know the Mercedes-Benz Manhattan showroom at 430 Park Avenue, at Fifty-sixth Street, as a Wright design? "Oh, we get quite a few people coming in off the street," says John McCormick, a sales consultant. "Usually they're artists and museumgoers who recognize the style."

The white-stucco and glass showroom was built in 1953 for Max Hoffman, a car importer and distributor, who also lived in a Wright house in Rye, New York. Restored in 1981 by Wright's firm of Taliesin Associated Architects, the showroom is equipped with some nifty features: a revolving floor (now slate gray instead of its original salmon color), and a mirrored version of the Mercedes-Benz logo built into its ceiling.

Sullivan's Skyscraper

Q. *I recently heard that the great American architect Louis Sullivan designed only one building in New York. True?*

A. Yep. And Sullivan, who was considered the founder of the Chicago School of architecture and responsible for many of that city's finer buildings, left his only mark on the city in a rather unusual spot: tucked away on the less-traveled segment of eastern Bleecker Street.

Sullivan, who helped create skyscraper design (a hallmark of early Chicago architecture), designed the Bayard-Condict Building, which was built at 65 Bleecker Street at Crosby Street in 1898. Standing twelve stories tall (yes, that was a skyscraper at the time), the building was considered a radical departure from the more ornate New York style, according to the *AIA Guide to New York City*. It sports a white terra-cotta fronting and is crowned by a sextet of angels supporting the cornice. (According to legend, the first owner, Silas Alden Condict, insisted that Sullivan include the angels in his design, despite the architect's protests.)

Sullivan never built another building in New York City; the exact reasons are unclear. According to *Architecture, Ambition, and Americans* (Harper & Brothers, 1947), by Wayne Andrews, rivalry and territorialism were rife between New York and Chicago architects and may have discouraged Sullivan, whom Frank Lloyd Wright referred to as his *"lieber Meister."* And he may have chafed at complications in constructing the Bayard-Condict that were caused by New York's conservative building codes, says the Blue Guide to New York.

Or, suggests Carl Condit, an architectural historian, the building may simply have been overlooked. "Who would expect," Mr. Condit says in the *AIA Guide,* "an esthetic experience on Bleecker Street?"

Rooftop Tanks

Q. *Why are wooden water tanks on top of so many New York buildings?*

A. It's a question of the pressure of urban life, or actually of the lack thereof.

Back in the 1880s, when buildings started growing higher than the city water pressure could reach, architects started pumping water to storage tanks on the roofs.

"Most every building over six stories has

them," says Thomas Ronayne, director of operations for Rosenwach Tank Company, who describes the tanks as really nothing more than a fixed reservoir from which the water—both drinking and fire supply—can flow downward.

Like barrels, they're constructed from either yellow cedar or redwood and girdled with steel hoops, and can last up to forty years with annual cleaning and lubrication. Many newer buildings retain their boxy silhouettes by concealing the tanks behind the façade or inside the superstructure.

But we're nearing the millennium, you say. Why not something more high-tech?

"Wood doesn't affect the taste of the water," Mr. Ronayne says, "and it has terrific insulating properties." And if the inner and outer lids are properly sealed—which, in the vast majority of cases, they are—the water is perfectly potable. Still, horror stories abound of things found where they ought not be—including dead pigeons and, once, a human corpse. Mr. Ronayne says with a groan, "You don't want to read about what we've found in there."

Tanks a Lot, Pop

Q. *As someone new to the city, I would like to know what the story is with these funky wooden water towers on top of so many buildings. Are any of them still used for anything or are they just relics?*

A. They're not relics. Just ask Wallace Rosenwach, who thinks they work all too well. His family's business, Rosenwach Tank Company, has been making wooden water tanks since 1896. And, he says, if his father and his father's father hadn't been quite such good craftsmen, he'd have more orders for replacement towers.

"They last too long," said Mr. Rosenwach. "This is not an item you throw out."

He says that most of the wooden tanks that you see on rooftops are operational, even though many date back to the 1920s or 1930s, the heyday of wooden tanks. Improvements in standard pump technology have made it possible to force water directly from the water mains into homes and apartment buildings with six floors or less. But for many moderate-sized buildings, it's still more efficient to use the tanks, which are filled by smaller pumps and then use gravity to provide water pressure. Wooden tanks are light and resilient, and require little care beyond the yearly cleaning mandated by the Department of Health.

The Rosenwach business is the last company in New York to manufacture wooden tanks. "Sometimes I think my father should have gotten into those Bic pens," lamented Mr. Rosenwach.

Literary Lighthouse

Q. *Is there really a Little Red Lighthouse at the foot of the George Washington Bridge as in the children's book, and can you go inside?*

A. The proud little tower that has lit up the imaginations of readers of Hildegard Hoyt Swift's *The Little Red Lighthouse and the Great Gray Bridge* is indeed in the bridge's shadow. On a clear day, it can be spied from sections of Riverside Drive and the Henry Hudson Parkway, and from some New Jersey towns atop the Palisades.

The only lighthouse on Manhattan, it stands on Jeffrey's Hook, a tiny precipice extending into the Hudson in Fort Washington Park, near 181st Street, where it was moved in 1921 after its previous life as the North Beacon at Sandy Hook, New Jersey, from 1880 to 1917. In 1947, the Coast Guard decided that the bridge itself was beacon enough and decommissioned the tower. It was put up for sale in 1951, but lovers of the 1942 book protested, and it ended up with the Parks Department, sorely in need of an overhaul.

Since the lighthouse's restoration in 1986, the Urban Park Rangers have held a yearly festival during which the 40-foot cast-iron tower is open to the public.

Red-Light District

Q. *Why do some tall buildings like the World Trade Center in Manhattan have what appear to be red aviation collision-avoidance lights on top and others do not? Is there any practical advantage to the lights?*

A. In theory, the Federal Aviation Administration must perform an aeronautical structure analysis on any building 200 feet or higher in the New York City area, according to Arlene Salac, the public affairs officer for the agency's Eastern region office in Jamaica, Queens. But for Manhattan, where a great many buildings are taller, potential airspace obstructions are designated this way: If a building is within 500 feet of a taller structure that has appropriate markings to warn an aircraft of its presence, it does not need to be marked.

That's why the Empire State Building and the World Trade Center have those red lights, and why the surrounding—and somewhat shorter—buildings may not. Pilots, by the way, must keep at least 1,000 feet above any tall building, and at least 2,000 feet to the side.

By Any Other Name

Q. *I heard that there was once a second Empire State Building. Is this true?*

A. Not only was there, there still is. Moreover, it predates the tall, famous one by some thirty years. The original Empire State Building is a nine-story structure at 640 Broadway (at Bleecker Street), built in 1897. Its name was derived from the tenant of the previous building at the site, the Empire State Bank, according to Christopher Grey, the real estate columnist for *The New York Times.*

When the 102-story Empire State Building opened in 1930, the one at 640 Broadway began to be known by its address alone. Today, the building's original name inscription is covered by a green sheet-metal piece reading "640." It is home to a hot-dog shop and residential lofts.

A Very Private Club

Q. *There's a building on Hanover Square, in the Financial District, with the words "India House" carved into its side. It seems ancient. What is it? An old consulate?*

A. The India House dates back to 1851, when it was built as a bank and then housed the New York Cotton Exchange. At that point, the area was still recovering from

the Great Fire of 1835, which destroyed all of what is now Hanover Square, according to the *AIA Guide to New York City*. Today, it is home to an eighty-one-year-old club, the India House, so called because many of the club's first members traded goods with the Far East. The club is private. Very private. A manager who refused to give his name would only say that it is "primarily a lunch club"—and no, the club has "no gym."

Tower Among the Trees

Q. *Driving along the Major Deegan Expressway, just before the George Washington Bridge, I can see a tower in the distance high among the trees. It has a strange pointed dome. What is it?*

A. The imposing structure is the Highbridge Tower, a watertower that as part of the Old Croton Aqueduct system used to help provide the city with its water. The system, which opened in 1842, brought water from a reservoir near Croton, New York, some 33 miles north of the city, via large iron pipes.

The 195-foot tower, topped by a 48-foot copper

minaret, was built at 174th Street on the
eastern bluffs above the city in 1872, according to documents from the Department
of Parks and Recreation. It contained a
47,000-gallon tank which, when filled,
guaranteed constant water pressure for
the burgeoning metropolis below. It
was in use until 1965 and from
1957 on contained a carillon
that chimed daily over the
local din.

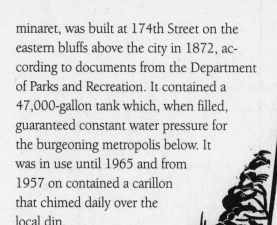

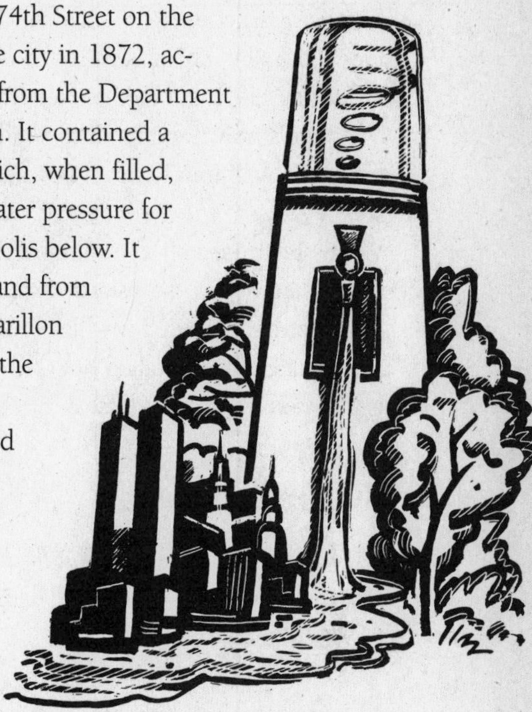

In 1984, a deranged
arsonist set the tower's
belfry on fire and
jumped to his death.
The tower under-
went a $900,000
restoration in
1988, including a
new copper belfry and weather vane. Plans to open the
top floors of the tower as an observation point for visitors
were never realized.

MONY Talks Weather

Q. *I was told that the odd blinking pole on top of the
MONY building in the West Fifties had some weather-related
function. Is this true?*

A. The star-topped pole atop the MONY building,
at 1740 Broadway (Fifty-sixth Street), is indeed more than
just decoration. Called the Weatherstar, it indicates the

weather prediction, said Charles Wasilewski, a spokesman for MONY, a financial services company, formerly known as Mutual Life Insurance of New York.

Here's how it works: If the lights are traveling upward, look for a warming trend; if down, it should be cooler; if steady . . . you get the idea. Put up in the 1950s, the Weatherstar used to feature more elaborate predictions with different colors to signal different weather conditions. That feature, however, was discontinued in 1988 when the digital clock was installed below the pole. The Weatherstar is updated every six hours.

30 Flrs, No Vu

Q. *If you look carefully at the skyline of lower Manhattan, you'll see a tall, windowless building. What is it, and why no view?*

A. The building, at 33 Thomas Street, is part of AT&T's giant Worldwide Intelligent Network, which is responsible for directing an average of 175 million phone calls a day, said Virginia Gold, a company spokeswoman.

The building, which is thirty stories tall, is filled with computers that switch and guide the electronic pulses of the human voice through the millions of miles of wiring that make up the nation's phone system.

"It's like the human body, and this is the nervous system," Ms. Gold said. "Its job is to respond to pressures and try to avoid congestion."

And like the nervous system, the building is a little sensitive to potential threats. The lack of windows at 33 Thomas Street staves off two of them. One is solar infiltration, a fancy way of saying that if the sun's rays are allowed to enter, they could make the interior too hot and cause this nervous system to burn out. Not having windows makes it easier to maintain a stable temperature, Ms. Gold said.

The second reason is protection from nature's wrath (i.e., hurricanes) or even more sinister forces, Ms. Gold said. She explained that a security advantage of a windowless building is that it is less vulnerable to terrorism or accidents.

The building at 33 Thomas Street is only one of more than one hundred switching points around the country. Nor is it the only such building in New York. Though Ms. Gold said "we don't like to get too specific for security reasons," she did say there was a counterpart in Rego Park, Queens.

Corner Paradise

Q. *At the corner of Greenwich and Charles Streets is a tiny white house. It's got an iron fence, a cobbled driveway, and a white gazebo in its beautiful green yard. I've coveted the place for years. What is this tiny slice of paradise's history?*

A. The wooden house at 121 Charles Street, now part of the Greenwich Village Historical District, has been around since the early- to mid-1700s, but not always at that site.

In 1968, it was trucked to its present site from Seventy-first Street and York Avenue, a distance of five miles through city streets, after being threatened with demolition, according to the Blue Guide to New York.

Originally built as a one-story back house, it gained a floor after the move, along with the yard and its wild roses, but it remains in roughly the same condition as before.

Alms for the Rich

Q. *On the west side of the Grand Concourse in the Bronx between 166th and McClellan Streets there is a gorgeous building that looks like a grand old mansion. What is it?*

A. It's a grand old mansion.

Next question. Okay, okay. Right in the middle of that stretch of anonymous apartment blocks on the noisy and treeless Grand Concourse is a nearly block-long French palace set in its own expansive park, guarded by a chain-link fence. The *AIA Guide to New York City* says it was built in 1928 by Andrew Freedman, who made millions in subway construction. After the 1907 financial panic, he had experienced the fear of losing his accustomed comforts and later established the mansion as a home for rich people who lost their wealth.

Fire Island

Q. *I was recently on the train to Boston, and sometime after we left the tunnel out of Manhattan, I noticed a strange set of red brick buildings on what must be the northeastern edge of Randalls Island. About four stood in a row, all alone, with no cars or people or anything around them. Is this an abandoned housing project?*

A. It's the Fire Department's training facility. Probationary firefighters go to school there and, among other things, learn how to put out fires in several of the nine buildings. All the buildings at the academy are constructed of poured concrete, faced with brick, and each is marked with an enormous number to help the new firefighters orient themselves.

To ease concerns about the environmental impact of ash and smoke, the fires are fueled by propane and controlled by a computer system—tem. The smoke is artificial, too. With a few exceptions, fires are started only in Building 2, known as "the burn building."

Justice on a Bridge

Q. *While downtown recently, I found myself between the criminal courts building and the new prison to the north. There is a bridge connecting the two buildings, on either side of which are mythological-looking bas-reliefs. Each scene has an inscription presumably designating what it portrays, but one is in Chinese and one is in Hebrew. Can you fill me in?*

A. The scenes are different versions of the same story, as portrayed by Richard Haas, who calls the site "the bridge of sighs."

"I wanted something that related to justice," he said, "and as a gateway between two communities."

The scenes depict the Old Testament story in which Solomon suggests dividing custody of a child between two women by dividing the child, and the Chinese tale of the Judgment of Bao-Chung, in which a child placed in a chalk circle is pulled between two women, Mr. Haas said.

The story of Bao-Chung focuses on an adoptive mother who finds and raises a child and then is challenged when the natural mother, a bad gal, reappears. It was the basis for the play *The Caucasian Chalk Circle,* by Bertolt Brecht. (For those of you in suspense, the loving mother gives up her claim in both stories.)

The inscriptions say "The Judgment of Solomon," in Hebrew, and "The Judgment of Bao-Chung," in Chinese.

Verdi and His Crowd

Q. *There is a lovely statue of the composer Giuseppe Verdi in (where else?) Verdi Square at Seventy-second Street and Broadway. There are a number of figures circling the base of the sculpture. Who are they?*

A. The four statuettes represent characters from Verdi operas: the jealous Otello (facing east), the foolish Falstaff (westerly), the proud Aida (looking north), and the noble Leonora from *La Forza del Destino* (gazing south).

Funds were raised for the monument through a competition run by Carlo Barsotti, the editor of an Italian-language newspaper, *Il Progresso*. The marble figures were created in 1906 by a Sicilian sculptor, Pasquale Civiletti, said Jonathan Kuhn, director of art and antiquities for the Department of Parks and Recreation.

What a Pig!

Q. *What is the significance of the statue of the boar in Sutton Place Park?*

A. "Generations of children and nannies have pawed the wild boar," said Parks Commissioner Henry J. Stern. "It's one of our most noticed sculptures, and it's a fierce example of animal art."

The statue, which is in the vest-pocket park where Fifty-seventh Street dead-ends at Sutton Place, is a replica of the bronze *Wild Boar,* which was completed in 1634 by the Renaissance sculptor Pietro Tacca, and which adorns a fountain in the Mercato Nuovo in Florence. Tacca modeled his bronze, commissioned by Grand Duke Cosimo II, on an antique marble work, as was customary.

Tacca's bronze, fondly known as Porcellino, is a favorite in Florence for its striking realism. To capture all of the animal's details, the sculptor kept a recently killed boar by his side while he worked, copying the texture of its fur, snout, and tusks.

Lurking for 114 Years

Q. *I often run in Central Park and I notice a strange black carving of a big cat (a cougar, perhaps?) crouched above the East Drive at about Seventy-sixth Street. It's partly hidden*

by trees, there's no pedestal, and
sighting it unawares can
give you quite a chill.
What is its history?

A. The bronze
kitty is called *Still
Hunt*. It was created by the
sculptor Edward Kemeys,
and Parks Department
records show it has been
scaring the spandex and its
predecessor off joggers and
skaters since 1881. Kemeys's
inspiration to sculpt animals
came while he worked as an ax
man with the Parks Department's corps of engineers in
the 1860s. He traveled
around the United States
in search of indigenous beasts to sculpt and
places to put his works.

His special talent seemed to lie with felines. *Still Hunt*
depicts an American mountain lion; Kemeys's two majestic African lions guard the Art Institute of Chicago's gates.

Found, in Grant's Tomb

Q. *At Grant's Tomb there is, among other peculiar
things, a small statue of a man on a horse with a name card on
it that reads "Paul Manship." As though we all know who that
is. So who is he?*

A. His name may not be familiar, but his work most certainly is: he's the sculptor who, during his heyday in the 1920s and '30s, created some of New York's most famous Art Deco pieces, notably the gilded Prometheus that overlooks Rockefeller Center's plaza.

His work also adorns the Paul J. Rainey Memorial Gateway at the Bronx Wildlife Conservation Center and the front of the former AT&T building in lower Manhattan.

In fact, *Armillary Sphere,* his enormous depiction of the zodiac created for the 1964 World's Fair in Flushing, inspired an outlandish act of art theft, said Jonathan Kuhn, the director of art and antiquities for the Department of Parks and Recreation. Some twenty years ago, by means of trucks and crews, as far as anyone can figure, eight of the twelve signs were hauled off. After playing detective, the Parks Commission was able to track down *Aries the Ram* and *Taurus the Bull* in 1990. One of the two pieces was exhibited at Flushing town hall for nine months beginning in September 1995, as part of an exhibition on the World's Fair.

As for that statue of Grant inside the tomb—it's actually a working model for a full-size statue, produced in 1928, said Eric Reinert, a museum technician for Manhattan Sites, which manages the tomb. The Grant Monument Association, which built the tomb, was in the process of raising money for the work when the Depression hit, and the statue was never completed.

The Fate of All Cash

Q. *At the north end of the Hudson River Park in Battery Park City there's a bizarre sculpture / chess garden with all these little bronze figures pushing pennies, among other things, into a tower shape in the fountain. There are some little dead figures buried in the piles of coins, and a bodiless head. What is it?*

A. It's called *The Real World* and it's definitely not the MTV show. It's the work of the sculptor Tom Otterness, whose fondness for the little doughboy figures is a trademark.

There are plaques, Mr. Otterness said, at the northern and southern entrances to the work. "But nobody ever sees them," he said. "They just step over them."

The piece was unveiled in 1992 and combines cartoonish whimsy with a comment on the fickleness of the financial businesses that literally shadow the park. Mr. Otterness says he likes to drop by to watch families explore the work.

"I go with my three-year-old daughter, Kelly," he said. "It's great to watch. The kids come up and say, 'Look, dead people!' and the parents go 'Eeeeechhhh.' And little kids go up and yell into the ear of the head that's lying down. It seems endless."

Mr. Otterness's next big public work: designs for the Fourteenth Street subway station on Eighth Avenue, slated for completion in 1999.

Q. *At 20 Vesey Street, between Church and Broadway, there is a building with four wonderful figures on the façade. Some of the figures look like monks. What's the story?*

A. Nowadays, the headline would probably read something like this: MONKS ON FRONT HAVE RUSHMORE TIES!

The building is the Garrison Building, the home of the *New York Evening Post* (predecessor of the *New York Post*) between 1907 and 1930. The building was built by the paper's owner, Oswald Garrison Villard, during the fierce days of the city's newspaper wars (there were fourteen daily papers in 1911), and the four statues on the façade are, according to the Blue Guide to New York, symbolic of the Four Periods of Publicity. (What those are we can only guess—maybe Anonymity, Geraldo, Oprah, Anonymity?) They were sculpted by Gutzon Borglum, the man who did Mount Rushmore, and Estelle R. Kohn.

Two Tripods, No Torch

Q. *At Bartel-Pritchard Square, which was once an entrance to Prospect Park, there are two very tall columns topped with tripods that, old-timers say, once were lit. What is the story behind the columns and those unlit tripods?*

A. Just like they said in college, it all goes back to the Greeks. The columns are one of the last projects completed by the architect Stanford White, who modeled their design after the Acanthus Columns of Delphi, before he died in 1906, according to Barbara Caldwell, director of cultural programs for Prospect Park. In Delphi, the columns were topped by fire during big events, like dramas or other entertainments. In Brooklyn, the columns were each topped by a tripod—a decorative nod to the Acanthus—and were lit even for nonevents like darkness falling. Ms. Caldwell couldn't say exactly when the tripods stopped being lit, though she guesses sometime in the mid-1960s when "some parts of the park were not getting a lot of attention."

Practical Firelight

Q. *What are the orange tube-shaped lights attached to streetlight poles?*

A. Boy, is Firefighter Francis J. McCabe glad you asked. It brought back twenty-year-old memories of teaching children about fire safety.

"That light indicates that somewhere within the four corners of that intersection," he said, "there's a fire-alarm box," either of the mechanical variety, where you simply pull a lever, or a voice-activated box. "You push a button," he said, "wait, and someone will say, 'This is the Fire Department, can I help you?'"

How many of these lights are there? "There should be a light for each one," Mr. McCabe said. And that adds up to 15,869: there are 1,999 in Manhattan, 2,251 in the Bronx, 4,513 in Brooklyn, 5,130 in Queens, and 1,976 in Staten Island.

You're Now Entering...

Q. *I'm always speeding past the Manhattan side arch of the Manhattan Bridge, so I can never really see what the sculpture on it represents. What is it?*

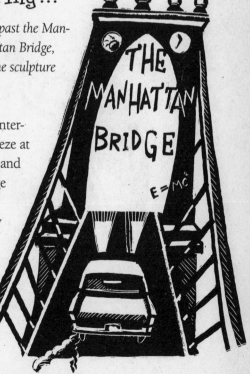

A. This is a little like entering the Twilight Zone. The frieze at the top is called *Buffalo Hunt* and was designed when the bridge was built, around 1910, by Charles Cary Rumsey, a feisty society type, sculptor, and noted polo player.

That's not odd. What's odd is what happened next. Newspaper files show that in 1934, Rumsey's wife, Mary

Harriman Rumsey, died of injuries sustained during a hunt, after her horse fell on her. Even more oddly, that was twelve years after Rumsey himself died, when the car he was riding in hit a bridge abutment. Can you hear the voice of Rod Serling yet? Rumsey's funeral was held in Buffalo.

Walking on Time

Q. *Is there really a clock embedded in a sidewalk in lower Manhattan, as my best friend says? If so, who takes care of it, and how do they handle the "spring forward–fall back" thing?*

A. The clock you have heard about sits in the middle of the sidewalk on the northeast corner of Maiden Lane and Broadway, in front of the William Barthman jewelry store.

"That's our clock," said Joel Kopel, the store's manager. Barthman does all the maintenance, which basically means polishing the crystal twice a year. The store's basement extends under the sidewalk, so it's fairly easy to reset the clock in the spring and in the fall.

Mr. Kopel says some kind of clock has been there "a minimum of eighty to ninety years"—including a wooden model, an electrical one, and the current quartz version. You know that saying about the streets being paved with gold? Well, the works for the Barthman clock were made by Cartier. Wipe your shoe leather on that!

Horseman, Pass By

Q. *Along my route to work, at 106th Street and Riverside Drive, is a statue of a military horseman on a riled steed. The nameplate reads "Franz Sigel." Who is this guy and why is there a statue of him?*

A. Franz Sigel was a "well-rounded guy," according to Jonathan Kuhn, director of art and antiquities for the Department of Parks and Recreation. To say the least.

During his life (1824–1902), Sigel was known as a revolutionary, a teacher, a Union general, a New York City bureaucrat, and the publisher of several German-language magazines. After graduating from military school in Karlsruhe in 1843, he led a rebellion against local authorities in his hometown of Sinsheim and was forced to leave Germany. He found his way to America around 1852 and in 1857 settled in St. Louis, where he taught mathematics and history at the German-American Institute and eventually became director of city schools.

When the Civil War erupted in 1861, Sigel enlisted with the Union forces and rose quickly to the rank of brigadier general. He led troops in the second Battle of Bull Run, but his most memorable engagement may have been the trouncing of his forces by a heavily outnumbered Confederate battalion during Grant's march on Richmond. After the war, Sigel briefly edited a German-language newspaper in Baltimore before coming to New York to become the city's pension agent and later its revenue collector. After his retirement, Sigel was publisher of *New Yorker Deutsches Volksblatt* and editor of *New York Monthly*. The bronze statue, a depiction of one of his more successful battles, was commissioned two years after his death and unveiled, in prominent view of Riverside Drive, in 1907.

Out of Forty-two, a Mere Six

Q. *All kinds of obscure subjects are commemorated by sculptures in this city—even a sled dog in Central Park. But how many statues of United States presidents are there?*

A. It's hard to say for the city as a whole, but the city parks—where memorial statues tend to gather—keep pretty good records. Only a half-dozen presidents have made the grade, according to Jonathan Kuhn, director of art and antiquities for the city's Parks Department.

There seems to be a mix of highly popular as well as more obscure presidents. Chester A. Arthur has a statue in Madison Square Park. George Washington is the most popular, with statues in Washington and Union Squares, at 114th Street and Morningside Drive, and at Washington Plaza in Brooklyn. Abraham Lincoln is remembered in metal in Union Square and at Grand Army Plaza in Brooklyn.

Ulysses S. Grant is portrayed at Grand Army Plaza and in Grant Square in Bedford-Stuyvesant. John F. Kennedy is memorialized at Grand Army Plaza, and Theodore Roosevelt rides immortally by the Museum of Natural History.

Bright-Eyed, Indeed

Q. *In Herald Square, there is a memorial tower with a clock and a few bronze birds. Is it my imagination or do their eyes light up?*

A. The sculpture, on Broadway between Thirty-fourth and Thirty-fifth Streets, was once attached to the New York Herald Building, which was erected in 1895 and came down in 1921.

In the 1940s, Aymar Embury II designed a base for

the piece, and up it went as a memorial to James Gordon Bennett, the Herald's founder.

The memorial depicts Minerva, the goddess of wisdom and invention, flanked by—deadline, anyone?—two bellringers (the monument is thus sometimes called the Bellringers Monument).

It also features a clock and two owls.

Now, to the point: The owls' eyes contain bulbs on timers. They do indeed light up.

The city's clock master, Marvin Schneider, has the job of keeping the birds' eyes beady.

A Soldier of Fortune

Q. *From growing up on Allerton Avenue near Bronx Park, I remember a statue of a Civil War soldier in the middle of the Bronx River, just south of Gun Hill Road, which at that time was a lovers' lane of sorts. Check it out, please.*

A. The granite statue, constructed in 1898 by John Grignola and quite typical for its time period, was once on the banks of the river just south of Gun Hill Road. Jonathan Kuhn, director of art and antiquities for the Parks Department, said that the statue was vandalized in 1965 and removed sometime after that for restoration.

To better protect it, it was then placed next to the Valentine Varian Historical House near Bainbridge Avenue in Norwood, the Bronx. Why not pop by and relive a few of your memories from lovers' lane?

Counting Horses' Legs

Q. *Is there some special significance to the different positions of the horses' legs in statues of men on horseback around the city?*

A. In the July 1950 issue of *Library Journal*, I. G. Grimshaw wrote that when one leg of the horse is raised, it means its rider suffered a wound in battle. In the book *Other Statues of Boston*, Alan Forbes says that a horse reared up on two legs indicates that the rider was killed in battle, and that a horse with four legs on the ground carries a rider who died of natural causes.

Yes, a Water Statue

Q. *There is a statue partly submerged in the water off the southern tip of Manhattan. What's it all about?*

A. The American Merchant Mariners Memorial was installed in 1991 by Marisol, an artist who goes by a single name, on a breakwater next to the Fire Department

Marine Company's Pier A, near Battery Place and Castle
Clinton in Battery Park.

Based on a photograph taken by a German submarine
commander, the bronze sculpture depicts three terrified
seamen aboard the sinking hull of the torpedoed ship
Muskogee, and a fourth crewman in the water reaching up
to be pulled aboard. The part of his body exposed above
the waterline changes with the tides, conveying different
impressions of hopefulness and desperation about his fate.
In the end, all four died at sea.

5 From Here to There

Half-Moons Revolving

Q. *Why does the Transit Authority so carefully paint white half-moons on every axle of every subway car? Are they measuring wear and tear? And why half-moons rather than the whole thing?*

A. Astrology plays no part in the subway operation. But the crescents help insure a safe ride, said Charles Seaton, a spokesman for the Transit Authority.

"The reason we paint them is simple," he said. "To make certain the wheel is rolling."

A subway car has eight wheels, any of which can lock or brake without stopping the entire train—a condition that the conductor would not be able to see or detect. But an outside observer can watch as the moons go round and round. The observers are the tower operators at the twenty-two subway yards, the gatekeepers who oversee the deployment of 5,803 cars.

The authority began painting subway wheels in the 1960s, and this is a standard railroad practice, Mr. Seaton said. Half the hub, the part around the axle, is white or yellow. Older cars have larger slivers along the flange, the wheel's outer circumference. If the entire wheel were painted, its motion would not be visible.

The Transit Authority does not rely solely on visual observation. "Subway cars are inspected every sixty-six days or 10,000 miles, whichever comes first," Mr. Seaton said. "The cars go an average of 80,000 miles between mechanical failures."

The Sound of Steel

Q. *Can't the Transit Authority do anything to quiet that shrill, ear-splitting screech produced by subway cars as they round a sharp turn?*

A. Not much. The New York City subway is a high-decibel beast of steel. What you hear are bell-like 880-pound steel wheels—bearing cars that weigh up to 90,000 pounds—scraping against steel rails.

The Transit Authority has made progress in recent years in shushing them, said Termaine Garden, a spokesman. In the 1980s, 282 areas of curved track were rigged with treadles that pump lubricating gel over the rail when a train enters the turn, he said. Older sections, like the South Ferry, Fourteenth Street, and Grand Central areas, tend to have sharper turns, Mr. Garden said, and those areas have received much of the noise-reducing technology. Motormen have been instructed to take certain curves more slowly.

The TA has even experimented with sound-dampening wheels with a rubber center, Mr. Garden said, adding that retrofitting the entire 722-mile system would cost too much. "But we're always looking at new technologies," he said with a sigh.

The Angle on Angels

Q. *At each exit of the Grand Army Plaza subway station in Brooklyn is a sculptured bronze plaque of an angel. Terra-cotta angel mosaics—one of which depicts angels flanking a subway car—grace the station itself. Can you explain the heavenly motif?*

A. When you leave the station, look up: the angels on the plaques and mosaics are intended to echo the two herald angels atop the Soldiers and Sailors Memorial Arch. The angels above the arch, which honors Union troops from the Civil War, were sculpted by Frederick MacMonnies. The angels in the subway station are the work of Jane Greengold, and were installed last year in the Metropolitan Transportation Authority's Arts for Transit program.

The installation, *Wings for the IRT: The Irresistible Romance of Travel,* evokes the original logo of the IRT: a subway car with wings.

Sidelining the Tram

Q. *Is the Roosevelt Island tram ever taken out of service because of weather conditions?*

A. Yes, but those occasions are few and far between. The two synchronized cable cars sit out severe electrical storms, or sustained north-south wind gusts that exceed 40 miles an hour, according to Michael T. Greason, spokesman for the Roosevelt Island Operating Corporation.

A recent day's punishing gusts were east-west and did not stop the tram from completing its 3,100-foot path from Fifty-ninth Street and Second Avenue in Manhattan to Roosevelt Island. Snow, rain, or hail don't slow the ride significantly.

But Mr. Greason said a lightning bolt could cripple the system, and strong winds blasting the sides of the cabins, though not actually dangerous, could rock them severely.

How often do events like these occur?

"Very seldom," said Mr. Greason, adding that the 18,300-pound cabins, which reach a peak altitude of 250 feet, are inspected daily. Emergency evacuations have been rehearsed since the tram opened in 1976. On January 27, 1998, a construction crane working on the Queensborough Bridge slammed into a Manhattan-bound tram car, injuring eleven people and suspending service until February 7.

Finger Tips

Q. *I've noticed subway conductors performing an odd ritual when the train stops in the station, just before the doors open. The conductor extends his index finger, and with a quick, small motion, seems to point at the station ceiling. What is this peculiar movement?*

A. Though it looks like an exceptionally subdued disco pose, the subtle pointing gesture is actually a safety practice imported from Japan. When a train stops in a station, conductors are supposed to look out the window and see a black-and-white-striped indication board directly above them before they open the doors.

The board, which is suspended from the station ceiling, tells them that the train is in the correct position and all cars are in the station.

In 1996, conductors opened doors while cars in the front or back of the train were still in the tunnel, or opened them on the wrong side of the train, at least forty-three times, according to a Transit Authority spokesman, Termaine Garden.

"That's forty-three times too many," he said. So the pointing practice, which is used by conductors in the Tokyo subway system, was instituted for New York's twenty-eight hundred conductors in September.

The slightly funky little movement "is for the conductor, not for the customers," Mr. Garden said. "The thinking is that it forces them to take an extra second, and in that second they can look up and make sure they see the board, and point at it, before they open the doors."

When Meters Click Off

Q. *How do taxi drivers get paid? I understand they rent their own cabs, but do rates vary? Do they pay in everything and then get a check at the end of the week, or do they take the cash?*

A. Drivers generally rent their cabs for twelve-hour shifts, usually five A.M. to five P.M. or vice versa.

Rates vary from garage to garage and also depend on day and time. Friday nights are the most expensive, with rentals being jacked up to about $110; Sunday nights the price drops to about $70. Drivers pay the rental fee up front, and then also have to invest in gas, which runs about $18 to $20 a tank. Thus, cabbies usually start the day (or night) at least $100 in the hole. At the end of the shift, cabbies return the cab, pay any late fees (cabbies can be charged $5 to $10 for bringing a car back ten minutes late), and walk off with the remaining cash. Which had better be more than $100, or they haven't even broken even.

Expecting a Ride

Q. *I heard in my Lamaze class that many New York cabbies won't pick up a pregnant woman carrying a suitcase. Apparently they are afraid that the woman is in labor and might give birth before she gets to the hospital. Is this true?*

A. The evidence indicates that most cabbies are happy to take pregnant women to the hospital, and those who don't face some pretty stiff penalties.

"A pregnant woman?" boomed Willie Bly, managing director of the League of Mutual Taxi Owners. "We'll always pick her up!"

The league, Mr. Bly said, represents the roughly thirty-three hundred owner-drivers of the more than twelve thousand medallion taxis—the ones most likely to lose income if their cabs became birthing rooms. He added that you have only to stand at a hospital entrance to see cab after cab arriving with mothers-to-be.

"Besides," Mr. Bly said, "I'm in this business a long, long time and I've never heard of anyone actually giving birth in the cab."

Section 2–50 of the Taxicab Drivers Rules of the New York City Taxi and Limousine Commission states unequivocally that cabbies must pick up the first passenger who signals them and take that passenger anywhere he or she wants to go in New York City. There are some justifiable grounds for refusing a passenger, but none of them are medical.

Not Everywhere, Signs

Q. *I've noticed that when subway stations are renovated or repainted, only about half the station signs are replaced on the columns that flank many of the platforms. Why?*

A. How many station signs do you need in order to know where you are? Though the image of endlessly repeating, identical columns is not without poetry, it is out of step with the Transit Authority's current sign philosophy.

In 1989, the Metropolitan Transportation Authority introduced new sign-display guidelines as part of a larger program to standardize graphics and reduce "visual clutter," according to a spokesman for the Transit Authority, Termaine Garden. Under the plan, station signs on platform columns, which are placed at a height where they can be read by standing or sitting passengers, will be left in place only on every second column.

The guidelines are imposed only in stations that are being rebuilt or refurbished, like the Broadway–Lafayette station on the A, B, D, and Q lines, or in stations where other signs are known to be causing confusion, like the Broadway–Nassau station on the A and D lines, Mr. Garden said.

Removed signs are donated to the Transit Museum or discarded, Mr. Garden said, and columns covered with porcelain tile will generally be restored with their signs intact. He added that the MTA hoped to have replaced signs in 80 percent of the system's 469 stations by the end of 1999, and be at work on the remaining ones.

Subway for Tinseltown

Q. *Recently, there was an F.Y.I. question about the Eighth Avenue and Forty-second Street subway platforms. That reminded me of something. Under the downtown platform, you can see another platform, very dark and seemingly unused. What is it? For service trains?*

A. Nope. It's for the movies. The platform is leased out by the Transit Authority to film companies wanting to re-create that unique New York City subway feel. Until the mid-1980s it was used for the train to Aqueduct Racetrack. Once you've got your platform, you can also rent a train and a crew to run it. It's quite affordable, as well: a four-car train, with conductor and train operator, said Termaine Garden, a Transit Authority spokesman, would set you back about $1,127. (Or about 750 rides on a real train.)

Illness in the Subway

Q. *I hate to sound callous, but why do sick passengers wreak such havoc on subways?*

A. The delays come from caution. When a passenger gets sick on the subway, the conductor of the train must call the information in to the operations control of the system, which then makes a call to the police and EMS. Employees of the Transit Authority don't have medical training, according to TA spokesman Termaine Garden, so when a passenger becomes ill, the only recourse is to move the train into the nearest station and hold it there

until the police or EMS officials arrive to care for and remove the passenger.

All of which, unfortunately, means delays for the trains
behind that one. Lots of them. One train stopped in a
station can cause delays for up to thirty other trains.

No Passengers, Please

Q. *Often, late at night, I see yellow subway cars with
bars on the windows riding the rails. What are these cars? And
why the bars? Is it some sort of mobile prison?*

A. Boy, would that make sentencing fun: "Ten years
on the prison train. And make that a local!"

In reality, the yellow cars are part of the Transit Authority's work equipment fleet, which transports the authority's workers, its tools, and, most important, its
money, said spokesman Termaine Garden.

The money train, as it's called, picks up cash and tokens from stations for delivery to an underground stop at the authority's Jay Street headquarters. Along for the ride is a phalanx of armed guards. How many guards? "I'm not going to tell you that," Mr. Garden said.

Those Dreaded Grates

Q. *The grates in the city's sidewalks seem to be deeply feared: it seems only a few brave souls tread on them. How long have they been there, and is there any reason we're so skittish about them?*

A. Some of the grates are for building ventilation, but most grates were designed to ventilate the subway tunnels in the dark ages before air-conditioning. They have been a fixture in city streets since the birth of the subway system in 1904. But it doesn't seem to be the age that worries people; it's the way they look. No matter how strong those thin grills are, they just don't look as solid as concrete sidewalks.

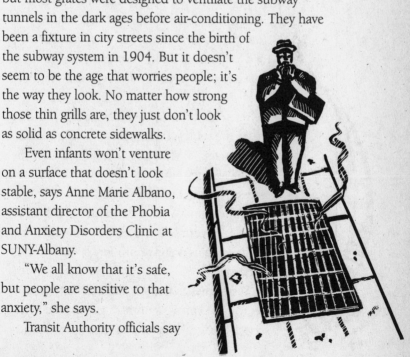

Even infants won't venture on a surface that doesn't look stable, says Anne Marie Albano, assistant director of the Phobia and Anxiety Disorders Clinic at SUNY-Albany.

"We all know that it's safe, but people are sensitive to that anxiety," she says.

Transit Authority officials say

people wearing heels (not to mention skirts; think of Marilyn) do need to look out, but under normal use, the grates are pretty safe.

There have been a few serious accidents involving grates. The most serious was in 1990, when a grate collapsed under the weight of a 2-ton generator, killing a homeless man. In 1988, a Brooklyn woman fell through one on Eastern Parkway. She suffered cuts and a broken pelvis, but recovered. The grate was found to have been weakened by gypsy cabs parking on it. And more recently, a grate collapse in SoHo injured nine people viewing an art exhibit.

Twisted Tracks?

Q. *The D train from uptown arrives at Rockefeller Center on the west track, and the F train from Queens on the east track. Between there and Forty-second Street the tracks cross, then at Broadway–Lafayette the tracks cross again. Why?*

A. It's easy to understand if you visualize the routes. (Hint: hands make great subway trains.) When you're facing downtown, the D comes into Rockefeller Center on the west (your right hand) because it's coming from the Upper West Side and the F comes in on the east (your left) because it's coming from Queens, explains Transit Authority spokesman Termaine Garden.

The D switches to the left tracks at Forty-second Street to run express, and the F goes to the right to service the local stops. (The express track actually runs under the local part of the way from Thirty-fourth to West Fourth.) After Broadway–Lafayette, the F heads east under Houston Street while the D swings down, and to the right of the F, to service Grand Street.

Buses without Riders

Q. *When public buses display the "No Passengers" or "Not in Service" signs, it is frustrating for would-be passengers not to know the reasons, especially when the buses pass by during rush hour. Why don't they take passengers along?*

A. The buses are probably "deadhead-ing," traveling empty from their depot to the start of their regular route or back to the depot at the end of their shift, Melissa Farley, a spokeswoman for the Transit Authority, said.

Why is this necessary? The city has nineteen bus de-pots scattered throughout the city where buses are stored and maintained. Keeping enough buses on the street sometimes re-quires elaborate maneuvering. (One deadheading route involves driving from a depot in Staten Island to West Fifty-seventh Street in Manhattan.) They don't carry passengers because it would slow the process and defeat the purpose of the trip. (Besides, imagine how long it would take to get from Fifty-seventh Street to Staten Island aboard a local.)

Slow on the Downgrade

Q. *Subway trains on the B and C lines traveling south always slow down considerably when passing the 135th Street station. Why is this?*

A. First off, you can take solace in the fact that trains coming from both directions slow when approaching 135th Street. The reason is that the station is in a depression in the island, meaning that when a train approaches from either direction, it encounters a downward slope.

Because the trains might build up too much speed (what with momentum and all) coming down the slope, the tracks are equipped with grade time signals, which force the conductor to slow the train to maintain a speed limit (posted inside the tunnels). If a train goes through a signal at too quick a clip, a "stop arm" trips a lever on the bottom of the train, bringing the whole kit and caboodle (cabboosle?) to a screeching halt.

Nonstop at Fourteenth Street

Q. *Why do the IND B and D express trains bypass Four-teenth Street when all other subway lines make Fourteenth Street an express train stop?*

A. It's a case of first come, first served. The station at Sixth Avenue was the last built along Fourteenth Street, opening in 1940 for D and F trains. When the decision was made in the mid-1960s to extend the BB service (as it was known) south from its end point at West Thirty-fourth Street, planners judged that the station was sufficiently served and already also included a PATH stop, explains Transit Authority spokesman Termaine Garden.

So the new express tunnel, to carry the BB and the D, was laid out underneath the station. B and D express service was inaugurated in November 1967, leaving the station at Sixth Avenue sadly local.

Now, Cabs Can Call You

Q. *What are those round yellow lights that protrude from the bumper, a little to the left of the license plate, of the new taxis?*

A. These are trouble lights that are available to cabdrivers who are in danger. If a driver is being robbed or threatened, he can trigger the light with his foot, which will cause it to flash. This is to alert police or others in the area that he is in trouble. Similar lights in the taxi's front grille are visible only when flashing. The Taxi and Limousine Commission recently mandated that all taxis carry these lights. Expect to see them on every cab in the city soon.

F Is for Culver

Q. *Why is the F train service in Brooklyn referred to as the Culver line? There is no Culver Street station in Brooklyn. Actually, there is no Culver Street or Avenue in the borough, period.*

A. Well, there's some history here. Below Church Avenue, the F line runs over a path once used by the old Coney Island and Prospect Park Railroad, a steam-powered railroad that began in 1875. It ran between Ninth Avenue and Twentieth Street and Coney Island. Since it was financed by Andrew Culver, it became known as the Culver line. Around 1899, when the route became electrified, it took on the name officially. The F train started service on its general path in 1914.

Higher Underground

Q. *In the BMT station at Thirty-fourth Street, the southbound platform is higher than the northbound one. Why?*

A. In 1918, when the BMT station was built, its southbound platform was built higher to accommodate a station of the Hudson & Manhattan Railroad Company, just below. In 1937, the Hudson & Manhattan station was moved south a block. After the old station was sealed— and sealed it remains—the southbound subway platform stayed where it was, on the principle that there's no need to fix what isn't broken.

Up Stairs, Down Stairs

Q. *Why is it that at Thirty-fourth Street subway stops at both Seventh and Eighth Avenues the express track isn't across the platform from the local track, forcing those who need to change trains to go up and down a set of stairs? The Atlantic Avenue station in Brooklyn has a similar problem.*

A. If you are the sort who dabbles in conspiracy theories, you will enjoy this answer. When these stations were built, the designers anticipated a lot of traffic because of the number of railroad companies with lines through Penn Station and Atlantic Avenue. In Penn Station, they placed the express tracks away from local ones, partly to control the traffic of passengers, partly to discourage people from switching from local trains to express trains, with the same goal in mind, said Transit Authority spokesman Termaine Garden.

Keeping Track

Q. *There are subway lines with numbers and lines with letters. Why?*

A. Numbers were first used in the 1920s on the BMT lines, and when the IND opened in 1932, it opted for letters. The IRT opened in the 1940s, and it used numbers. All of this was fine; since each line was separate, there was little confusion. When the systems were unified in 1960, the BMT changed to letters to eliminate the conflict with the IRT, which shared some of the numbers.

That Subway Sway

Q. *Why are the metal "straps" in buses and subways designed to swing?*

A. They don't swing, they spring, said Termaine Garden of the Transit Authority. When the subway opened in 1904, the cars were equipped with leather straps that gave easily, so passengers would not slip and fall when the train moved. In the 1930s, trains got metal grips, like the ones you see today, which contain springs so that the "strap" will still swing as the cars sway.

The Bus Stops There

Q. *Why are bus stops in Manhattan almost always placed beyond traffic lights rather than at the lights? It seems to be a waste of passenger time as well as fuel, since the bus must usually stop twice: once at the light and again at the bus stop. Can this actually be deliberate?*

A. It isn't a conspiracy to make you miss your bus. It is done for safety reasons, says the city's Department of Transportation. If buses stopped at the lights, she explained, people crossing the street in front of or behind a bus could enter a blind spot of the bus driver or of other drivers, and might be hit as a result. You might not agree with this theory, but the department plans to relocate any bus stops that are in fact placed at traffic lights.

Gratitude for an "S" Turn

Q. *The Flushing No. 7 line seems to run from Grand Central to Times Square along Forty-second Street, yet at some point near Fifth Avenue it makes a sharp S-turn. What is it avoiding?*

A. That line runs along Forty-first Street, which is where you stand underground when you wait for it. The

S-turn is made to steer clear of the Times Square–Grand
Central Shuttle train.

Safety Locks

Q. *I notice that many doors between the subway cars on
the N, Q, and R lines are locked. I suppose this is intended to
limit the number of injuries incurred by people who ride between
the cars, but what are passengers to do if there is a fire, or if a
hatchet-wielding madman gets on? How are the doors
unlocked?*

A. The cars of these particular trains (as well as
those of the E, F, and A lines) are 75 feet long, said Termaine Garden of the Transit Authority. When they turn
corners, huge gaps are created between cars, and passengers could easily fall into them.

Regarding your dread of subterranean calamities, Mr.
Garden said, "The questions raised are valid, but fortu-
nately none of that has ever happened on those lines."

But should they occur, fear not. Train crews can open
all locked doors electronically.

Subway Cars by Colors

Q. *Have you ever noticed that subway cars seem to be
color coded? On the No. 1 train I rode today, for instance,
there was a red bar below the numbers; on a No. 2 train across
the platform, the bar was blue with a yellow diamond in the
middle. Curiously, the last car of that train also had a large
gray or green circle next to the bar. What's the purpose of the
color codes?*

A. The color bars denote the maintenance shop ("car barn," in transitspeak) from whence the car has come. There are thirteen such car barns, and this accounts for what you are seeing. Circles, diamonds, and other shapes affixed to cars indicate the type of equipment it is carrying.

The Third, Deadly, Rail

Q. *So tell me, is the third rail really electric? If it is, how do track workers get their jobs done?*

A. The third rail on every New York City subway track is electrified with 600 volts of direct current. A "shoe beam" picks up the current and transfers it to the train, providing it with the electricity necessary to make it move.

What would happen if you touched the third rail? You would be dead.

Segments of the rail are turned off so that track workers can service an area, and third rail fatalities are rare. Most victims have been people riding between the cars or homeless people taking shelter in the subway, rather than workers.

Expert advice: Do not go down on the track.

Upside and Downside

Q. *Why is there a downtown No. 6 subway stop at Broadway–Lafayette in Manhattan, but no uptown stop?*

A. This station was never designed to be a transfer point, but in fact that is what it has become, though only halfway. The downtown No. 6 train stop at Bleecker Street allows access to southbound trains at Broadway–Lafayette, but because of the station's layout, there is no access to northbound trains. Annoying, simple truth.

Those Slamming Doors

Q. *Why is it that every time people are stepping off the local IRT train the express train across the track is slamming its doors, almost as if it were waiting there just to taunt and vex them?*

A. If the doors of the local train open before the express doors close, the express train should then wait. But sometimes the conductor is behind schedule.

In theory, the uncomely behavior of the conductor is really just his way of saying, "Pardon me, I am a bit pressed, and there is another express train right behind me."

Wired in the Old Days

Q. *I often see road crews with equipment and heavy machinery marked "Empire City Subway Company" digging up the streets of Manhattan. What does this company actually do?*

A. Since 1891, it has built and maintained the underground ducts—once called "subways"—in Manhattan and the Bronx. That was the year New York City (which then consisted of the two boroughs) hired the Empire City Subway Company to bury the city's low-tension wires below the street, according to a spokesman. Until that time, a thickening web of wires had been strung above the streets on wooden poles. Empire City Subway dug up the streets and installed the ducts through which all low-tension communication cables for the two boroughs have been threaded ever since. Today the company owns, leases, and maintains 12,000 miles of 4-inch conduit beneath the city streets. The ducts—which are dug over, under, and around underground utilities—carry cables for telephone and cable TV companies. Empire City rents the ducts to outside companies by the foot, but does not usually install cable. Empire City Subway also owns ten thousand manholes, where the cables are spliced and routed into surrounding buildings. Covers for these manholes are stamped "E.C.S.Co.Ltd." The company, a subsidiary of Bell Atlantic, employs about 300 people, and most of its work is in Manhattan below Fifty-ninth Street. Occasionally the company's diggers unearth an Empire City Subway duct of yesteryear—still in use—made of iron, clay, or even wood.

Subway "Bing-Bong"

Q. *What are the musical notes that signal the closing of the subway car doors, and what is their origin?*

A. Subway riders have been playing "Name That Tune" for years, but the answer is in the ear of the beholder. Transit Authority officials aren't sure of the key but say the interval of the "bing-bong" is a descending major third—like going from an E to a C—the same one found at the beginning of Beethoven's Fifth Symphony and George Gershwin's "Summertime." But it is doubtful that the TA specified the notes that summon travelers aboard, says Gene Sansone, the assistant chief mechanical officer in the equipment, engineering, and technical support division. The first cars to use the chimes—the R-44s—were acquired in 1972, and the music came with the doors, which were manufactured by the Vapor Corporation of Chicago.

6 The Vanishing City

The Fire Last Time

Q. *My grandmother, who is seventy-nine, tells me that when she was a child on the Lower East Side, on the eve of every election men would gather in the street and start bonfires with scraps of wood. What was this about?*

A. The bonfires were rallies, organized by the ward heelers of Tammany Hall to get out the vote, said James P. Shenton, a professor of history at Columbia University.

"The ritual was inherited from the Irish, who used to mark grand occasions by setting bonfires across the hills, notifying people to come out and do what they were sup-

posed to do—celebrate, raise hell, whatever was necessary," he said. Tammany Hall, the political machine that shaped Democratic politics in the city for generations, was dominated by Irishmen from the 1850s on.

The Lower East Side, long a Tammany stronghold, would have been predominantly Jewish when your grandmother was a child, but the tradition began to wane only after the death of longtime political leader Charles Francis (Frank) Murphy in 1924, Professor Shenton said.

Until then, he said, on election eves, "the Lower East Side could have seen several dozen bonfires. You would have seen the same thing further uptown in Chelsea, Hell's Kitchen, the Italian Village, and in all probability up in Harlem, too.

"The men, when they showed up, would be walked over to the local saloon for some free beer or other intoxicating beverages. Most saloons offered a buffet, provided by the local leader. You had your beer, your sandwich, the kids running around—the environment was like a neighborhood carnival."

Where Have You Gone, Verrazano Street?

Q. *Something called Verrazano Street appears on my old map of Manhattan, running east from Seventh Avenue South to the intersection of the Avenue of the Americas and Houston Street and cutting across Carmine and Downing Streets. The actual street, however, is not to be found, nor does it appear on current maps. Did it ever exist?*

A. "Verrazano Street" was conceived as an approach to the Lower Manhattan Expressway, a sprawling super-highway that would have connected the Holland Tunnel to the Williamsburg and Manhattan Bridges via Broome Street and the Bowery, obliterating much of lower Manhattan's loft district in the process. The highway and "Verrazano Street" were never built.

The idea of an arterial link between New Jersey and Long Island had been around since the Holland Tunnel was completed in the 1920s. Robert Moses, the powerful chairman of the Triborough Bridge and Tunnel Authority, proposed it to Mayor Fiorello La Guardia in 1940. The highway was included in the City Planning Commission's master highway plan the following year, and by 1947 the first working drawings for the project were complete. Money for the project remained scarce, however. Though defeated by the Board of Estimate in 1962, the plan was revived the following year under Mayor Robert F. Wagner and drawn on the official city map, allowing the city to begin buying property and condemning buildings along the proposed route.

By Mr. Moses's estimate, the $100 million expressway would have displaced 1,972 families and 804 businesses as it carved its way across lower Manhattan. Community opposition, especially among the artists who had begun to live in the cast-iron loft buildings of SoHo, gained momentum and political support. In 1969, under Mayor John V. Lindsay, the board finally voted to have the plan removed from city maps. The city later sold "Verrazano Street" back to the various lot owners.

About That Arch

Q. *Barely visible behind the auto repair shops on Broadway at 215th Street is what appears to be a full-size Roman triumphal arch. Quod hoc sibi vult?*

A. What does this mean? you ask. *Tempori parendum*—one must change with the times. The arch was originally the gateway to a lavish estate built on top of the hill.

In 1851, the Seaman family bought a 25-acre hillside parcel between 214th and 217th Streets, which included a number of marble quarries along the old Kings Bridge road. Marble from these quarries was used to build a mansion, and at the base of the hill, a monumental entry arch, 35 feet tall, 40 feet wide, and 20 feet deep. An old photograph shows that the gateway's pristine façade on Broadway contained a pair of niches for statuary and, beneath an elegant cornice, two inset panels that flanked the central vault.

The estate later passed to the Drake family, then to a contractor who used the arch as a business office, according to Christopher Gray, an urban historian. Since early this century the arch has been surrounded by low brick buildings, serving as the entryway first to car dealerships and, later, auto repair shops. Apartment buildings have occupied the site of the old Seaman-Drake estate since it was sold in the 1930s.

Since about 1960, the arch's central vault has led directly into the garage of Jack Gallo's auto body shop. Mr. Gallo says the inside of the arch, now bricked over, was once inhabited by the gatekeeper for the estate, and in later years was used by a social club. Though obscured today by a cacophony of signs and shops, it remains a quietly astonishing sight.

That Old Club of Mine

Q. *Among some artifacts from my childhood I found a small, tattered card declaring my membership in the "Sidewalk Superintendents' Club" of Rockefeller Center. I don't recall the club, and my childhood memories all take place in Canarsie.*

A. As we figure it, one day late in 1938 or 1939 you visited Rockefeller Center with your parents. As you passed the giant excavation site for the Eastern Airlines Building (now 10 Rockefeller Plaza), between Forty-eighth and Forty-ninth Streets, you paused to watch the steam shovels at work. But rather than peering through a knothole in the fence, you joined a small throng within a 100-foot-long viewing shed directly overlooking the construction site. A huge coat of arms bearing the Dutch motto *De beste stuurlui stan aan wal* ("The best pilots stand on the shore") decorated the entrance, and a uniformed guard handed you a membership card as you stepped onto the terrace.

Ten thousand cards like yours were handed out after the club opened, with much ballyhoo, in November 1938. Rockefeller Center was financed by John D. Rockefeller Jr., and according to a 1938 news release by the center's public relations department, Rockefeller paused on his way to his office one day to observe the work from the entrance to a truck ramp. A watchman, failing to recognize him, unceremoniously ordered him off the building site with a gruff "Keep moving, buddy."

Determined to give the public a better chance to marvel at the construction of his vast midtown complex (this is still the news release talking), Rockefeller conceived of the Sidewalk Superintendents' Club for construction enthusiasts and "curbstone kibitzers" like yourself. Members could even receive an autographed copy of a photograph of their favorite steam shovel operator. We're just guessing, but you probably thought it all was nifty, or keen, or whatever you said back then.

Summer Days

Q. *I understand that there was once a popular beach resort and amusement park on the Queens shoreline between Bowery Bay and Flushing Bay. What became of it?*

A. It became La Guardia Airport. But from 1886 until the 1920s, Bowery Bay Beach—later renamed North Beach—was a seaside haven for thousands of working-class families from Manhattan, Long Island City, and Brooklyn. Once known as "the Coney Island of Queens," the resort was financed by William Steinway, the piano manufacturer, who hoped to provide a wholesome retreat for the workers from his nearby factory, and George Ehret, owner of the Hell Gate Brewery in Yorkville, according to Jeffrey Kroessler, a historian at Long Island University.

The shady hillsides and clear water of the bay were augmented by bathhouses, saloons, and landscaped picnic groves. During North Beach's heyday between 1895 and 1915, electric lights, amusement piers, and thrill rides were added, and fireworks displays, vaudeville acts, and ragtime music sweetened the atmosphere. Although families and church groups visited to swim or picnic during the day, at night North Beach became a less reputable

destination, where single young men and women drank beer, danced, and caroused, Mr. Kroessler said.

Attendance at North Beach declined rapidly after Prohibition closed the dance halls and saloons, and the bathing beaches of the bay became too fouled by untreated sewage to make swimming appealing, Mr. Kroessler said. In the late 1920s part of Bowery Bay was filled to provide runways for the Glenn L. Curtiss Airport, and by the late 1930s North Beach had disappeared beneath the city's second municipal airport, later renamed for Mayor Fiorello H. La Guardia.

Underground Trolleys

Q. *In the 1930s, I used to travel with my mother by trolley from Brownsville to the Lower East Side, to spend Passover with my grandparents. Our trip ended at the underground trolley terminal under Delancey Street. Any idea what became of it?*

A. The Delancey Street Trolley Terminal is still there, said Termaine Garden, a spokesman for the Transit Authority. It is partly visible from the eastbound subway platform of the J train at Essex Street. The terminal served the five or six trolley lines that crossed the Williamsburg Bridge.

The loop-shaped terminal, approximately the size of the Essex Street subway station, closed in 1948, when buses replaced trolley service throughout the city. The B39 bus traverses the bridge now.

Mr. Garden said Transit Museum staff members occasionally lead tours of the terminal, but there are no plans for its restoration. "It's an artifact," he said, "a remnant of an earlier transportation era."

Lobby Light Show

Q. *In the 1950s, the lobby of a Madison Avenue office building had a high, sloping ceiling of dancing multicolored lights. Day and night, the display changed patterns, colors, and textures as passersby watched, mesmerized, from the street. Where exactly did this light show occur?*

A. Sooner or later, someone was going to ask about the Rollo-Color lighting system, which stopped pedestrians in their tracks when it was installed in 1951 at 383-385 Madison Avenue, between Forty-sixth and Forty-seventh Streets. The flamboyant developer William Zeckendorf, head of Webb & Knapp, demonstrated his philosophy of "adding ideas to real estate" by including the "lobby of light" in his renovation of the company's staid 1923 office buildings, which he joined with a single lobby.

Designed by a British lighting engineer, Rollo Gillespie Williams, the 1,200-square-foot honeycomb ceiling—through which shone the light of 1,920 lamps—swept boldly up to a height of three stories at the glassed-in entrance. Built for $125,000, the Rollo-Color apparatus could create five hundred hues and tints of light in forty-eight independently programmed zones, in timed or static patterns of squares or stripes.

"These newly renovated office buildings, unified by this lobby of light, have become the most talked-about, stared-at buildings in New York," *Architectural Forum* said in 1952. A photoelectric cell increased or reduced the brilliancy of the illumination according to changing daylight conditions. The Rollo-Color ceiling cost $10,000 a year to operate.

Webb & Knapp went bankrupt in 1965 after losing millions on the Freedomland amusement park, and the building has been at the center of an epic struggle for development rights since the 1980s. It has been empty for more than ten years, but the honeycomb ceiling is still visible.

Bushwicks, Not Bush

Q. *I've heard that there was once a baseball field called Dexter Park where I live in Woodhaven, Queens. Who played there?*

A. Barnstorming teams with players like Babe Ruth and Lou Gehrig. Negro League teams like the Brooklyn Royal Giants, Kansas City Monarchs, and Homestead Grays. And scrappy semiprofessional teams like the Brooklyn Bushwicks, the park's legendary home team. Dexter Park, which in its prime held 15,500 fans, sat on 10 acres just north of Jamaica Avenue on the Brooklyn-Queens border, according to Robert F. Eisen, a historian of New York semipro baseball.

It was built in 1885 on the site of the Union Course racetrack and named after a champion trotter, he said. By the 1900s it was home to a number of semipro teams like the Dexter Parkers, working-class teams whose players knocked around the horsehide on the weekend. A famous advertisement on the outfield wall read, "Don't kill the umpire— Maybe it's your eyes."

Legend claimed that a horse was buried beneath the

right-field grass. "Nonsense," Mr. Eisen said. The powerful Bushwicks played at Dexter Park from 1918 until the park's demise in the mid-1950s. "They were a blend of young ballplayers on the way up and professional players on the way down."

Lefty Gomez of the Yankees and Dazzy Vance of the Dodgers both pitched for the Bushwicks in the twilight of their careers. Big, beery crowds packed the park for Sunday doubleheaders, when the Bushwicks would face dazzling Negro League teams with players like Jackie Robinson or Satchel Paige, or barnstorming all-stars, or lunchbucket guys from Bay Ridge or Glendale. Mr. Eisen said the Bushwicks often outdrew the Brooklyn Dodgers. He confessed that he finagled his way into Dexter Park many times, once by carrying the bags of a visiting pitcher named Dizzy Dean.

A Dry Patch

Q. *I have heard my Staten Island neighborhood in Westerleigh called Prohibition Park. What is the origin of this rather dour nickname?*

A. By some accounts, the first liquor distilled in the United States was brewed on Staten Island in 1640. Later, things took a sobering turn. In 1887 the National Prohibition Party bought a wooded 25-acre tract in the center of what is now Westerleigh and dubbed it Prohibition Park. Occupying the area now bordered by Watchogue Road and Demorest, Maine, and Wardwell Avenues, the shady precinct served as a summer haven for teetotalers and a focal point for the local temperance movement. Another

temperance community flourished in New Dorp. The
three-acre Westerleigh Park is all that remains of the area's
once-abundant greenswards, but street names still honor
the party's presidential candidates of that censorious era,
like Clinton B. Fiske and John G. Woolley. Willard Avenue
is named for Frances E. Willard, leader of the Women's
Christian Temperance Union. Other streets pay homage to
once-dry states like Ohio, Virginia, and the Dakotas.

A Long Way Down

Q. *After years of studying the Parachute Jump while
lying on the beach at Coney Island, I haven't been able to figure
out how the ride actually worked. Did it spin?*

A. No, it dropped. The Coney Island landmark,
about 270 feet tall, was erected in Flushing Meadows for
the 1939 World's Fair, where it shared a lakeside site with
rides like the Drive-a-Drome, the Stratoship, and the
Bunny Hug. The device was designed by James H. Strong
to train paratroopers.

The World's Fair model was a mushroom-shaped red
behemoth, emblazoned with the words "Life Savers
Candy," and was bedecked with the sweets in red, yellow, and green neon. Dripping with steel cables and guy
wires, the Parachute Jump originally held eleven gaily
colored parachutes—kept permanently open by metal
rings—each with a pair of seats underneath, surrounded
by a protective cage. After paying forty cents, riders were
strapped into their seats and pulled straight up to the
top by cables.

The trip up took about forty seconds—the ride's real

scare-time. Then, after the standard brief moment to re-
flect on life's uncertainties, an automatic release started
the drop, the parachute billowed, and riders whooshed
down to earth in about ten seconds, guided by more cables
and cushioned from below by shock absorbers beneath
the seats. After the Aquacade, it was the second-most-popular
attraction at the amusement area of the fair, according to
1939: The Lost World of the Fair (Free Press, 1995), by David
Gelernter.

The 170-ton structure was moved to Steeplechase
Park, just off the Coney Island boardwalk at Sixteenth
Street, in 1941. There it sank slowly into bittersweet obso-
lescence along with the rest of the park, which closed in
1964. The Parachute Jump stayed open until 1968, when
an inspection found that its weathered cables were unsafe.

Thrills and Romance

Q. *Down the way from the Cyclone roller coaster at
Coney Island, in Steeplechase Park, is another old roller coaster
that looks as though it's from the same era. What's the story?*

A. That's the Thunderbolt, the scene of screams,
dreams, and, it turns out, romance. This 1925 roller
coaster predates the Cyclone by two years; during Coney
Island's heyday, the steel-framed Thunderbolt rivaled the
wooden Cyclone in speed and scare factor, said John Manbeck, the Brooklyn historian.

The Thunderbolt was built and run by George H.
Moran, who willed it to his son Fred in 1965. As popular
as it was, the house underneath it may have attracted even
more attention: you might recognize it from scenes in the

1977 Woody Allen movie *Annie Hall*. But for more than forty years, it was the scene of an extraordinary real-life story. The house was the home of Fred; his girlfriend, Mae Timpano; and his mother, Mollie. Though Fred and Mae were a couple for four decades and lived together, they never married, acceding to Mollie's worries about an interfaith marriage.

"He was Jewish, and I was Catholic," said Ms. Timpano, sixty-nine, who now lives in Bensonhurst. "After Fred's brother died in World War Two, he didn't want to hurt her again." Fred Moran died in 1982, and the Thunderbolt stopped running a year later. Ms. Timpano finally moved out in 1988.

What was it like to live under a roller coaster?

"The days were noisy," Ms. Timpano said. "But at night it was like living in the country." She added: "It didn't bother us. We were very, very much in love." The house was gutted by a fire in 1991, and the developer who now owns the property, Horace Bullard, said plans for the site, which he would not discuss, were on hold.

Sweeping Statements

Q. *One morning back in 1989, as I waited in my parked car, a street-sweeper rolled up behind me and, to my astonishment, the inimitable voice of Mayor Ed Koch came blasting over a loudspeaker, scolding me and telling me to move my car immediately. How long was this grating message broadcast by city trucks?*

A. "It was novel, it was unique," a spokesman for the Department of Sanitation, Lucian Chalfen, said

of the short-lived experiment in extremely direct government. "But as with anything, it had its place, it had its
time." Introduced in May 1988, the recorded message
was broadcast from the mechanical brooms for fewer
than three years, until Mayor Koch was, er, swept from
office by David N. Dinkins in 1990. But it was fun
while it lasted: "This is Ed Koch, your mayor. You
know the Sanitation Department can't sweep this street
if you don't move your illegally parked car. Please get it
outta here."

The Sanitation Department introduced mechanical
brooms and alternate-side-of-the-street parking regulations in the 1950s, and it has struggled ever since with
illegally parked cars, each of which forces the sweepers
to leave about 30 feet of curb unscoured. Another Koch-
era weapon has survived: the Day-Glo green, so-called
ugly sticker, which since 1987 has been affixed to passenger windows of obstructing cars. The continuous
mayoral message was the idea of Vito A. Turso, then a
spokesman for the Sanitation Department. It was broadcast over the same 100-watt speakers used by fire trucks
and police patrol cars, which were gradually mounted on
all 450 of the city's mechanical brooms, according to Mr.
Chalfen.

The admonition was broadcast in all five boroughs, he
said, including Staten Island—where alternate-side-of-the-
street parking regulations didn't even exist. "It was quite
effective," he said.

No Microbrewery This

Q. *I have a clear 12-ounce bottle I found years ago in my backyard in Brooklyn Heights. On the bottom it says "Horton Pilsener Brewing Co., 460 W. 128th St., New York." Can you tell me about this brewery?*

A. The brewery was built by the Yuengling Brewing Company in 1876, in the village that was then known as Manhattanville—a dense, industrial enclave in the deep valley between Morningside and Hamilton Heights near the Hudson River. Nearby were the D. F. Tiemann pigment factory (from which Tiemann Place takes its name), a worsted mill, and the first buildings of Manhattan College.

The giant red-brick brewery included a swimming pool and opulent parlors for entertaining dignitaries, who included King Edward VII of England. More buildings and equipment were added after the brewery was purchased by the Bernheimer & Schwartz Brewing Company in 1903, and a 1911 advertisement for the beer depicts a brewing complex stretching from 127th Street to 129th Street along Amsterdam Avenue.

Prohibition closed up the brewery in 1920, and the sprawling parcel was purchased by the Horton Pilsener Brewing Company, which resumed production after Prohibition was repealed in 1933. Though the plant closed long ago, many of its buildings remain in commercial use.

Macy's Origins

Q. *Until a few years ago, the word "Macy's" and a red star were faintly visible over the doorway of the narrow nine-story building at 56 West Fourteenth Street. Was this the original site of the "world's largest department store"?*

A. That red star should look familiar. Though the original storefront was actually around the corner, this building was part of Macy's early and rapid expansion before construction of its Herald Square store and the move uptown in 1902.

Rowland Hussey Macy, a Nantucket Quaker, was born in 1837, and at age fifteen went to sea aboard the *Emily Morgan,* a whaling vessel bound for Cape Town and the South Pacific. Macy returned four years later with about $500 in savings—and a five-pointed red star tattooed on his forearm. After a succession of speculative disappointments and merchandising failures in Boston, Macy opened his first New York store—R. H. Macy—in 1858 at 204 Sixth Avenue, between Thirteenth and Fourteenth Streets, north of the city's established dry-goods district. Within a few years, he began to use the red star from his whaling days as his trademark.

Macy's introduced such commercial innovations as a money-back guarantee, fixed prices, and cash-only sales, and sewed made-to-measure garments in a factory on the premises. The business prospered. By the time Macy died in 1877, the store had expanded into a complex of eleven connected buildings on Thirteenth and Fourteenth Streets, including No. 56, and offered a vast selection of merchandise sold in different "departments." The No. 56 storefront is now occupied by a cut-rate Macy's descendant, 99-Cent City.

History to Chew On

Q. *To my delight and astonishment, my favorite chewing gum from childhood—Black Jack—suddenly reappeared at newsstands a couple of years ago, after an absence of many years. Then it disappeared again. What's going on?*

A. Sorry. The American Chicle Company stopped manufacturing Black Jack in the 1970s, a century after the gum first appeared in New York. Chewing gum, a New York invention, was first manufactured in 1870 by Thomas Adams in a warehouse on Front Street. Called "Adams New York Gum No. 1," it was made from chicle, a form of sapodilla tree sap chewed in the Yucatan and Guatemala.

Mr. Adams had tried unsuccessfully to use the chicle to manufacture rubber for car-

riage tires, but his chewing gums enjoyed great success, and they soon replaced the chewable paraffin wax that was then available. Licorice flavoring was added to create Black Jack.

History does not record when the first wad of used Black Jack landed on a New York City sidewalk, or who stepped on it. In 1899, Adams merged with six other gum manufacturers and became the American Chicle Company. In 1923 the company moved its factory and headquarters from Forty-fourth Street in Manhattan to Thomson Avenue in Long Island City, where Black Jack and other popular gums were produced beneath giant rooftop "Chiclets" and "Dentyne" signs.

An explosion and fire rocked the factory in 1976, and American Chicle left the city in 1981. The former factory is now part of the International Design Center. Since 1986, the licorice-flavored gum has been periodically reintroduced as a nostalgia item, explained Jeff Baum, a spokesman for the Warner-Lambert company, which has owned American Chicle since 1962. Black Jack was last shipped "a couple of years ago," Mr. Baum said, adding that though the company has no plans to produce the gum again, that remains a possibility.

Old Cold

Q. *Many prewar apartment buildings around the city have old signs stating that they are "equipped with General Electric refrigerators by Rex Cole." Obviously, electric refrigeration was quite a draw to apartment seekers—but who was Rex Cole?*

A. The name Rex Cole was a household word back in the 1920s and '30s, when refrigerator salesmen drove the city's icemen out of business. The General Electric Company produced its first electric refrigerator in 1926 and asked Mr. Cole, already an effective promoter for a lighting subsidiary, to distribute the product in New York.

He started with four employees and by 1931 had more than one thousand, in fifteen branches around the city. In that banner year his sales were $15 million. Many of the sleek Rex Cole showrooms, along with the fixtures and furniture, were designed by Raymond Hood, the innovative architect of the McGraw-Hill and Daily News Buildings. Most featured a sparkling white G.E. refrigerator atop the building, towering glass windows, and cool, modern interiors where the newest models were displayed in elegant austerity.

According to articles published after Mr. Cole's death in 1967, many thought "Rex Cole" was a trade name, one that perhaps meant "king cold," and were surprised to learn there was an actual person selling those refrigerators.

The Widget News

Q. *I recently overheard some old-timers chuckling over a newspaper called The Widget, which was published in New York in the 1960s. What on earth were they talking about?*

A. The New York *World Journal–Tribune,* a short-lived daily formed when three venerable New York newspapers merged in 1966. With tabloids like the New York *Daily News* and *Daily Mirror* winning instant popularity after World War I, many of New York's older dailies—

some of which had begun publishing before the Civil War—had already merged by the 1940s: *The Herald* and *The Tribune* in 1924, *The World* and *The Telegram* in 1931, and *The Journal* and *The American* in 1937. In 1950 *The World-Telegram* merged with *The Sun*. Strikes by several newspaper unions in the 1960s began to topple the city's remaining dailies. The *Mirror* declared bankruptcy in 1963; in 1966 *The Journal-American* and *The World-Telegram and Sun* combined with *The Herald Tribune* to form the hopelessly hybrid New York *World Journal–Tribune*, which was immediately nicknamed Widget by a doubting public. A four-month strike delayed the paper's debut until September 12, 1966. The Widget folded in May 1967.

Little House in Midtown

Q. *Years ago—it might have been in the 1930s—a modest wooden house was built at Park Avenue and Fortieth or thereabouts, then removed a year later. I can't recall why a home was built on such an expensive site, only to be torn down. Can you help?*

A. Yes, indeed. The little two-story Georgian house was built during the Depression as a "national demonstration of what the dollar will buy in the construction field," and stood for over a year, according to reports in architectural publications of the day. Christened America's Little House, it was built in 1934 for only $8,000 on one of the costliest housing sites in Manhattan, amid luxury apartment houses at Park Avenue and Thirty-ninth Street.

Designed by Roger H. Bullard and Clifford C. Winde-hack, the eight-room cottage was commissioned by a housing-industry organization called Better Homes in America, and was one of several model homes constructed in New York in that era, when large-scale development was rare. No wonder you remember the house: Mayor Fiorello La Guardia broke the ground, Eleanor Roosevelt laid the hearthstone, and CBS used it to broadcast three radio programs a week. More than 166,000 people paid ten cents each to visit before it was demolished. In June 1936 another short-lived home was built on the site, the all-steel House of the Modern Age, designed by William Van Alen, architect of the Chrysler Building. It was demolished that November.

The Vanishing Stairs Case

Q. *As a child long ago, I seem to remember mounting a grand staircase, much like that of the Metropolitan Museum, to enter the Brooklyn Museum. Am I mistaken, or were the stairs removed?*

A. There were indeed stairs there. The broad flight of steps, a defining feature of the 1893 Beaux Arts museum design by McKim, Mead & White, was removed in 1934. Riddled with structural and logistical problems, the staircase was declared unsafe in 1930, three years after the completion of the museum's East Wing, according to a 1988 essay on the museum by Joan Darragh, the museum's vice director for planning and architecture.

In 1934, Philip N. Youtz, director of the museum and a reform-minded modernist architect, began to reconfigure the museum. An avowed enemy of the processional architecture typified by the McKim, Mead & White plan, Youtz criticized the stairs as imposing and unsound. He argued that a street-level entrance would symbolically render the great Greco-Roman-style museum more "democratic" and accessible to the public.

The long stairway up to the portico was removed, and with it a formal yet animate public setting from which to enter or leave the building. All five finalists in a 1986 competition to renovate and eventually expand the museum included plans to reintroduce the grand stairway. The winning plan, by Arata Isozaki & Associates of Japan and James Stewart Polshek & Partners of New York, is currently being built in stages by the museum, but no date for the construction of a new staircase has been announced.

A Soda Label Fizzles

Q. *I'm a longtime fan of Dr. Brown's sodas, including the little drawings on the cans, which depict familiar landmarks of old New York. I recall that a can once featured the Third Avenue El, but I couldn't find it at the store. Was that flavor discontinued?*

A. Not the flavor, just the drawing. Dr. Brown's sodas—including the popular black cherry and cream sodas and the legendary celery-seasoned Cel-Ray—have been bottled and sold for 127 years in New York, where they are a fixture in many hearts and most delicatessens. But the current labels go back only about twenty-five years, to when they were designed by Herb Lubalin, said Murray Pollack, a spokesman for the Canada Dry Bottling Company of New York, which until recently owned Dr. Brown's.

Each of the six Dr. Brown's flavors was packaged with a New York vignette—all taken from old prints—to emphasize the brand's origins in old-time New York, Mr. Pollack said. Cream soda was adorned with the Statue of Liberty, Cel-Ray got the Brooklyn Bridge, and orange got the old Grand Central Terminal. Root beer got an old ice-cream parlor, ginger ale got the Astor Hotel, and the black cherry showed a station on the old Third Avenue Elevated line. But the el station, Mr. Pollack said, was deemed to be too obscure an image for non–New Yorkers, and was soon replaced by the Central Park carousel. He could not explain why the Astor Hotel—a regal Times Square establishment that was torn down decades ago—was kept.

Track Action

Q. *Last spring, when the surface of Broadway between 110th and 125th Streets was milled off for repaving, some sections of rusty old iron tracks were revealed. In some areas, there appeared to be a third, grooved rail between the other two. What were they for?*

A. These tracks were once used by streetcars of the Third Avenue Railroad System, which ran up Broadway from the turn of the century until the line closed in the late 1940s. Fare was a nickel on the red-and-white streetcars, which ran from First Avenue across Forty-second Street, up Broadway to 125th, then over to a Hudson

River ferry landing. They were converted from horse power to an electric conduit system around 1898, according to Joseph Brennan, a railroad and subway enthusiast.

Overhead trolley wires were forbidden in most parts of Manhattan, Mr. Brennan said, so power lines for the streetcars were placed underground, in the form of a pair of T-shaped rails set in the middle of the tracks, which were charged with 500 to 600 volts of direct current—the "third rail" that you saw. The streetcars made contact with the electrified conduit via a sliding collector that extended from beneath the car. The elaborate track-and-conduit assembly ran over 2 feet into the earth, Mr. Brennan said, and there was simply too much buried concrete and cast iron to tear up completely when the system closed. The tracks you saw disappeared when Broadway was resurfaced recently.

However, Mr. Brennan points out that a never-paved-over section of the Third Avenue crosstown line is on permanent display, on Twelfth Avenue between 125th Street and St. Clair Place, under the Riverside Viaduct.

Smoke on the Water

Q. *I read that an early automobile speed record was set at a raceway right here in Brooklyn. Where?*

A. In the days when gritty, goggled drivers in cloth caps hunched over their steering wheels roared around wooden tracks in cars that looked like soapbox racers, auto speed records were set at the Sheepshead Speedway in Sheepshead Bay. The speedway, a high-banked 2-mile racing oval, was built in 1915 along Ocean Avenue off

Jerome, on the former site of the Coney Island Jockey
Club Race Track. The track, like several others of its time,
was constructed entirely of wooden planks—two-by-fours
cut from Georgia pine and laid smoothly end to end—
which made "incredible" speeds of over 100 miles an hour
possible long before asphalt-paved speedways became
common.

During its brief heyday, the Sheepshead Speedway was
considered one of the fastest tracks in the world, earning
the nickname the Shrine of Speed. In its first race, on October 9, 1915, Gil Anderson set a world record, barreling
around the track in a Stutz for 315 miles at an average
speed of 102.6 miles an hour. On September 22, 1917,
fifty thousand spectators watched breathlessly as Louis
Chevrolet, the pilot and car designer, set a track record of
110.4 miles an hour in a car called a Frontenac. While dirt
and brick tracks of that era lasted much longer, the
Sheepshead Speedway closed in 1919 and was demolished in 1923. In 1924 the area was divided into four
thousand lots, which were auctioned off in six days.

Grid Yankees

Q. *My granddad likes to talk about a football team
called the New York Yankees that used to play up in the Bronx.
Is he making it up?*

A. Trust Grandfather. At least five New York Yankees
football teams made their homes in Yankee Stadium. The
first played its inaugural season in 1926, and included
the Galloping Ghost, Red Grange, as running back. When
the fledgling American Football League ceased operations

after only a year, the team disbanded. Until the New York Giants moved to Yankee Stadium in 1956, any new league that sought to challenge the National Football League established a team there hoping to borrow some of the Bronx Bombers' luster.

Yankee teams played in 1936, 1937, and 1940, under two different AFLs; both AFLs folded. In 1927 the young NFL even fielded its own Yankee team, which went 7-8-1, and then 4-8-1 in 1928. The team then disbanded. In 1946, the new All-American Football Conference included a dominant New York Yankee team. These Yankees—wearing navy-blue-and-silver uniforms, in contrast to the baseball Yankees' pinstripes—won divisional crowns in 1946 and 1947. The rangy Yankee halfback Orban (Spec) Sanders led the young league in rushing and scoring both years. He also played defense and was the team's punter. In 1949 the Yankees absorbed their local AAFC rival, the Brooklyn Dodgers. The team folded at the end of that season when the NFL absorbed the league. In 1950, the NFL's New York Bulldogs became the Yanks—and disbanded after two seasons.

Mohawks and Steel

Q. *I know that Mohawk Indian ironworkers helped build New York skyscrapers and bridges early in this century, and I always heard that it was because they had no fear of heights. Is that true? And are there still Indians in this line of work?*

A. Mohawk Indians make up 12 to 15 percent of ironworkers in the city, just as they did in the 1920s and 1930s, according to R. Victor Stewart, a spokesman for

Iron Workers Union Locals 40, 361, and 417. "There are Mohawks working on the Queensborough Bridge right now," he said. As for a fear of heights, the subject is not generally discussed among ironworkers, Mr. Stewart said, because none of them have it—Mohawks or anyone else. "There's a question on the job application that says 'Are you acrophobic?' " he said. "No one answers yes."

Kahnawake and Akwesasne Mohawks from upstate New York and Canada were the first to learn the trade, taking dangerous jobs no one else wanted on the elevated steel beams of railroad bridges and steel constructions along the St. Lawrence River in the late 1800s, Mr. Stewart said. "After they had developed the skills," he said, "it was natural for them to move to where the iron work was, in New York City."

Mohawks have helped build virtually every skyscraper and bridge in the city this century, including the Empire State Building, the George Washington Bridge, and the World Trade Center. Mr. Stewart explained that work "on the high steel" still requires exceptionally close communication. Many Mohawks, bound by cultural pride in the trade, still work together in crews, he said, explaining, "When you're five hundred feet up in the air in a twenty-mile-an-hour wind and they're bringing you a five-thousand-pound steel beam to hook in, you want to make sure your partner knows what you're going to do."

Planted in Memory

Q. *When I was a child back in the 1950s, I seem to recall shaking hands with Mr. Peanut in Times Square. Was I dreaming?*

A. No. The Mr. Peanut you recall was an employee of the Planter's Peanut store at 1560 Broadway. The store and its brilliant 15,000-bulb Mr. Peanut sign were Times Square landmarks in the years immediately following World War II, according to Richard D. Reddock, author of a book on Planter's Peanut memorabilia. He said that the store, largest in a national chain, closed around 1960. "You had glass display cases, a roasting machine with a Mr. Peanut sitting on top, a large 10-foot papier-mâché Mr. Peanut, a cast-iron Mr. Peanut scale, and in the back, a couple of costumes," Mr. Reddock said. The Mr. Peanut costume—white spats, cuffs, and gloves, a black cane, and a hard plastic peanut "shell" and top hat—would be worn by a tall, slender male employee of the store the entire workday, he said.

"He wasn't anything special . . . except some people had a feel for it." For the same wages as the store's other employees, Mr. Peanut wandered up and down Broadway in front of Planter's, posing for photographs, pointing to the store with his cane, and occasionally dispensing bags of peanuts, Mr. Reddock said. Sadly, Mr. Peanut was not allowed to speak.

A Casino in the Park?

Q. *While browsing through an old guidebook, I saw a reference to the Central Park Casino. Was there a gambling joint in the park, and if so, where?*

A. There wasn't a casino in Central Park. There was the Casino. The Casino was a swank, high-priced restaurant situated where Summerstage makes its home today. It was built in 1864 by Calvert Vaux as a "Ladies Refreshment Salon," and was converted into a "quiet little night club" in the early 1920s by Sidney Solomon, a restaurateur, according to *The Power Broker* (Knopf, 1974), Robert A. Caro's epic biography of Robert Moses, the parks commissioner. It was a favorite hangout of James Walker, the flamboyant 1920s mayor, and had a silver-and-maroon dining room, a glass-walled ballroom, and an orchestra that would play "Will You Love Me in December?" anytime the Mayor entered the room.

It was just this type of extravagance—and bad blood between Mr. Moses and Mayor Walker—that led to the Casino's demise in 1934. Mr. Moses argued that the prices were beyond the reach of the average citizen and thus the restaurant should be removed. Mr. Solomon countered that his friend the Mayor was the target of a Moses vendetta. After a series of legal machinations, a state appeals court ruled in favor of the Power Broker. Twenty-four hours later, in a flurry of jackhammers and settling dust, the Casino was gone.

The Other Avenue A

Q. *While browsing through some dusty books of yore, I found a passing reference to a building at East Ninetieth Street and Avenue A. This puzzled me, since the only Avenue A I know is in the East Village. What was Avenue A doing uptown?*

A. The name Avenue A, now given to fourteen oh-so-grungy-but-fashionable blocks in the East Village, once applied to the whole of what is today Sutton Place and

York Avenue, stretching north from East Fifty-third Street all the way to East Ninety-third Street.

Laid out in the 1811 Commissioner's Plan, which imposed a grid pattern on the city's streets, Avenue A was simply a line on a map until 1813, when the street actually opened, according to *The Iconography of Manhattan Island, 1498–1909* (1916; Arno Press, 1967), by I. N. Phelps Stokes. (The gap between Fourteenth Street and Fifty-third Street is explained by the geography of the island: Kips Bay and Turtle Bay, which were actually bays in 1811 and not just neighborhood names, cut off Avenue A as planners extended the line north.) The upper portion of Avenue A became known as York Avenue in 1928, named in honor of Sergeant Alvin C. York, World War I hero and later a successful Tennessee farmer, according to *The Street Book* (Hagstrom, 1978), by Henry Moscow. The Sutton Place portion was named for Effingham B. Sutton, a California gold prospector in 1849 and wannabe real-estate mogul who developed property along the southern stretch of the uptown Avenue A in the 1870s.

Houses That Brew Built

Q. *At the corner of Bushwick Avenue and Willoughby Avenue in Brooklyn, there are two interesting buildings across from each other. On the east side is 670 Bushwick, a dilapidated, turreted mansion, and on the west, 680 Bushwick, another old, crumbling, forbidding-looking home. Neither appears to be in active use, and both seem out of place in this row house–dominated 'hood.*

A. Those are two of the houses that brew built. "The history of Bushwick has been the history of brewing," says the *AIA Guide to New York City,* which attributes the large number of nineteenth-century breweries in the area to the surge of German immigrants following "unsuccessful uprisings in the Fatherland in 1848 and 1849." In fact, Bushwick—which is one of Brooklyn's oldest towns, incorporated in 1660—attracted so many brewmeisters that the area around Scholes and Meserole Streets became known as Brewers' Row.

Included in this brew crew were William Ulmer, who built the stolid mansion at 670 Bushwick in 1885, and Claus Lipsius, whose widow, Catherine, commissioned the Italianate mansion ("strangely windowed" the *AIA Guide* says) at 680 Bushwick in 1886. The days of beer and finely honed German design have passed. Both houses have long since been sold to other, decidedly un-sudsy owners and are presently unoccupied and in decay. The Ulmer residence was, most recently, home to a medical office. The Lipsius mansion housed a monastery.

The Waldorf's Oscar

Q. *I recently bought a 1,000-page antique cookbook published in 1896 called, quite simply,* The Cook Book, *by "Oscar" of the Waldorf. So, who was Oscar?*

A. "Oscar" was the legendary Oscar Tschirky, who for fifty years around the turn of the century reigned as the maître d'hôtel at the Waldorf-Astoria. Born in Switzerland in 1866, Tschirky arrived in New York with his mother on May 14, 1883, and the next day went to work as a busboy at the Hoffman House off Madison Avenue, according to *The Waldorf-Astoria: America's Gilded Dream* (Evans, 1991), a history by Ward Morehouse III.

But busing wasn't his thing. Besides, he had fallen in love with the sight of Lillian Russell eating at Delmonico's, and a week later he was working as a waiter there. In 1893, he was hired as the headwaiter at the Waldorf, which had recently opened and was the grandest joint in town. When he was asked for letters of recommendation, he produced only one, which included the signatures of Diamond Jim Brady and, of course, Miss Russell.

Tschirky was an institution through 1943—a 1934 roster listed him as "Host of the Waldorf-Astoria," right behind the manager, treasurer, and president—when he took an advisory position with the hotel until his death in 1950. Why should you care? Though he never cooked, Tschirky is credited with inventing staples of American cuisine like Waldorf salad and eggs Benedict.

The Tree of Hope

Q. *My mother grew up in Harlem and I vaguely remember her telling me something about a "tree of hope." Was it real? If so, where was it, and what was its significance?*

A. The tree once grew on the center island of Seventh Avenue and 131st Street, across from the old Lafayette Theater, which for three decades after its construction in 1910 was the nation's leading black theater. Entertainers who had fallen on hard times performed in front of the tree, believing that it had power to bring good luck, says Marcella Thum in the *Hippocrene U.S.A. Guide to Black America* (Hippocrene, 1991). The tree fell victim to urban renewal and was cut down.

A second tree on the same site was donated by the tap dancer Bill "Bojangles" Robinson in the 1930s, and he had a brass plaque embedded in the sidewalk with the inscription "The Original Tree of Hope Beloved by the People of Harlem—You asked for a tree of hope so here it is, Best wishes," followed by his signature. The second tree was also cut down, and was replaced by an interpretive sculpture by the artist Algernon Miller in 1972. But the tree still serves as inspiration: its stump remains a fixture on the stage of the Apollo Theatre, at 253 West 125th Street, where would-be stars rub it for luck.

The "Suicide Curve"

Q. *At Columbus Avenue and Cathedral Parkway there is an old six-story apartment building with a curve that would let a train track turn 90 degrees. Is this where the Ninth Avenue El's famous "suicide curve" ran from Ninth to Eighth Avenues?*

A. The people at the Transit Museum can't produce any gory tales of trains that careened off the tracks at that hair-raising turn, which was indeed part of the so-called suicide curve. But the tracks, which were torn down more than fifty years ago, left their imprint on the area's architecture. A serpentine curve twisted from Ninth Avenue (renamed Columbus) eastward to Eighth Avenue (later Central Park West). Built through a grassy, undeveloped section of the Upper West Side, the el, on completion, spurred residential and commercial construction along its corridor.

The resulting neighborhood was built to fit—one story for those buildings lurking underneath, and angled walls for those within shouting distance of the steam engines—perhaps as near as 4 feet.

Showtime Showdown

Q. *What happened to the Harlem Opera House that Oscar Hammerstein built?*

A. Showtime at the Apollo ultimately did it in. Oscar Hammerstein—not to be confused with his lyricist grandson, Oscar II—was a gutsy, stogie-chomping speculator who garnered the title "the father of Times Square" after he developed music halls and theaters in the area. In 1889, in a daring leap uptown, he opened the Harlem Opera House at 209 West 125th Street in hopes that the neighborhood would become the next bastion of the upwardly mobile (with disposable income for nightlife).

According to the Schomburg Center for Research in Black Culture, it was the first theater built north of Central Park, and Hammerstein operated it for several years as a legitimate opera house until the D. F. Keith vaudeville chain bought him out. After Harlem became a mostly black neighborhood, the policy switched in the 1930s to black entertainment, and patrons jumped to a different swing band each week. But the owners made a fatal mistake: they inaugurated those famous Wednesday-night amateur hours. And the Apollo Theatre raised the curtain on an identical format in 1935.

The two battled it out for a year, and the Apollo won. The Harlem Opera House showed movies until 1959, when it was demolished for a bowling alley. A business school and a health club are there now.

Terminal's Hideaways

Q. *A friend told me that a whole other world exists above the old waiting room of Grand Central Terminal—one of tennis courts and posh apartments. What's the story?*

A. Your friend is a little off on the location of the apartment, but there was one and it was posh indeed. In the 1920s, John W. Campbell, the president of the Credit Clearing House, had an office and pied-à-terre, modeled after an Italian villa, near the terminal's southwest corner. The duplex survives, with its two-story ceiling, walnut paneling, travertine walls, oak floors, and leaded-glass windows. And don't forget the wine cellar.

But put away your checkbook—it's not for rent. The tycoon's hideaway eventually became the headquarters for Metro-North's police department, and is now a signal control center. But as the terminal itself gets a makeover, the apartment will be removed from such mundane matters and restored to its original splendor as part of a new restaurant. The tennis courts, two of them, are directly above what was the main waiting room on the terminal's south side. The cavernous space was used for CBS television studios in the 1950s and these quarters are now leased by the Trump Organization and called, yes, the Tennis Club. Court time sets you back $95 an hour during the week, or $75 on the weekend.

NFL on SI?

Q. *The Giants' and Jets' poor football seasons have forced me to look to the past for solace. In rummaging through* *a football encyclopedia, I saw mention of a 1930s team in, of all places, Staten Island. Is this true? Was Staten Island ever big league?*

A. Oh yes, and to make it even sweeter, it stole the team from Brooklyn. During the Depression, from 1929 to 1932, the Staten Island Stapletons were proud members of the National Football League. The team was taken over by the Stapleton Athletic Club after a Brooklyn franchise, owned by C. C. Pyle, dissolved, according to the 1945 book *Football: Facts and Figures,* by Dr. L. H. Baker. The team's fortunes were not much better than those of this year's Giants (5–10, at time of writing) or Jets (3–12). Its best season (5–5–2) was in 1930.

The team's only real star was the quarterback, Bob Campiglio, who set a league record for running 504 yards in 104 attempts in 1932. A year later, the team, and the record, were gone.

Hailing from Herkimer

Q. *On a recent visit to see my grandfather in the Bronx, he referred to me as a "Herkimer Jerkimer." I think he was trying, jokingly, to call me, well, stupid. But I'm not sure. What does this mean?*

A. A Herkimer Jerkimer? Why, that's a local yokel, you rube.

"Herkimer Jerkimer" is city lingo for our less urbane countryfolk, according to *The City in Slang: New York Life and Popular Speech* (Oxford University Press, 1993), by Irving Lewis Allen. New Yorkers started to use the phrase in the 1940s, when "jerk" became part of urban argot. The "Herkimer" part of the snub refers to the upstate town of Herkimer, New York, 15 miles southeast of Utica, and, seemingly, a rustic breeding ground for country bumpkins. (According to city slickers, that is.)

Destruction of Temple

Q. *To the south of One Liberty Plaza (east of the World Trade Center) is a street sign that reads "Temple Street." The problem is, there's no street to be found, just Liberty Park. Was there a Temple Street here at one time, and if so, what happened to it and when?*

A. Temple Street was a block-long street running north from Cedar Street to Liberty Street between two large blocks of insurance company buildings, according to *The Iconography of Manhattan Island,* by I. N. Phelps Stokes. The street probably dated from the eighteenth century. When developers demolished the buildings in 1972 to make way for the park, they demolished the street as well. The sign was remounted after the development was complete.

The sign wasn't the only holdout. A Chock Full o' Nuts restaurant on the southeast corner of the plaza (between the ghost of Temple Street and Broadway) refused to give up its lease, and stood while the eleven stories above it and everything around was torn down. Its owners finally acceded in 1980 and allowed the building's destruction.

So ended the last business that could use Temple Street as part of its coordinates.

High Line History

Q. *What is that raised roadway, completely overgrown with tall grass, that crosses Tenth Avenue at about Fourteenth Street and runs along the avenue, through the buildings along the way?*

A. History! The overpass and the raised viaduct that run parallel to Tenth Avenue are what remain of the New York Central Railroad's High Line, a freight railway that served manufacturers along the route, according to Paul Fritz, a subway motorman and train historian. The High Line was opened on July 2, 1934, and replaced a ground route that existed as far back as 1849. It ran from the yards at Thirty-third Street down through the manufacturing and meatpacking districts to West Houston Street, stopping at sidings along the way to load and unload merchandise.

As manufacturing in the area slowed, southern portions of the High Line were demolished to make way for housing. The last train ran on the tracks in 1980—carrying three boxcars of frozen turkeys. In 1991, a five-block stretch along Washington Street was taken down amid protests from locals wanting to keep the High Line, and its history, intact. The remains, which you see, are owned by Conrail.

Moored on High

Q. *I heard that blimps once docked at the top of the Empire State Building. Is this true?*

A. Make that *blimp,* singular. When the landmark skyscraper was built in 1931, it was indeed designed as a blimp terminal. The balconies surrounding the top of the building's sixteen-story metal finial, now the 102nd floor, were equipped to secure and dock the dirigibles as well as to house ticket stands and loading docks. After the building was opened on May 1, 1931, and its mooring mast declared safe, it took four months before a blimp actually moored there. On September 16, 1931, *The New York Times* reported that a small privately owned blimp had docked for all of three minutes before taking flight. (This was after it circled for a half hour in 40-mile-per-hour winds, attracting quite a crowd of gawkers and tying up traffic below.)

Two weeks later a Goodyear blimp dropped a bundle of newspapers, but it failed in an attempt to dock in near-perfect conditions the next day, according to *The Encyclopedia of New York City.* After other docking failures, the mooring tower was abandoned in favor of a safer, more profitable venture: sightseeing.

Changed Exchanges

Q. *Does the phone company still use or issue exchange letters (like BUtterfield 8) to identify telephone number prefixes? And if so, is there any way to get a list of all the telephone exchange letters and their corresponding areas in New York City?*

A. The answer to your first question is: 66. (That's NO.) Telephone exchange letters, once a source of pride (and sometimes snobbery) among the city's callers, finally went the way of the dodo in the middle-to-late 1970s, said Dave Frail, spokesman for NYNEX. But it wasn't without some squawking. The demise of the letters, which paid tribute to streets and neighborhoods as well as prominent families and historic figures, began in 1960. In 1960, Fredrick R. Kappel took over as the CEO of AT&T (the 236 of 288) and decided to switch to an all-number system to ease direct dialing and directory information, according to *Telephone* (Harper & Row, 1975), a history of the phone, by John Brooks.

Early experiments with all-numbered prefixes in Council Bluffs, Iowa, went just fine. The trouble began when AT&T started to try to take away the letters in bigger cities. In San Francisco, phone users were so outraged they formed the Anti-Digit Dialing League and filed lawsuits to prevent the change (people really liked their letters). An October 1962 editorial in *The New York Times* in support of the league noted disdainfully that AT&T "wants nothing but numbers, just numbers—digits, just digits."

By the end of 1962, AT&T had a public relations fiasco on its hands and slowed down the plan to change the system, issuing all-number numbers to new customers only. Thus, letter exchanges were still being listed in city phone books as late as the late 1970s. (BUtterfield 8, made famous by the 1935 John O'Hara novel and the 1960 film starring Elizabeth Taylor, referred to numbers in a stylish area on the Upper East Side.)

Though less present in the lexicon now, the exchanges

are still used by some New Yorkers. No current maps or listings exist, Mr. Frail said, but if you check the front of any phone book before the change (available on micro-fiche at the New York Public Library), you can find a list of the lost letters.

"Billy's" Bawdy Roots

Q. *On the southwest corner of Avenue of the Americas and Twenty-fourth Street is Billy's Topless Dance Bar. Above the sign is a cement block in the building that says "The Corner 6th Avenue." On the other side one says "The Corner 24th Street." "The Corner" is also cut into the cornice. Was this the name of the building?*

A. This small red-brick building is all that remains of one of the most popular entertainment spots in the Gay Nineties. Built in 1879, it was called The Corner, and was the beer hall annex to Koster & Bial's Vaudeville Theater / Concert Hall, where Victor Herbert conducted his forty-piece orchestra. In *City of Eros: New York City, Prostitution, and the Commercialization of Sex, 1790–1920* (W. W. Norton, 1992), Timothy J. Gilfoyle writes: "John Koster, the proprietor of the popular Koster and Bial's, admitted that were the law enforced (on prostitution) he saw no other way of doing business than to shut up at once."

In 1896, Koster & Bial did close, and entered into a brief partnership with Oscar Hammerstein II at his Thirty-fourth Street Manhattan Opera House (on the present site of Macy's). Milton Anthony, who runs Billy's Bar, says he still considers the establishment "The Corner"—only now, "it's Billy's corner."

Daffydils of Old

Q. *The old song "Lullaby of Broadway" contains the line "the daffydils that entertain / at Angelo's and Maxie's." What were the daffydils and where were Angelo's and Maxie's?*

A. First, the daffydils. Joe Franklin, the former television host and a living encyclopedia of show-business trivia, says that "daffydils" was a "pet word for chorus girls," who often performed in the night clubs and restaurants with floor shows (known as "peacockeries," according to a 1935 article in the *Times*) that flourished in midtown after the repeal of Prohibition in 1933.

Angelo's and Maxie's, on the other hand, may have been stretches of the imaginations of Al Dubin and Harry Warren, who wrote the song for a number in Busby Berkeley's 1935 movie musical *Gold Diggers of 1935,* about a party girl's fall from grace. The song was resurrected for the 1980 musical *42nd Street.*

Mr. Franklin said that while "Angelo's" might have referred to the ninety-five-year-old Italian restaurant on Mulberry Street, "Maxie's" was just a convenient fiction to provide a rhyme for the preceding line: "The rumble of the subway trains / the rattle of the taxis." Irv Lichtman, deputy editor of *Billboard* and musical historian, agrees with Mr. Franklin, though he thinks there might have been an Angelo's restaurant in midtown somewhere. To further occlude the mystery, a 1935 phone directory actually lists a Maxie's restaurant at 109 Chrystie Street and an Angelo's restaurant at 160 Pearl Street.

Bronx Swing and Slalom

Q. *Maybe it's the heat, but my mind is on a winter ques-tion: I know that people sometimes cross-country ski in Van Cortlandt Park in the Bronx, but have people ever taken advan-tage of some of those hills for a little downhill action?*

A. Oh yes, and if you timed it just right, you might have been able to ski and play nine holes all in one go. Van Cortlandt Golf Course, at one hundred the nation's oldest public course, used to be home to the city's only public downhill ski course, according to Parks Department records. In 1961, the first slope was carved out below the south end near the present-day sixteenth hole. By 1964, there were snowmakers, rope tows, and a grandstand for spectators (not to mention Bronx cheers for beginners). The Big Apple's alpine event didn't last long, though. The popularity of winter golf caused the slopes to close in the mid-1960s.

Take the El to Japan?

Q. *Me and my peers (all native New Yorkers in our mid-fifties) disagree about where each of the Manhattan elevated trains was and when they came down. (One squabble involves a tale about the Japanese buying scrap and using it during World War II.) You could settle a lot of fights by giving us a definitive answer.*

A. Elevated trains once ran, as part of the IRT sys-tem, up Second, Third, Sixth, and Ninth Avenues, as well as over the streets in lower Manhattan, said Paul Fritz, a subway motorman and train historian who has created a comprehensive map of subway lines throughout the system's history. The els' disappearance, hastened by improving technology and the unification of the city's system, began in earnest with the abandonment of the Sixth Avenue elevated line in 1938 and its demolition a year later.

It was that demolition and its timing in relation to the 1941 attack on Pearl Harbor that sparked the myth of subway steel being used by the Japanese war machine, said Clifton Hood, author of *722 Miles: The Building of the Subways and How They Transformed New York* (Simon & Schuster, 1993). "It's not true, but its amazing how that story persists," chuckled Mr. Hood, who said the rumor was so pervasive during the war that Manhattan Borough President Stanley M. Isaacs commissioned an investigation. It found that the scrap had not made it into enemy

hands, though according to Mr. Hood, other scrap metal from around the country was bought by the Japanese before the war.

As for the Sixth Avenue scrap, a large portion was bought by two men (one from San Francisco, one from the Bronx) who paid $80,000 for some 20,000 tons of steel, according to the December 1938 issue of *The Bronx Home News*. The Board of Estimate approved the sale over the objections of the Bronx Borough President, who was concerned about the scrap being used by (you guessed it) enemy forces. The piecemeal demolition of the elevated lines continued. By 1942, the Second and Ninth Avenue lines were gone. The Third Avenue El lasted until 1955.

Tribe of Democrats

Q. *On the Upper East Side, there's a tiny street called Cherokee Place, just east of York Avenue. What's the story of its name? Indians? Jeeps?*

A. How about politicos? Cherokee Place, which runs from East Seventy-sixth Street to East Seventy-eighth Street, a half-block east of York Avenue, is the namesake of the Cherokee Club, a former political clubhouse on East Seventy-ninth Street, according to the Blue Guide to New York. Built around the turn of the century, the club, at 334 East Seventy-ninth Street, was a branch of the powerful Democratic patronage mill run out of Tammany Hall, and its handsome design was symbolic of the clout of local Irish-American politicians.

The club had all the trappings associated with back-room politics, according to Brent L. Brandenburg, a preservationist who documented the building, including a big portrait of Boss Tweed, power broker and embezzler extraordinaire, inside the door. Marked by floral motifs and two giant bas-relief Indian heads above the doorway, the Cherokee Club was demolished after an effort to make it a New York City landmark failed in 1976. But its influence is still evident in the neighborhood: along with Cherokee Place, there is the local Cherokee Post Office as well as the landmark Cherokee apartments on East Seventy-seventh Street. And influence, after all, was the name of the game.

Deciphering a Slogan

Q. *For years, an odd slogan was visible from the Queens approach to the Queens-Midtown Tunnel. It appeared to have been stenciled or painted on the outside of the overhead roadway and it read, "Wheels over Indian Trails." The words have since been eradicated, but I often wonder about it. Who painted it, and where did it go?*

A. The cryptic message that long adorned the overpass of the Pulaski Bridge at the tunnel approach was the work of the artist John Fekner, who painted the message in tribute to the thirteen Indian tribes that once lived on Long Island. Mr. Fekner, who is now the director of the computer graphics program at the C. W. Post campus of Long Island University, painted the piece (in artspeak: spray paint on concrete, $3^1/2'$ x 25') with the help of two friends under cover of night during the summer of 1979.

The friends held on to Mr. Fekner while he leaned over the edge of the bridge to paint several giant stencils. The slogan was intended to give commuters something "to think about while stuck in fumes and gas and smog," he said. The bridge is just a few hundred feet from the ancient meeting ground of the Mespat Indians (who gave their name to Maspeth).

The message remained untouched for eleven years, until Earth Day 1990, when Mr. Fekner, feeling the piece had run its course, painted over it. But the words "Wheels over Indian Trails" apparently stuck with people: the slogan has popped up in the choruses of at least two punk rock songs.

The Ruins on Roosevelt Island

Q. *At the southernmost tip of Roosevelt Island, there is the abandoned shell of a four-story building. These ruins are sometimes illuminated by a series of floodlights carefully placed to create a rather dramatic effect. What's the story here? What was the building? Why is it lit on some nights and not on others? Are there any future plans for the relic?*

A. As in a well-structured play, the dramatic effect is supposed to facilitate an even more dramatic effect. (This will make sense—patience!) The lighting of the Smallpox Hospital, a New York City landmark dating to 1856, is an attempt by the Friends of Roosevelt Island Landmarks to attract attention to the ruins. Why? Because the nonprofit group is trying to raise $200,000 for a permanent display, which could be viewed from Queens as well as from Manhattan. (The current display, accomplished with several old "tin-can" floodlights, has been on most every night since February 1995, said Lynne Abraham, spokeswoman for the Friends. Before that, the ruins were lit about once a month, usually on holidays.)

The hospital, which was designed by James Renwick when Roosevelt Island was also the site of a prison as well as of hospitals for the tubercular and the insane, has fallen into dangerously bad shape and is not open to the public. Plans for stabilization depend on new financing.

The Nineteenth-Century Ghetto

Q. *I have often read about the Five Points area of Manhattan in histories of New York City. Can you pinpoint it on a modern map?*

A. Five Points, a nineteenth-century slum described variously as "an abode of atrocious crime" and a place where once "evil passions made their playground," was located about where the southwest corner of Columbus Park in Lower Manhattan is today. Kenneth Holcomb Dunshee, who wrote *As You Pass By* (Hastings House, 1952), a survey of the city's historic districts, placed Five Points at the intersection of Orange Street (now Baxter), Anthony Street (now Worth), and Cross Street (what's left of it is now Mosco Street).

The result was a star-shaped convergence of streets and buildings, the corners of which gave the name Five Points to the area. It was just east of a freshwater pond called the Collect, which was a magnet for water-hungry tanners and brewers, and their money-hungry laborers, at the end of the eighteenth century. In the 1790s and 1800s, business and population grew around the area, and the Collect's waters were gradually fouled and filled with garbage.

By 1811, according to the Blue Guide to New York, it had disappeared altogether. But the local neighborhood hadn't. Five Points had become a squalid square populated by destitute immigrant families, gangs, and seamy characters drawn by local saloons and other "nests of iniquity," according to the 1893 *King's Handbook to New York*.

A five-story brewery building that stood where the County Courthouse is now was particularly infamous. During the 1840s, legend has it, it housed up to twelve hundred people at a time—and was equipped with a dirt basement just right for sudden, surreptitious burials. The brewery was demolished in the early 1850s, and by the turn of the century, with the construction of wider streets and a new square, the *King's Handbook* could proclaim Five Points "generally improved sanitarily and socially" and a home to "industrious working people."

Capital Criminals

Q. *Who was the last person executed in the city?*

A. When Eddie Lee Mays, a convicted murderer, was shipped "up the river" to the electric chair at Sing Sing Correctional Facility in Ossining, New York, on August 15, 1963, he became the last New York County inmate to be executed. But according to Larry Fleischer, who teaches legal history and law and literature at the Graduate School of Liberal Studies at New York University, Daniel Lyons was probably the last person to be executed within the city. A murderer, he was hanged at the New York County Jail, more commonly known as the Tombs, in 1888, shortly before a law prohibiting executions in the city took effect. But he was comparatively lucky. Mr. Fleischer reports that until 1835, when public executions were officially banned, prisoners were sometimes paraded over a 2-mile course down Canal Street to the execution site, where they were met by a waiting throng eager to witness the deed.

All-Star Pack Rats

Q. *I recently saw a movie review by Ed Koch in which he wrote: "The two uncles are Collyer Brothers types, living in an apartment packed with old newspapers." My question: Who were the Collyer Brothers?*

A. In the first half of this century, the Collyer brothers, Homer and Langley, were perhaps the most famous eccentrics in New York, a pair of recluses who lived in a booby-trapped, junk-stuffed, and yes, Mr. Koch, newspaper-packed brownstone until their mysterious demise in 1947, according to *Manhattan '45* (Oxford University Press, 1987), by Jan Morris.

The Collyers moved into 2078 Fifth Avenue (at 128th Street) in 1909. Homer, the older brother, worked as a lawyer, and Langley was a concert pianist. Throughout their lives, though, their residence was off-limits to anybody but themselves. (They forswore gas, electricity, and every other modern convenience.) Homer was rendered blind and bedridden by a stroke in 1932, and the Collyers withdrew further. Langley left the house only to buy groceries for his brother, though he sometimes went on daylong runs to Williamsburg for whole wheat bread.

Though the tabloid press speculated about their worth, the Collyers managed to remain safely sheltered. Until they died. On March 21, 1947, *The New York Times* reported, the police received a strange phone call from someone saying Homer was no more. Police tried to break into the house. No luck. They tried axes. Something still blocked the way. Finally, they managed to force a second-floor shutter open. Inside they found the late Homer, sitting straight upright in a gray bathrobe. Downstairs, firemen made it through the front door to find their way blocked by thousands of neatly bundled stacks of newspapers. What they did not find was Langley.

The mystery persisted for more than two weeks, as the authorities cleaned out an estimated 120 tons of debris, including fourteen grand pianos. The house was labyrinthine, with tiny passages between towers of stacked books, boxes, and papers, periodically rigged with wire and bucket booby traps. Ah, those booby traps. It was on April 8 that they finally found Langley, dead about a month, decomposing under a crushing stack of newspapers, apparently a trap gone wrong. He lay about 10 feet from where his brother, left without his caretaker, had died. Thus, the Collyers, front-page news in the spring of 1947, became part of the lexicon—and the very papers that they knew so well.

Scoping Out Shoes

Q. *In the 1940s my mother took my brothers and me to a shoe store for special orthopedic shoes on Third Avenue. I was very young, but I remember they had a huge rectangular box, which we climbed up on. There was a "viewer" somewhat like binoculars. We looked down and we could see the bones in our feet. What was the box called?*

A. That box was a fluoroscope, and the reason you don't see them anymore is because they weren't the safest contraptions. Dr. Bill Rossi, a podiatrist and former editor of *The Boot and Shoe Recorder,* says the fluoroscopes, which used X rays to view bones, were in vogue in children's shoe shops around the country immediately after World War II. Generally about 3 feet tall, with slots at the bottom to slip your feet into, they were used to convince parents of a shoe's fit—a selling point that occasionally backfired.

"It was a curse, because most shoes don't fit perfectly," Mr. Rossi said. "The flaws in the shoe design would show up." More serious concerns about the liberal use of X rays also arose.

Improvements in technology have given the device a renaissance in medical circles, but don't expect shoe stores to stock up anytime soon.

Taft to Michelangelo

Q. *What ever became of the Hotel Taft? My grandparents honeymooned there in the 1930s and my parents stayed at the Taft in 1967, but I find no record of it now. Apparently, a big band radio show was broadcast from the top of it.*

A. The Taft, at 777 Seventh Avenue, between Fiftieth and Fifty-first Streets, built to cater to the Broadway tourist crowd, has seen more than its share of drama in its lifetime. Built as the Hotel Manger in 1926, it stood twenty stories, had 1,432 rooms, and was Manhattan's third-largest hotel. Right around the corner from the Roxy Theater, it was often host to big bands, including George Hall's orchestra on the rooftop and the Vincent Lopez band, which broadcast a weekly radio show out of the Taft Grill for more than twenty-five years. It was also unfortunately popular with suicides, including a midnight jumper in 1954 who shocked a rapt crowd estimated at five thousand people when she leaped to her death.

Another potential jumper was coaxed to safety in 1957 by a passing priest. (The crowds, ever present, went wild.) The Taft hit hard times in the 1970s and was gutted in 1985. It was remodeled, and reopened as the Grand Bay Hotel in 1986. It is now home to a new hotel, the Michelangelo.

A Colonial Memory

Q. *Just off Kings Highway in Brooklyn is what looks like an ancient farmhouse that is still a residence. It's at the intersection of Avenue P and Kings Highway, on East Twenty-second Street. The mailbox bears the faded words "Bennett House" and, unique in that neighborhood, there is no sidewalk in front. What gives?*

A. The house is the last remnant of the Bennett family, the first Brooklynites and a presence in the borough for four centuries. Adrianse Bennett was the first person to buy land in Brooklyn, dealing with the Mohawk Indians in 1636 for a parcel in Gowanus. About two hundred years later, a descendant, Cornelius Bennett, was also looking for a house and came upon the Dutch-style farmhouse that is now on East Twenty-second Street.

The farmhouse, built for the Wyckoff family in 1766, was the centerpiece of a 100-acre farm running from the house south to the ocean. Cornelius bought the house in 1835 and kept it in the family for another four generations, weathering such inconveniences as the incorporation of Brooklyn into New York City (which resulted in the breaking up of the 100 acres) and various attempts by the upstart city to throw pavement around the house.

One attempt resulted in the house's being lifted and turned from its original orientation, facing south, to a westerly view to allow for the construction of a street. Another attempt, to pave a sidewalk in front of the house, was thwarted by Gertrude Ryder Bennett, the last direct descendant to live there, who called in the Landmarks

Preservation Commission to prevent concrete from blemishing the area in front of her white picket fence.

The concrete still stops at the property line along East Twenty-second Street. The current owners, who bought the house after Ms. Bennett died in 1982, are not Bennetts but have kept the interior intact, right down to the two names scrawled into panes of glass, apparently left by two Hessian soldiers during the Revolutionary War: "Toepfer Capt of Reg de Ditfurth" and "MBach Lieutenant v Hessan Hanau Artilerie." (Spelling wasn't the Hessians' strong suit.) It is not open to the public, but is sometimes included in tours by the Brooklyn Historical Society.

Thanksgiving Begging

Q. *When I was growing up in Bay Ridge, Brooklyn, in the 1950s, little was made of Halloween trick-or-treating. Instead, we went out, dressed as Indians or ragamuffins, on Thanksgiving morning, to ask neighbors: "Anything for Thanksgiving?" We were given coins, apples, nuts, candy, etc. This would last till about noon. Can any "old Brooklynite" comment on the custom of Thanksgiving begging? How widespread was it? How did it start? Why did it end?*

A. Its exact beginnings are hard to pinpoint, but it probably dates back to at least the early part of the century, says Professor Jack Santino, an expert on holidays at the Department of Popular Culture at Bowling Green University. Mr. Santino has spoken to Jewish and Italian Brooklynites who remember such holiday begging in their immigrant communities as far back as the early 1920s, and he believes it may date back even further.

The tradition, he says, probably stems from a European tradition of symbolic begging on holidays, a custom still palpable in trick-or-treating on Halloween, begging for pennies on Guy Fawkes Day, and even in Christmas caroling. Mr. Santino says that the booty from Thanksgiving begging was sometimes shared with the less fortunate in communities, but the begging was never really integrated with the idea of Thanksgiving.

Brooklyn, with a large European immigrant population, was a natural breeding ground for this custom, which probably was practiced on Thanksgiving simply because it was an already established American holiday. The custom died out as trick-or-treating became more popular after World War II, though a Ragamuffin Parade, established in 1966, is still active in Bay Ridge. The parade, usually held on the last Saturday of September or the first Saturday of October, attracts thousands of children in costumes, and more than a few ragamuffins.

Bong, Boink, Ding

Q. *Years ago when I went into a department store in New York City I used to hear this sound I liked: bong, bong, bong. What was this for? And how come I don't hear this today in department stores?*

A. The bong, bong, bong—or the bong, bing, boink, pause, ding—that could be heard in almost all of the department stores around the city was a paging system in the 1960s and '70s called Autocall, said Barbra Lewinsky, a spokeswoman for Bergdorf Goodman, who asked around until she found store employees who remembered the system.

They told her that every manager was assigned a code. For example, the cosmetics counter manager may have been assigned two beeps, a pause, and a bong. If someone wanted to reach that manager, the person would call the store operator, who would in turn project the sounds over the speaker system. The manager would know to pick up the phone and find out where the page came from.

"It was a forerunner to the beeper systems that are now in place," she said.

It seems that none of the major department stores in Manhattan still use this system, but for those fans of the binging (however few you may be), it may still be used in some of the older department stores around the country, Ms. Lewinsky said. And there's always the doorbell.

Anniversary Day Lives

Q. *During the early- to mid-1940s, public school children in the five boroughs enjoyed a holiday called Anniversary Day, which commemorated the founding of Brooklyn Sunday schools. I remember parades and banners and ice cream, but recently Anniversary Day seems to have disappeared. What is the history of this holiday and why was it discontinued?*

A. It has not disappeared. Howard Topoff, professor of psychology at Hunter College and lifelong Brooklyn resident, says Anniversary Day, more commonly known as Brooklyn Day, began in 1829 as a Protestant Sunday school festival. In a 1984 article on the Op-Ed page of *The*

New York Times, Mr. Topoff said that somewhere along the line, it metamorphosed into a day to celebrate the founding of Brooklyn. And in 1959, the Board of Education extended the holiday to cover the founding of Queens. Though parades and banners might not be in abundance, the holiday, usually celebrated on the second Thursday in June, closes schools in Brooklyn and Queens.

Masonic Mysticism

Q. *There's a building on West Seventy-third with these huge globes on its front that light up and give off a strange Gothic effect. What's the story of the globes, and the rest of the building?*

A. The building at 253 West Seventy-third Street is actually a kind of glorified clubhouse, one of several built in the area during the 1920s and '30s. Called the Level Club, it was commissioned in 1924 by a Masonic fraternal club called the Levellers, which was waging a friendly competition with the Shriners over who would build the nicer fort. Designed to be "the finest Masonic club in the world," the building served as a hostel for visiting Masons, and when it finally opened in 1927, it included an enormous banquet room, an Olympic-sized pool, a gymnasium, a fifteen-hundred-seat theater, and a roof garden.

Masonic symbolism fills its architecture. Bruno Bertuccioli, author of *The Level Club: A New York Story of the Twenties* (Watermark Press, 1991), writes that the front façade was designed in the image of King Solomon's Temple, a central symbol in Masonic tradition, and that the bronze globes (actually planets adorned with water lilies) are supposed to symbolize earthly love. Despite all the Masons' middle-class mysticism, the Level Club went into bankruptcy in 1930. Since then the Level Club has functioned as a hotel, an SRO, and the headquarters of Phoenix House, which operates a network of drug treatment centers. In 1982, it was bought by West Side Associates and renovated as a residential condominium. It is listed in the *National Register of Historic Places*.

Forgotten Kips

Q. *I recently moved to Kips Bay Towers and am eager to know whether there is or ever was a real Kips Bay.*

A. There was, and there isn't. The city's official map from the early 1800s shows Kips Bay dipping west past First Avenue between Thirty-seventh and Thirty-fifth Streets. Jeanie Sakol, a historian for neighboring Turtle Bay, said that in the mid-1600s, a Dutchman named Jacobus Kip established a large estate in that area. He called it Kipsberry or Kippenburgh. Later generations of Kips decided to name the bay after themselves. What's there now? The FDR Drive and some train tunnels. Of Kips Bay, Ms. Sakol said, nothing remains "but the name."

Recalling Ladies' Mile

Q. *Way back in the labyrinth of my mind I seem to remember my mother taking me to a store called Siegel Cooper. Is this a figment of my imagination or a tribute to my memory?*

A. If you were living in New York before World War I, it is a tribute. If not, perhaps you are simply psychic. The Cooper-Siegel Dry Goods Store was an emporium along Ladies' Mile, in a neo-Renaissance-style building at 616–632 Avenue of the Americas between Eighteenth and Nineteenth Streets. Designed by DeLemos & Cordes, a prominent architectural firm of the 1890s, the store was referred to by its owners, Henry Siegel, a Chicago merchant, and Frank H. Cooper, as "The Big Store—A City in Itself." It opened on September 12, 1896, and 150,000 shoppers jammed Sixth Avenue, as the thoroughfare was officially known until 1945, to get in. Cooper-Siegel closed during World War I. The building is now leased to a variety of commercial tenants.

Indispensable After All?

Q. *There is a building at Christopher Street and Waverly Place that has been vacant for quite some time, with the sign "Northern Dispensary" on it. Do you have any info?*

A. The 165-year-old dispensary was once the primary source of health care for thousands of poor New Yorkers. The building sits on a small triangular patch bounded by Christopher Street, Waverly Place, and, in one of New York's most delectable geographic oddities, Waverly Place again. (Waverly Place splits in two at the building's easternmost point.) A southern dispensary, located near Town Hall, was founded in 1791 to provide basic medical services to the indigent. In 1824, residents of what was at that time the city's northern edge (Greenwich

Village and Chelsea) decided their area needed a place to care for the less fortunate.

After working in a variety of temporary lodgings, the clinic's organizers moved into the new building in 1831 and served a steady stream of sick stewards, hacking valets, and droopy dockworkers. (Not to mention morose poets: Edgar Allan Poe stumbled in with a nasty cold in 1837.) The dispensary remained in business, in various forms, until 1989, when its final incarnation, a dental clinic, closed after being criticized by the Human Rights Commission for refusing care to people with AIDS. BRC Human Services, a nonprofit organization, is seeking to convert the building into housing for homeless people with AIDS.

Local Island-Hopping

Q. *I happened to be doing a little pleasure boating the other day and noticed an odd overgrown little island just north of Rikers Island, with some very interesting ruins on it. What's the story?*

A. It begins back in 1614, according to Lloyd Ultan of the Bronx County Historical Society, when a Dutch sea captain named Adriaen Block (after whom Block Island was named) was exploring and mapping the area around the Harlem River and Long Island Sound. He found two little similar-looking islands and called them *gesellen,* Dutch for "the brothers." They came to be known as North and South Brother Islands. The ruins on North Brother are the remains of the Riverside Hospital for Communicable Diseases, a city-owned asylum established in 1885. Its most famous resident was Mary Mallon, the cook who became known as Typhoid Mary. She died there (of a stroke). North Brother has its place in history for another reason: it is a grave marker of sorts for Little Germany, a stretch of the East Side from Houston Street to Fourteenth Street. On a June morning in 1904, the *General Slocum,* a steamboat filled with residents of Little Germany, beached there in the captain's desperate attempt to save the passengers from a roaring fire. Many died in the fire; hundreds tried to jump from the stern but drowned when they leaped into water 30 feet deep. The death toll was more than one thousand, and Little Germany dispersed, with survivors moving back to Germany or up to Yorkville. In the mid-1950s, the island was home to a school for teenage addicts. In the '80s, plans were abandoned to build a prison (as you note, the island is quite near Rikers Island). Currently, its main function is to confuse pleasure boaters.

The Ghost Marina

Q. *I live in the Sherman Creek area of Inwood, and have noticed an abandoned marina on the Harlem River, at Tenth Avenue and Dyckman Street. There must be about thirty smashed-up boats in this grim nautical graveyard. What happened?*

A. The little inlet, a marina since at least the 1920s, filled with sediment over the years, and in the late 1970s and early 1980s arson wiped out most of the remaining piers and boathouses. "Now you can probably walk across it at high tide," said Dennis C. Reeder, the director of the Washington Heights and Inwood Development Corporation. In its heyday, which probably lasted through the 1950s, the little marina was home to about sixty boats and at least five boat clubs, including the Bohemian, the Lone Star, and the Atalantic. The New York University crew had a boathouse there. But the marina silted over with sewer outflow, so dredging posed ecological problems, Mr. Reeder said. And as the clubs lost interest in long-term leases, and the piers and boathouses burned down, many owners just left their boats behind. They remain to this day, unmanned and useless, sailing atop the muck at low tide.

Print Is No Hallucination

Q. *My wife and I have a print of a favorite Georgia O'Keeffe painting,* New York Night *(1929), which depicts the Manhattan skyline above a long avenue shimmering with tiny headlights. The foreground is dominated by a dark, castlelike tower with a large, rose-shaped window near the top. For many years we have searched New York for this strange building. Does it still exist? Did it ever?*

A. It's the Beverly Hotel, at East Fiftieth Street and Lexington Avenue. In November 1925, Georgia O'Keeffe and the photographer Alfred Stieglitz moved into an apartment on the thirtieth floor of the Shelton Hotel (now the Marriott East Side), on Lexington Avenue between Forty-eighth and Forty-ninth Streets. O'Keeffe left the windows uncurtained, and the light-filled living room, which faced north and east, became her studio. *New York Night* is a painting of Lexington Avenue as O'Keeffe saw it looking out from her studio in 1929, when the peculiar-looking twenty-six-story Beverly, then only two years old, obscured much of the streetscape. Nonetheless, in a 1976 catalog of her work, O'Keeffe wrote of the painting that Lexington "looked, in the night, like a very tall thin bottle with colored things going up and down inside it." Between 1925 and 1929, O'Keeffe completed more than twenty paintings, pastels, and drawings of various New York skyscrapers and views of the East River from the Shelton. The skyscraper paintings from this period, virtually the only time O'Keeffe focused on New York as a subject, dramatize the soaring verticality of the exuberant, ambitious city of the 1920s in a precise, hard-edged style. Several depict buildings at night, their windows aglow. *New York Night,* by the way, is on display in Lincoln, Nebraska, in the Sheldon Memorial Gallery at the University of Nebraska.

Theater Alley District

Q. *In lower Manhattan between Ann and Beekman Streets is a dingy corridor called Theater Alley. Was this once a theater district?*

A. After the first amateur theaters were built on Nassau Street and near Broadway about 1732, the theater district crept north, becoming more commercial and more cosmopolitan. In 1798, the city's first fully appointed and elegantly built theater, the New Theatre, opened on Park Row, which became a center of theatrical activity during the early nineteenth century. The theater was later known as the Park, and its stage door opened onto the street now called Theater Alley. The Park Theatre was designed by Joseph Mangin, a French architect who with John McComb later designed City Hall. According to Mary C. Henderson's book *The City and the Theatre* (James T. White, 1973), the Park was the city's first theater with a permanent company, and it engaged the greatest English actors of the day. While a handful of theaters like the Park and the Chatham Gardens clustered around Park Row, by the mid-1820s larger theaters were built on Broadway near Houston Street and on the lower Bowery, including the Vauxhall Garden Theatre, the Bowery Theatre, and Niblo's Garden. The Park Theatre burned and was rebuilt several times, but more populist entertainments took root in the theaters and concert halls along Broadway and the Bowery, catering to the city's swelling population of immigrant workers. By 1848, when the Park Theatre closed for good, the Park Row area was rapidly becoming the center of the city's newspaper industry.

Shoes for Show Folks

Q. *Looming over Times Square, on the north side of Forty-sixth Street just east of Broadway, are four statues of great actresses from the 1920s in some of their most famous roles. Above them is an inscription saying that "famous show folks" bought their shoes at this shop. What was the shop, and who put up those statues?*

A. Israel Miller, a shoemaker from Poland, arrived in New York in 1892 and began making shoes for theatrical productions. His designs were popular with many vaudeville performers, who turned to him to produce their personal footwear. In 1911 he opened a small store in a brownstone at 1552 Broadway, at Forty-sixth Street, which he soon expanded into the adjacent property at 1554 Broadway, as well as to the showrooms on the upper floors of both buildings.

When he acquired long-term control of the property in 1926, Miller unified the buildings' façades, using marble with granite trim, and bronze fittings around the showcase windows. The wall along West Forty-sixth Street, beneath the cornice, bears the inscription "The Show Folks Shoeshop Dedicated to Beauty in Footwear." Niches were added along the wall to honor four of New York's then-favorite actresses. Miller released a public ballot to pick actresses in drama, musical comedy, opera, and film.

The winners were: Ethel Barrymore as Ophelia, Marilyn Miller as Sunny, Rosa Ponselle as Norma, and Mary Pickford as Little Lord Fauntleroy. Mr. Miller commissioned Alexander Stirling Calder to make these sculptures, which were unveiled on October 20, 1929. In 1990 the organization Save the Theaters, seeking landmark status for the façade, prepared a report for the Landmarks Preservation Commission with this information. Landmark status was denied.

Signs of the Times

Q. *Wasn't there a time when each borough had different-colored street signs? When did they become uniform, and what are the exceptions?*

A. It is true, street signs were once color-coded by borough. Queens signs featured blue lettering on white signs, Brooklyn had white letters on black signs, the Bronx was white on blue, and Manhattan and Staten Island were both black on yellow.

In the late 1970s, Federal funding laws began to require uniform signage, and so every borough went to green with white letters. There are exceptions. When a street name changes, it will get a blue sign with white lettering placed above the green sign. In historic districts, all the streets in the district have terra-cotta (a.k.a. brown) signs. And in places such as along the river in Williamsburg, old street signs can still be spotted, rusting reminders of days gone by.

7 Tell It to the Judge

Stretch Limo Intrepid

Q. *I live in Little Italy, where it's not uncommon to see superstretch limousines, turning from one narrow street to another, actually driving up on the sidewalk. Is there a legal limit to the length of these land yachts?*

A. New York City does not restrict bad taste per se. But part of Section 385 of the New York State Vehicle and Traffic Laws states: "The length of any single vehicle, inclusive of loads and bumpers, shall be not more than 40 feet. . . ." (Buses, fire vehicles, semitrailers, and construction equipment are excepted.)

A sedan limousine from the factory is usually about 18 feet long, while a typical stretch limo, created by slicing a car in two and inserting a midsection, is about 22 feet.

If the "stretched" part—measured from the rear edge of the original front door to the front edge of the original rear door—exceeds 100 inches (a little over 8 feet), the builder has to certify that the limo meets additional safety requirements, according to Thomas D. Apple, a spokesman for the New York State Department of Motor Vehicles.

Companies offering stretch and superstretch limos in New York rarely venture beyond the twelve-seat, 120-inch-stretch zone—there are few reputable builders—but an informal poll revealed that a handful of 32-, 34-, and 40-footers are out there.

Mr. Apple said there are no restrictions on where the superstretch limos may be driven. "But I can't imagine driving something like that in the city," he said. "In some neighborhoods, you'd be all over the sidewalks."

Pigeon Feeders Beware

Q. *Is it really against the law to feed pigeons?*

A. Only if you're causing them to gather in enormous numbers.

"We neither encourage nor discourage the feeding of pigeons," said a spokesman for the Department of Health, John Gadd. But where pigeons congregate in sufficient numbers, in an area where people live and eat, it can create a public health nuisance, he warned.

Most complaints about pigeon feeders, Mr. Gadd said, are made in the summer, when the Department of Health gets up

to twenty calls a week. Many, he said, involve people feeding pigeons from their apartment windows, which is considered unsanitary. Where a public health nuisance—a misdemeanor under Article 3.11 of the city's health code—is found actually to exist, the Health Department will usually issue a warning.

If that warning is ignored, a feeder can receive a summons leading to a fine of up to $1,000, Mr. Gadd said. "I'm not aware of a large number of these fines being collected," he added.

Milk Money

Q. *I've seen warnings on milk crates around the city with a warning that the illegal use of the crate is punishable by "fine and/or imprisonment." How much of a fine or imprisonment are we looking at if we dare use a milk crate for a seat?*

A. Hold on to your seat. After a warning, you would face a maximum fine of $300 for the first violation and up to $600 for a subsequent violation. But inspectors from the state's Department of Agriculture and Markets are unlikely to impose that fine. Intended to prevent the unauthorized use of crates among milk dealers, the regulations were instituted in 1922 and are investigated only when there are complaints.

But department officials can't remember the last time they've received a complaint.

The department does enforce its regulations on the deposit on crates that apply to dairies and wholesale customers like grocery stores, restaurants, and hospitals. The minimum deposit is $2 upstate and fifty cents in the metropolitan region; the dealer is supposed to collect the deposit from the buyer at the time of delivery.

The deposit regulation helps reduce the loss of cases, which cost $2.50 to $3 to produce. The rules also work toward fair competition by requiring identification of the case—"clearly printed, embossed, inscribed or otherwise permanently marked"—and the collection and refund of the deposit.

Officials do not recall the specific events that prompted the adoption of the regulations in November 1974, and the records of the proceedings are not available. But the section on violations reveals a rough-and-tumble business, in which competitors borrow, steal, and destroy crates or offer concessions and rebates to wholesale customers—practices that increase the cost of doing business and raise milk prices for consumers.

The acting director of the division of dairy industry services and producer security, Charles Huff, says auditors check for documentation on deposits and issue warnings to violators. But illegal concessions relate to many factors and "are practically impossible to detect," he said, and "are hard to prove."

You can buy plastic crates at discount stores. Considering all the possible costs, they are a bargain at $5.

Keeping a Head Count

Q. *In theaters, restaurants, nightclubs, and cabarets throughout the city, I see signs declaring that occupancy by more than a certain number of people is "dangerous and unlawful." How is this number derived, and why is it posted?*

A. You've heard of someone yelling "Fire!" in a crowded theater? This number is the legal size of the crowd.

Before issuing a place-of-assembly permit for a club, restaurant, or theater, the Department of Buildings calculates the appropriate "occupant load" by dividing the entire floor area of the room by 12—the number of square feet per person considered necessary for orderly evacuation in case of a fire, according to Buildings Department officials.

Display of a conspicuous, well-lit "occupant load" sign is one of several fire safety measures that went into full effect in 1980 under Local Law No. 41, known as the city's "Blue Angel" law. Aimed primarily at social clubs, discotheques, and nightclubs, it was passed after a fire behind the stage at the Blue Angel nightclub at 123 East Fifty-fourth Street killed seven people on December 18, 1975.

Though the deaths were attributed to a delay in reporting the fire (employees tried for almost a half hour to extinguish the blaze with glasses of water and milk before summoning the Fire Department), inspectors found that exits were blocked by furniture and that the club was operating without a permit of assembly or a certificate of occupancy.

Under the Blue Angel law, plans showing seating arrangements, fire alarms, emergency lighting, and locations of all aisles and exits are required before a place-of-assembly permit is approved.

Liquid Law

Q. *In response to drought conditions, Mayor Edward I. Koch ended the practice of restaurants' automatically serving water to customers. (Customers would have to ask.) The drought is long over. Occasionally I will get water without asking. Was this policy ever officially rescinded?*

A. The water indeed flows more freely these days, but the law says you're still supposed to ask for that glass. As of 1991, when the water-on-request restriction became Section 20–10 of the Rules of the City of New York, any restaurant that doled out water at will was subject to a fine of $100, which could jump up to $500 for repeat offenders.

With New York's reservoirs nearly filled to capacity, the water rule isn't being enforced as rigorously as it once was. But it's a regulation that's strictly enforced during a drought. And it's good practice in general, city officials say, stressing that the idea behind the law is to promote conservation of our natural resources.

No Idling About!

Q. *Is there a law governing how long a car can idle in the street? I see cars with their engines running, spewing out exhaust all over.*

A. Think twice before pulling over for a sprint into the local deli. The Department of Transporta-

tion dislikes polluters as much as you do, and it has a way to discourage drivers who insist on sullying the air. Section 4–08 of the New York City Traffic Regulations says vehicles may idle no more than three minutes while parking or standing. But there's a big "unless": it's all right to idle if you are loading or unloading. A summons can cost anywhere from $220 for a first-time lapse to $875 for a repeat offense.

The hefty summonses go mostly to trucks and buses, city transportation officials say.

Vanity near Fifth

Q. *There is a large apartment house on the south side of Eighty-seventh Street that is approximately 150 feet east of Fifth Avenue yet has the address 1049 Fifth Avenue. No part of the building touches Fifth Avenue. So how did they acquire this address?*

A. In New York City, a building is not required to touch a certain street in order to use the name in its address. This address, and there are many others like it, including buildings on Park and Madison Avenues, is known as a vanity address. (Doesn't Fifth Avenue just sound better than Eighty-seventh Street?)

Approval by the borough president's office is needed, though. Lisa Daglian, who served in the office under Ruth Messinger, said that many vanity address requests come from new construction, but that the borough president's office does not encourage address changes. "You can't order these addresses like vanity license plates," Ms. Daglian said.

Vineyard to Deli

Q. *I noticed wine for sale in a deli on Second Avenue at Ninth Street (The Village Farm) the other day. When did delis get to start selling wine?*

A. Well, if you looked closely at the label, you'd probably see that what they were selling was a "wine product," not wine.

Delis are allowed to sell alcoholic beverages if the alcohol content is 6 percent or less, under the New York State Alcoholic Beverage Control Code, which has hardly changed since its post-Prohibition passage in 1933.

Most beverages with that low an alcoholic content are beers, but a growing number of "wine products" also fit in the category. Some are things that didn't exist until recently, like wine coolers. As those became more and more popular, and delis started carrying them, it was just a matter of time before delis added some other wine products with low alcohol content. At the Village Farm, the wine is kosher, and listed at 6 percent alcohol. (Most wines are usually somewhere between 9 and 13 percent alcohol.)

Stoops to Conquer

Q. *When I come home many nights there are people sitting on my stoop in front of my building. Is this illegal? Is there anything I can do?*

A. Stoops are the private property of the owner of the building, according to the Legal Bureau of the Police

Department, so anyone else (even a tenant) sitting on it is technically trespassing.

But here's the catch. If the person sitting there hasn't been notified that he's trespassing it's very hard to get an arrest, let alone a conviction. (The notification could be a sign or the owner saying something—tenants aren't owners, so their word doesn't mean anything.) So you can get the owner to post a sign, or you can buy the building so you can yell at the stoop sitters yourself. Otherwise, there's no real legal action to be taken.

However, there's a big however. You can, in a great New York tradition, complain. If someone calls the police, police officers say, it is up to the officer to determine whether to shoo on the person.

If the person is creating a disturbance, the officer will ask him or her to move or quiet down. And, in the most severe case, the officer can issue a summons.

Dining Out with Pets

Q. *Is my dog or any other pet allowed in a restaurant?*

A. No animal, with the exception of Seeing Eye or hearing dogs, is allowed to be in a New York City restaurant, even if the table in question is outdoors. Even cats, at one time exempted because of their reputation as reliable mouse and rat exterminators, are now barred from setting up shop in any restaurant.

Head full o' Nuts

Q. *I find the smell produced by nut vendors unbearable. At noon each day, a vendor parks outside our office window, and the smell rises up from his cart and fills the office. Have I any recourse?*

A. The New York City Air Pollution Control Code states that "establishments cannot emit an odor that interferes with the comfort of an individual in their home or office."

Now others may love the smell of nuts—or lilacs or barbecued ribs, for that matter—but if it drives you crazy, it may well be a violation of the code.

City environmental officials say that food vendors in the past have set up shop near office air vents, which spread the cart's scents throughout the building. They suggest that if this is the case, you should contact your local police precinct. If it takes no action, or if the vendor refuses to move, you should call the police.

The Glory of "NYP"

Q. *All around the city I have seen cars with license plates that are marked with a small diagonal "NYP." I have also spotted signs that prohibit parking for all vehicles except those with these plates. Who are these drivers, and why do they rate reserved parking?*

A. "NYP" stands for New York Press. The plates are issued by the Department of Motor Vehicles to New York City's journalists. They allow members of the working press to park in designated zones near places like Madison Square Garden and the courthouses. The police also issue dashboard signs for the press that allow parking in other spots.

But don't rush down to the Department of Motor Vehicles with instant career aspirations and suspended-alternate-side-of-the-street-parking dreams: a news organization must apply for the plates or provide written proof that an applicant is a working journalist in its employ.

The department also issues permits and plates for parking zones for doctors (marked with M D) and diplomats (DIPLOMAT), as well as various government employees.

Where to Go

Q. *What laws, if any, pertain to the use of rest rooms in stores? In some places, one is told flatly that there is no rest room. In large stores, they are under lock and key.*

A. Rest rooms are required in all public buildings with twenty or more seats that received permits after 1977. None of these places, including restaurants, are obligated to let anyone other than patrons use the rest rooms. But if they let one nonpatron do so, they cannot discriminate against others and must let in anyone who asks to use the rest room.

Limits of the Law

Q. *Is there any such thing in New York as a citizen's arrest?*

A. Yes, but don't go thinking you're an ad hoc member of your local precinct. A police officer can make an arrest based on probable cause. But under the law, citizens can make arrests only when they witness a crime, and using only the force necessary to subdue a suspect. In a city where more people than you'd like to know about are armed, the police don't encourage this sort of thing. After all, there's always 911. Now suppose you're feeling a bit fed up and sassy, and you want to arrest someone for, say, littering. Put your handcuffs away: littering is a violation of the civil code, not of the criminal code, and the law says hands off.

New York Arcana

Optical Exclusion

Q. *On a recent trip to the tropics, I often saw rainbows and realized, somewhat sadly, that I rarely see them here in Manhattan. Why?*

A. We see few rainbows because they are optical phenomena requiring specific lines of vision in order to be discerned, and in Manhattan these lines are almost completely obstructed by buildings.

The conditions that produce rainbows are most common in the summer, when brief showers occur and there are breaks between storm clouds where the sun can shine through, said Fred Gadomski, a Pennsylvania State University meteorologist.

Rainbows are usually seen in the late afternoon, when prevailing winds sweep storms toward the east and the sun is low on the western horizon. If you face the receding rain to the east while the sun shines directly behind you, the sunlight will strike the water droplets, where it will be refracted into its constituent colors and reflected back to you in the form of a rainbow if you are looking at the point directly opposite the sun's position.

In Manhattan, even where one can find a wide dome of sky, particles suspended in the city air make the bands of color more difficult to discern, Mr. Gadomski said.

Pollution, he said, scatters and dims sunlight before it can reach distant rain droplets, and although it doesn't prevent the prismatic effect from taking place, the weakened rainbow is further obscured by haze in the air.

All in all, a tough town for rainbows.

New York-itis

Q. *What are the physiological effects associated with living in New York?*

A. First, the bad news: hearing loss, high blood pressure, and respiratory problems.

A report from the Natural Resources Defense Council, an environmental group, states that particulate air pollution in the city causes more than four thousand premature deaths each year, mostly due to lung disease. In the South Bronx and East Harlem, asthma afflicts people at eight times the national average.

Workers in the city's many poorly ventilated high-rises and older buildings must also contend with closed-building syndrome, says Dr. Sue Richman, a staff physician at the Mount Sinai School of Medicine and the Irving Selikoff Occupational Health Center. The syndrome can cause flu-like symptoms, she says.

City noise, including screeching subways and screaming sirens, has been linked not only to hearing loss but also to a transient increase in blood pressure, Dr. Richman says.

Dr. Paolo Toniolo, a professor of environmental medicine at the New York University School of Medicine, says that at midday, ozone levels are higher as the sun interacts with elevated exhaust levels from an abundance of traffic. Ozone can irritate the respiratory lining and cause bronchitis. "Exercising at midday may be one of those most dangerous things to do," he said.

Finally, the good news (sort of). Dr. Toniolo says that while health concerns shouldn't be minimized, the overall effect of living in the city on mortality is minimal. "People

in cities tend to live at least as long as people in the coun-
tryside," he said. Rural populations have a different set of
problems, including pesticide and fertilizer runoff in water
supplies and chemical contamination in food sources.

No Free Sunblock

Q. *I heard that it's tougher to get a tan in the city because the sun's rays are deflected by particles of pollution in the
air. Is this true?*

A. This one gets a good chuckle out of the
meteorologists at Penn State's Weather Communi-
cations Center.

"That's an interesting concept," says
Lee Grenci. "New Yorkers think even
their pollution is good."

The rumor, he said, probably arose
because a prominent urban pollutant is
ozone. Ozone, in the upper levels of
the atmosphere, provides protection for
the planet's dwellers by deflecting and
absorbing ultraviolet radiation. And it is
that radiation that tans, burns, and can, in
the extreme, cause cancer.

Mr. Grenci said that the ozone floating
around the lower atmosphere may deflect some
UV radiation, but not enough to make getting too much sun
difficult. "Anyone who goes out sunbathing thinking he's
protected by pollutants," he said, "is asking for bad things."

Skillet Street

Q. *How hot can New York City streets really get during the summer? Hot enough, for instance, to actually fry an egg?*

A. The temperature on an average New York City street during a hot summer day can probably reach 150 degrees Fahrenheit, says Lee Grenci, a meteorologist at Penn State. But the temperature of any specific street depends on how much or how little its surface reflects sunlight, he explained.

Dark asphalt streets, for example, are hotter than those paved with pale concrete, because the darker pavement reflects less light and absorbs more heat.

According to *Kitchen Science* (Houghton Mifflin, 1981), by Howard Hillman, an egg begins cooking, white first, around 145 degrees—though the optimal temperatures for gourmet-quality frying start about 70 degrees higher.

So, yes, on a hot day you probably could fry an egg on Fifth Avenue, but ordering in would probably be quicker. Not to mention tastier.

A final note: it is a lot easier to freeze an egg on a city street, since eggs freeze at about 29 degrees. Unfortunately, there don't seem to be any evocative sayings on that subject.

Sweepers That Push

Q. *What is the point of street sweepers? I followed one the other day (not by choice, mind you) and watched it kick up some dust and sweep a small pile of refuse a foot and a half farther into the street. Within seconds, the passing traffic blew the refuse back to the curb. Explain, please.*

A. Here is how these sweepers (or "mechanical brooms," as the Department of Sanitation calls them) are supposed to work: Two circular flat brooms spin around and sweep trash into the path of a pickup broom, which in turn whisks it all onto a kind of conveyer belt that lifts the trash into the "hopper," or body of the machine. Occasionally, these machines squirt a little water on the street, for good measure.

What you probably saw was a broom with a faulty or poorly adjusted pickup broom, which was not sending the trash to the hopper, said a spokeswoman for the Department of Sanitation. Often these machines are damaged by the streets themselves, which are hard on the brooms. But they are routinely checked before the workers head out.

A Little Matinee History

Q. *How did Wednesday become matinee day?*

A. Theater producers, allowed eight shows a week before having to pay enormous amounts in overtime, have generally spread out the performances for maximum profit. That used to translate into six nights (humanely giving the cast a day off) and two matinees. With one matinee dedicated to copious weekend crowds, that left midweek for the other.

But it wasn't always Wednesday, said Price Berkeley, publisher of the weekly *Theatrical Index*. The influential Theater Guild, whose stars included the Lunts, Shirley Booth, Lillian Gish, Helen Hayes, and Ethel Barrymore, preferred Thursday, and only in the '50s, when the group's power waned, did Wednesday become more common.

The Landslide of 1869

Q. *Noting that Mayor Guiliani won the 1997 mayoral election with 57 percent of the vote, I wondered who won the city's most lopsided mayoral victory ever.*

A. According to *The Encyclopedia of New York City,* the most resounding victory occurred in 1869, when A. Oakey Hall, a Democrat running virtually unopposed, took 98.4 percent of the vote. More recently, Edward I. Koch, running on the Democratic and Independent tickets in 1985, won 78 percent. Carol Bellamy took 10 percent on the Liberal Party line, and Diane McGrath, the Republican candidate, had 9 percent.

Why Gracie's Mansion?

Q. *Who decided that the mayor of New York should live in Gracie Mansion?*

A. Gracie Mansion was built in 1799 as the country house of Archibald Gracie, who was a merchant down on Whitehall Street. And yes, the Upper East Side was "country" then for someone whose main digs were on State Street across from Battery Park.

Gracie used his sixteen-room house, an elegant example of Federal domestic architecture, to entertain Alexander Hamilton, Washington Irving, and various French royals. But Gracie's shipping business went belly-up during the War of 1812, and in 1819 he was forced to sell the house.

The city bought it in 1887 and used it as the Museum of the City of New York, reports the Blue Guide to New York. It became the official mayoral residence in 1942, when Fiorello H. La Guardia took one look at the other leading possibility, a seventy-five-room French-style chateau on Riverside Drive, and said in horror, "What, me in that?"

The Story of Sixth Street

Q. *Sixth Street between First and Second Avenues seems to have wall-to-wall Indian restaurants. How did this come about? What was the first Indian restaurant on the block?*

A. It all began back in 1968, when Manir Ahmed and his five brothers, emigrants from the part of India later known as Bangladesh, craved some home cooking.

They noticed a Japanese restaurant for sale at 320 East Sixth Street, bought it—kitchen, tables, and all—for $1,800, and started using it for family meals. Passersby often mistook them for diners in a restaurant, and soon the Ahmeds thought, Why not? Thus, Shah Bagh was born.

Two years later, the brothers opened Kismoth, at 330. Both places eventually closed; Kismoth later reopened under new ownership. Mitali, at 334, is now the oldest restaurant on Sixth Street still operating under continuous ownership. It was opened in 1973 by Abu S. Ahmed, a former waiter at an uptown joint, and no relation to the Ahmed brothers.

The brothers recognized their dream to "make an Indian street" by 1981. But Abu Ahmed says he was drawn to the area primarily because of the low rent, which started out at a whopping $75 a month. Combined with an abundance of available space and the neighborhood's international flavor, it was a recipe for success.

Apparently, other entrepreneurs agreed. Mr. Ahmed says the street now has about twenty-two Indian restaurants, and on a good weekend, he estimates, they draw five thousand to six thousand diners.

While some of the restaurants' owners live in the area—Manir Ahmed still lives on Sixth Street—others, like Abu Ahmed, prefer to separate work and play, opting to live within the large Indian community in Jackson Heights, Queens.

A Lesson in Numbers

Q. *Does the numbering of public schools have any pattern whatsoever? If there's a P.S. 41, does that mean there's also a P.S. 40 and a P.S. 39? And are there schools with the same numbers in different boroughs?*

A. Well, there's not really a pattern, but the system does have some logic.

Alex Doulis, an associate education analyst in the Board of Education's Office of Strategic Planning, said that when a new school is constructed, the board starts with the assumption that it will be assigned the next available number in the district. So where there's a P.S. 41, there should indeed be a P.S. 39 and a P.S. 40.

In theory, that is. Sometimes a school requests a number out of sequence, say to match its street address. Or a school across the street from P.S. 1 might ask for 11.

The board checks the district to make sure that there isn't already a school with the same number and that the number isn't in the pile of "dead" digits from closed schools.

Then a resolution is passed by the community school board and sent to the Central Board at 110 Livingston Street in Brooklyn. If the Central Board approves it, the school gets its out-of-sequence number.

Mr. Doulis stressed the importance of this process because, in terms of record-keeping, the number is the equivalent of an individual's social security number. But it's not as unique as a fingerprint. Since the numbering is by district, all five boroughs could indeed have identically numbered schools.

Why Police Wear Blue

Q. *What is the history behind the color blue for uniforms for the New York City Police Department? Why was it chosen?*

A. The department's official colors are blue, white, and green. Blue was chosen as the uniform color largely for practical purposes, said Officer Dominick Palermo, assistant curator of the Police Museum at the Police Academy in Manhattan. "Sometimes you have to change a flat tire," he explained. "It is much easier to get grease off of blue than white. Also, the color blue has meanings, such as courage and strength."

The uniform, modeled after that of the British police, was adopted in 1853.

New York officers resisted it at first, opting instead for street clothes and an eight-point star that identified them as police officers, because they thought the uniforms looked too British (not such a popular group in New York at that time).

Those Voice Ads

Q. *Why are people always placing classified ads on the back page of* The Village Voice *that say "Thank you St. Jude."*

A. St. Jude is the patron saint of hopeless cases, and prayers are made to him in the event of a huge loss or problem. Once a prayer is answered, one is obligated to make a public prayer of thanks, as in a newspaper, both to let others know that they too can pray to St. Jude and to insure that he or she can be helped again sometime.

Pool of Dreams

Q. *I often gaze at the Central Park Reservoir and dream of taking a dip. Have people ever been allowed to swim there? Now that it's no longer part of our water supply system, is anyone making plans along those lines?*

A. Simply put: no and no.

The billion-gallon, 40-foot-deep reservoir was built in 1862 to supplement the city's water supply, and it remained a part of the water system until late 1993, when fear of contamination intensified. Swimming was prohibited.

It is still under the domain of the city's Department of Environmental Protection, though the Parks Department is scheduled to take over the 106-acre site in 1999.

Various ideas—some calling for nothing to be done, others for conversion to recreational use—have been discussed, according to Parks Commissioner Henry J. Stern, but nothing resembling a plan has emerged.

Anybody wanting to use the reservoir for anything other than a pleasant backdrop, he added, "will have to wait till the calendar begins with a two."

City of (Wise) Fools

Q. *How did New York come to be known as Gotham?*

A. According to legend, Gotham was a town in England that became known as the place of "wise fools" when its inhabitants tricked King John out of setting up house there. When the king's men came riding through town to scout the location, the residents simply behaved like madmen. The royal retainers rode off and a saying was born: "More fools pass through Gotham than remain in it."

Washington Irving is believed to have been the first to call New York Gotham; in his periodical *Salmagundi,* which he published between 1807 and 1808, he deployed the name as a comment on his sophisticated, if pretentious, contemporaries.

Sisters of Charity?

Q. *About those women dressed in habits who sit in chairs in the subway panhandling: Are they really nuns?*

A. Some of them are. New York has a few religious communities that practice begging as a means of fulfilling the vows of poverty. There are also women who dress up in costumes and pose as nuns to collect money.

There is a way to check their authenticity. Mary Moore, a spokeswoman for the Archdiocese of New York, explained that only the archdiocese's Vicariate for Religious Issues can approve begging. The office issues an annual mendicant card with an official seal, and only about five sisters apply for it each year. A nun must carry this card at all times to beg.

Lucky Bucks

Q. *I always thought the dollar bills I see taped to cash registers in stores and restaurants were the proverbial "first dollars" the businesses earned upon opening. But sometimes I see several bills, in different denominations, clustered near the registers. What exactly is this custom?*

A. The custom is anything but exact, but based on a highly informal survey the bills are symbolic "payments" made by friends and family when the businesses open, and serve as a salutation and benediction.

Oksun Kim, a Korean-born cashier at the Lexington Grocery off Seventy-ninth Street, pointed to two $20 bills and a $100 bill, all signed by their donors in ballpoint pen and taped to the fake wood paneling by the cash register. "They are just . . . to bring good luck," he said with a shrug.

The practice has been around as long as anyone asked could remember, and is said by many to be Korean or Chinese in origin, though here it is practiced by small-business owners of every imaginable ancestry. In a single recent afternoon, evidence was heard of Vietnamese, Greek, Colombian, and Iranian businesses displaying the bills.

In New York, of course, social customs are borrowed, bent, and reconfigured as they move across ethnic and cultural boundaries. Shops and restaurant owners around town display $10, $20, or $100 bills—upside down, sideways, or upright—on registers, behind them, or across from them. "You can put it any way, but always near the register," said Robin Mui, president of the Chinese Journalists Association in Chinatown. "It's for good luck, but it's also to tell the money to keep on coming."

Psst! Some Chess?

Q. *I've often wondered this when I see the chess hustlers in Washington Square Park: How good are they?*

A. Victor Frias, an international master who has been watching the players in Washington Square Park for fifteen years, likens the hustlers there to pool sharks.

"They're good enough to hustle, good enough to take the money of unsuspecting customers, but not good enough to be professionals," Mr. Frias said.

A professional, like Mr. Frias, makes a living by playing in tournaments and exhibitions and giving lessons.

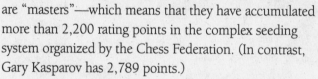

Of the approximately eighty-two thousand players ranked by the United States Chess Federation, only six hundred or so are "masters"—which means that they have accumulated more than 2,200 rating points in the complex seeding system organized by the Chess Federation. (In contrast, Gary Kasparov has 2,789 points.)

Mr. Frias says that of the fifteen or so hustlers who frequent the park, probably three or four might be able to qualify as masters. But he also warns that the hustlers are considerably stronger when playing speed chess, where each player has only five minutes to play the entire game.

He adds that many of the players who play the hustlers expect to lose. "The hustlers are funny, they talk well, and the players are playing for fun," said Mr. Frias, who knows many of the regular chess sharks, like "Sweet Pea" and "Uncle Ralph," by name.

"But if I go, they wouldn't play me," he said.

Police Tanks

Q. *I've heard that the Police Department's arsenal includes armored tanks. Yikes! When are they used?*

A. Almost never. The department's two tanklike vehicles—50,000-pound armored personnel carriers from the Korean War era, stripped of their weapons—are used on rare occasions to rescue officers or civilians pinned down by gunfire or to take officers through areas threatened by bullets or other projectiles, according to Sergeant Cory Cuneo, a spokesman for the police. They are also occasionally used to push down obstructions, Sergeant Cuneo said.

Called emergency rescue vehicles, or ERVs, they have been used by the Emergency Services Unit, the department SWAT team, for more than twenty years, Sergeant Cuneo said. The lightly armored vehicles, which reach a top speed of about 35 miles an hour, can stop all handgun rounds and 99 percent of rifle rounds, Sergeant Cuneo said, and they can carry ten people. With or without a cannon, a muscular blue-and-white tank that says "NYPD" on the side is a sight that is not quickly forgotten.

In May 1995, protesters in

the East Village were astonished when a rescue vehicle took officers to the sealed doors of two buildings on East Thirteenth Street that squatters had occupied. Some critics later described the operation as a blitzkrieg.

"The main drawback to the ERVs is that it's difficult to move them around," Sergeant Cuneo said. They are stored at Floyd Bennett Field in Brooklyn, he said, and are transported on a flatbed truck. The department is increasingly relying on armor-plated four-wheel-drive vehicles, so-called peacekeepers, which can be driven like a car.

"It cuts down your response time significantly," Sergeant Cuneo said.

Lowering the Bridge

Q. *Now that warm weather has arrived, the roadway across the Verrazano Narrows Bridge seems slightly less arched than during the winter. Am I imagining things?*

A. No, the roadway is actually lower.

Considering its awesome size and weight—more than a million tons—the Verrazano Narrows Bridge, which opened in 1964, is surprisingly animate. The delicate tracery of its four steel cables and 2,048 steel ropes contracts when cold and expands when hot—enough to lower the 248-million-pound roadway about 12 feet in the summertime. The change, according to Frank Pascual, director of public information for MTA Bridges and Tunnels, is visible to the discerning eye.

The road sits atop a skeleton of sixty 400-ton box-shaped steel frames, each the size of a suburban house, which are linked by a series of expansion joints that mesh at intervals like intertwined fingertips. This allows the 4,260-foot span, suspended an average of 230 feet above the chilly Narrows, to flex and change shape while the bridge's 690-foot towers do not move.

Political Gastronomy

Q. *Why are there so many restaurants with combinations of Chinese and Cuban chow in New York? Are there a lot of Chinese people in Cuba?*

A. Indeed, lots of Chinese people who weren't fond of Communism took off for more capitalistic places—which aptly describes Cuba before Castro. Many headed there hoping to continue on to the United States. Once in Cuba, a large number of Chinese opened restaurants, including local fare on their menus.

Relatives followed relatives, adding to the Chinese population. But in 1959 Castro took over, and to many of the Cuban Chinese, he looked like Mao all over again. The United States took in large numbers of refugees from Cuban Communism, Chinese among them.

These restaurants were once found mostly in Hispanic neighborhoods like Washington Heights; Elmhurst, Queens; and upper Broadway. As the numbers of Cuban Chinese grew, so did the number of these eating spots, which are now mainstays in many neighborhoods throughout the city.

Semiclassical Motto

Q. *What is the origin of the motto inscribed on the frieze of the post office at Eighth Avenue and Thirty-fourth Street? I've heard that the architect of the building made it up.*

A. Not exactly. The quotation on the 280-foot frieze—"Neither snow nor rain nor heat nor gloom of night stays these couriers from the swift completion of their appointed rounds"—is a free rendering of a passage in book 8, chapter 98 of the history of the Greco-Persian wars by the Greek historian Herodotus (484–420 B.C.); the chapter recounts the Greeks' defeat of the Persian invaders at the battle of Salamis in 480 B.C.

In the passage, Herodotus describes the mounted couriers of King Xerxes of Persia, known for their fidelity and determination. But according to the U.S. Postal Service, the loose translation from the original Greek was the work of the architect, William Mitchell Kendall, a young partner at McKim, Mead & White, who designed the sprawling edifice, built from 1909 to 1913 over the Pennsylvania Railroad tracks. While seeking a quotation with the appropriate gravitas to stretch above the twenty Corinthian columns of the stern two-block façade, Kimball—the son of a classical language instructor—stumbled on the passage in Herodotus. But the three English translations he examined lacked euphony, as did the one provided by George Herbert Palmer of Harvard: "No snow nor rain nor day's heat nor gloom hinders their speedily going on their appointed rounds." So Mr. Kimball simply twisted the Palmer version around.

Though the Post Office Department approved the quotation for Kimball's sprawling building, it is not the official motto of the Postal Service, nor is it generally found on other postal buildings.

Hold the Pepper

Q. *In Yankee Stadium there is a sign, visible during televised games, that reads, "No Pepper Games Allowed." What is a pepper game, and why isn't it permitted?*

A. A pepper game is a sort of pregame warm-up that involves a guy, a bat, and four or five teammates who stand 10 to 20 feet away from him, pitching balls.

Each player takes a turn throwing balls to the batter, who hits ground balls to another player. The basic idea is to hit the ball in a different spot each time, controlling the bat when faced with pitches from the extreme left to the far right. Some speculate that "Pepper" may come from the phrase "to pepper the ball down the line." The Yankees prohibit pepper games because such games can be danger-ous—a foul can go into the stands and hit a spectator.

One Alarm, Two Alarm

Q. *Local news always reports on fires by referring to the number of alarms they produce, but no one has ever explained what the numbers mean. Is it the number of trucks responding? Number of firefighters involved?*

A. Both. A one-alarm fire, for instance, requires eleven pieces of firefighting equipment (called units) and 55 firefighters; a two-alarm takes twenty units and 100 firefighters, and so on through five alarms, which require forty-three units and 217 firefighters. A little more number information: a 10–75 is a working fire, and a 10–76 is a fire occurring in a building that is ten stories or more high.

It is hard to say which of these fires is most common; in Brooklyn there are a lot of brownstones that often flame up one-alarm style, but then again, in Bushwick there are many row frame houses where fires spread quickly, and so more units are often needed pronto. Lofts in lower Manhattan produce similar fires and often need more fighters to cover the huge areas.

Underground Radio

Q. *For years, my car radio faded as I entered the Brooklyn–Battery Tunnel, remaining silent for the duration of the trip. Now it plays from one end to the other. What happened?*

A. The Metropolitan Transportation Authority let Bell Atlantic Nynex Mobile, a NYNEX subsidiary, install something called a leaky coaxial cable along the entire 9,117-foot length of the tunnel. The cable, about twice as thick as a typical television cable, acts as a continuous, insulated antenna that receives AM, FM, emergency band, and two-way radio signals inside the forty-seven-year-old tunnel as well as allowing mobile phone and beeper use.

The MTA's emergency and traffic management abilities are clearly enhanced by the cable, and Bell Atlantic Nynex Mobile is certainly pleased to enable customers to place more telephone calls and not have them cut off by a trip into the tunnel (about 55,000 trips are made through the tunnel every day).

The Queens–Midtown Tunnel has also been wired for sound. The good news is, that allows for a few extra minutes of radio listening. That, of course, is also the bad news.

Library's Roman Math

Q. *Why do the inscribed dates at the New York Public Library have four consecutive identical Roman numerals (XXXX or CCCC) when they should, we were taught, be written otherwise (XL or CD)?*

A. Roman numerals are read in sequences and groups. Thus VIII (8) is understood as 5 + 3. Abbreviations, like IV (4) or IX (9), entered the numerical lexicon in the late Roman period and are a form of subtraction, or "backward counting," according to Karl Menninger's *A Cultural History of Numbers* (MIT Press, 1969).

The Roman system of counting and numbering was never uniform. In fact, Professor Menninger writes: "The Romans used a system of numerals so crude and cumbersome that it is hard to see how it could be a product of the same culture."

Nonetheless, Roman numerals became the "official" way of writing in Western Europe in the Middle Ages, in contrast to knots, notches, stones, and other imprecise peasant number symbols. "In medieval Latin the full form of the numeral was written out as often as the abbreviation," Professor Menninger writes.

The New York Public Library's method of inscription is as inconsistent as that of medieval scribes. "How appropriate," said Bob Sink, the library's archivist. The library's 1902 cornerstone at Forty-second Street and Fifth Avenue reads MDCCCCII, for 1902, rather than the more common abbreviated form, MCMII. Yet, the inscription for the 1895 founding of the New York Public Library uses the abbreviated form, MDCCCXCV.

Despite a wealth of correspondence about the wording of inscriptions between John Shaw Billings, the library's founding director; Carrier & Hastings, the architecture firm; and others, there was no mention of Roman numerals. "Even the Mayor had to sign off on it," Mr. Sink said. "I'm not sure if we're inconsistent or following an unstated rule."

The Slant on Stripes

Q. *A British friend recently said the stripes on my tie "ran the wrong way." Indeed, the stripes of our ties sloped differently,* *his regimental stripe from top right to left, my Brooks Brothers rep stripe from top left to right. Any particular reason?*

A. Unlikely as it sounds, Brooks Brothers reversed the direction when it introduced its striped neckties early in the century, in an effort to spare American customers from accusations that they wore English club ties to which they were not entitled. Other retailers did the same.

Brooks Brothers was established in New York in 1818 by Henry Sands Brooks, father of five sons: Henry, Daniel, John, Elisha, and Edward. In 1890, Francis G. Lloyd, who later became company president, introduced the first English-style silk neckties to the United States. Shortly thereafter Brooks Brothers began producing ties in striped patterns borrowed from English sporting clubs and regiments, a company spokeswoman said. Today the store always carries thirty basic stripe-and-color combinations, each based on the five old Brooks patterns, classics with names like No. 1, No. 2, and No. 3.

The Scent of Memory

Q. *After a haircut and a shave, my barber splashes my face with a pale green liquid called Lilac Vegetal that, though soothing, has a musty floral scent that reminds me of my grandfather. Why do I still see it in so many New York barbershops?*

A. Tradition? The Edouard Pinaud Company, a Parisian fragrance manufacturer, began producing Lilac Vegetal in New York City in 1878, according to David Woolf, executive vice president of American International Industries, which makes the fragrance now. In 1927, Pinaud even built a seven-story showroom and laboratory on East Twenty-first Street. About ten years ago American International acquired the Clubman line of male grooming products, which included Lilac Vegetal.

And oh, that . . . distinctive fragrance! "When a man splashes on Lilac Vegetal, it brings back memories," Mr. Woolf said. "The barbershop. That first haircut. Your father, or your grandfather. The older you are, the more you've smelled it."

The cologne, which has always been sold to barbershops and athletic clubs, "was made from natural ingredients including lilac and ambergris until they became difficult to find or harvest, in the 1960s," Mr. Woolf said. Lilac Vegetal is now produced from artificial ingredients in Los Angeles, and is not advertised. It is found, however, in drugstores throughout the city and is perhaps the most inexpensive men's cologne on the market. This might help explain why your barber still uses it.

Signs of Nature

Q. *On the Belt Parkway in Brooklyn, near Canarsie, there are signs that say "Wildlife Crossing–Next 6 Miles." In thirty-four years, I've never spotted anything wilder than a squirrel. What are these signs talking about?*

A. The ducks, geese, and other fauna of Jamaica Bay. The signs were posted by the New York City Department of Transportation in early 1996, said a spokesman, Brice Peyre, after complaints that small animals, particularly waterfowl, were trying to cross the Belt Parkway between Cross Bay Boulevard and Knapp Street. This stretch

of highway passes through Floyd Bennett Field, Bergen Beach, Canarsie Beach Park, and Spring Creek Park, all part of the Gateway National Recreation Area.

Nearby is the Jamaica Bay Wildlife Refuge, a shallow tidal wetland established in 1953. Its 9,155 acres include two freshwater ponds and each year host more than 320 species of shorebirds, ducks, geese, wading birds, owls, and songbirds. At the end of summer, huge flocks of migrating shorebirds congregate in the area, and in late October and early November, flocks of snow geese pass through. The diamondback terrapin is also common. Efforts to clean Jamaica Bay in the 1980s met with surprising success, Mr. Peyre said, and robust conditions at the refuge might account for the increase in animal sightings.

Marvelous Addresses

Q. *It seems that many Marvel comic book superheroes live in New York City. What are their addresses? Can they drop in on one another?*

A. Since the modern Marvel era began in 1961, the city itself has been a character in almost every story.

Stan Lee and Jack Kirby, legendary creators of many of Marvel's sensitive, troubled superhumans, were both born in New York, and the company's offices have always been here.

Thus, Spider-Man lives in Forest Hills, Queens; the Fantastic Four live at the fictive Four Freedoms Plaza in east midtown; and Daredevil lives in Hell's Kitchen. The Avengers own a mansion at 890 Fifth Avenue (that nonexistent address would be on the site of the Frick Collection), and Doctor Strange, Earth's Sorcerer Supreme, dwells at 177-A Bleecker Street in the Village (there is a 177 Bleecker, a not-so-strange apartment house). And yes, in Marvel's mind-bending version of Gotham, Spider-Man can not only drop in on Daredevil at his apartment, he can also visit the artists at Marvel and complain about his story line.

Frosty the Soot Man

Q. *When it snows, my children lift their little faces to the sky and stick out their tongues to catch the falling flakes, just as I did as a boy. But I didn't grow up in the Bronx. Is falling snow safe to eat in New York?*

A. You couldn't keep a child from tasting snowflakes even if you wanted to, and a few on the tongue won't hurt anyone. In fact, you might taste a few flakes yourself.

But consumption of mittenfuls of city snow should probably not be encouraged, according to the city's Department of Environmental Protection.

Snow is formed at an altitude of 5,000 to 15,000 feet, when water vapor freezes around a speck of dust or dirt or other particle and ice crystals form, said Todd Miner, a meteorologist at Pennsylvania State University. In cities, factory and transportation exhaust are the primary sources of particulate matter, which can include soot, dust, and particles of iron, copper, nickel, or lead. It is possible, therefore, for a snowflake to "pick up" and transport soot and other minute contaminants that may be suspended in the air, he said.

"These snowflakes tend to be a little bit dirtier than those you would find in the country," said Mr. Miner, who admits that he enjoys a bit of the fresh stuff himself on occasion. Just remember to keep the portions small. And as for the stuff that's been on the ground for a few days . . . don't ask.

Coin Collection

Q. *I sometimes see a man cleaning the reflecting pool in front of the Vivian Beaumont Theater in Lincoln Center, and sweeping up all the coins tourists have tossed in. What is the value of all those coins? Who gets the money?*

A. What the public donates, it gets right back, center officials say. The money is collected, cleaned, and deposited directly into an operating account used for maintenance and upkeep of the plaza.

The fountain and pool are thoroughly cleaned, drained, and swept every two months. The coins—mostly pennies—usually total $50 to $100.

A Standup Hairdo

Q. *After spending an afternoon in the East Village, I have a question: What do you put in a Mohawk to make it stand up? Can you sleep on one?*

A. The care and feeding of a Mohawk? It's best to consult an expert, like Tolve.

He is a performer and the general manager of Manic Panic, a former East Village punk boutique and now a hair-color and cosmetics company. Tolve has worn a Mohawk since 1982, when neckties were skinny and made of leather.

He says the timeless, spiky effect can be achieved by putting just about anything in your hair that is gooey and dries hard. And that's it. "Once you make it stand up you don't generally have to worry about sleeping on it," he said.

And from his own anecdotal evidence, Tolve said Mohawk wearers use all manner of superhold hair sprays, gels, stiffeners, and fixatives, as well as Krazy Glue, Knox gelatin, egg whites, and sugar water, in copious amounts, to achieve the desired rigidity. Users saturate the hair with a generous amount of goo and, while hanging the head upside down, blow-dry the hair in place until it is completely stiff. But test the fixative first, he said: some can flake, and others can irritate the eyes or cause an allergic reaction.

For the Mohawk wearer in a hurry, waxy pomades can replace blow-drying, Tolve suggested. And he said keeping the scalp clean-shaven on either side of the plume of hair was the key to a Mohawk of distinction.

"The closest you can get with standard clippers is not acceptable to me," Tolve said. "A straight razor is best, but a standard razor is safer. I'm better than most; I shave every two or three days."

Visit U Thant? You Can't.

Q. *There is a forlorn little spit of land in the middle of the East River, by the United Nations, called U Thant Island. Other than seagulls, the harbor police, and the Coast Guard, is anyone allowed to visit?*

A. Only followers of Sri Chinmoy, who are allowed on the city-owned island once or twice a year to maintain it, according to the New York Harbor Police. Anglers, picnickers, and protesters will be put to shore.

The island, less than half an acre in size, was originally a small, parlous outcropping known as Man-o'-War Reef. At the turn of the century, it was heaped with rocks and soil removed from a trolley tunnel begun under the river. In 1906, the tunnel was completed by August Belmont, who used it for the IRT. The island took his name, and is still called Belmont Island on many maps.

In 1977, a group of United Nations employees who meditated with Sri Chinmoy, a Queens-based mystic, had the island rechristened in honor of the Burmese diplomat U Thant, who was the third secretary general of the world body, from 1961 to 1971.

Security around the U.N. has tightened in recent years, and island visits have all but ceased, said a member of the Sri Chinmoy group. The Coast Guard keeps a 57-foot tower with a blinking green navigation light at the island's southern end.

As Viewed from Above

Q. *Assuming darkness and a clear sky, are the lights of New York visible from space?*

A. Mario Runco Jr., an earth scientist who grew up in the Bronx and Yonkers, had just flown his third mission as a specialist aboard the space shuttle *Endeavour.* He said yes, he could see the city just fine.

"New York at night is plainly visible," he said. "You can see geometric shapes and linear features very well." The shuttle orbits 200 to 300 miles above Earth.

"You can see the outline of Central Park," Mr. Runco continued. "You can see the highways across the Bronx. You find Yankee Stadium, you find the Harlem River, you go upriver you can see Van Cortlandt Park Lake.

"As a matter of fact, I've attempted to find my house," he said.

But compared with other cities, said Dr. Neil deGrasse Tyson, a director at the Hayden Planetarium, New York is somewhat dim. That's because it is a "stacked" city, where the vast majority of people live in apartments and work in offices clustered and piled on top of one another in multilevel structures. And though we see it twinkling down here, almost none of that indoor illumination spilling out of windows escapes into space.

Dr. Tyson says the kind of light that really shows up in space comes from streetlamps and highway lights. New York does have plenty of those—Manhattan streetlamps alone pump about 1 million kilowatt-hours out into space every night. But it is the sprawling suburban areas, where there might be a streetlamp for every private home, that really stand out.

Bubble, Bubble...

Q. *It's early March, and for some reason my favorite beverage—New York city water, straight from the tap—has taken on a milky hue in recent weeks. Why the change?*

A. The calls start around this time every year.

The city's Department of Environmental Protection is quick to point out that the cloudiness does not pose a health risk, nor does it affect the taste of the water. But late every winter, city water comes out of the tap full of tiny air bubbles. The bubbles quickly dissipate, but the cause is not fully understood.

The water originates in the eighteen reservoirs and four lakes of the Croton, Catskill, and Delaware water systems north of the city, which are replenished by rain and snow. Routine maintenance of the reservoirs and monitoring operations at this time of year can alter the route and the source of water drawn for the city, "churning it up," and accounting for the increased aeration. Another possibility is that water from the reservoirs, now at its coldest after months of winter, is warmed as it travels to the city in the system's aqueducts, resuspending dissolved bubbles of air. Hmmm.

Current Affairs

Q. *Why do Circle Line sightseeing boats travel around Manhattan counterclockwise? The other way, they'd save the best—the Brooklyn Bridge and Statue of Liberty—till last.*

A. Because of a tricky bit of navigation at Manhattan's northwestern tip, at Spuyten Duyvil.

"It's much easier to come out of Spuyten Duyvil Creek into a rushing body of water"—the Hudson River—"than to go the other way," said Chris Calhoun, operations manager for the Circle Line, whose boats start and finish their loops at Forty-second Street and the Hudson. Boats circling Manhattan must pass beneath the Spuyten Duyvil railroad bridge. The center section of the low swing bridge pivots on a tower and rotates, opening a 100-foot-wide channel for boats on either side.

"It's very difficult to navigate large vessels such as ours between the piers of the bridge while going from the Hudson—which has a very heavy traveling current—into a calm current such as the Spuyten Duyvil," Mr. Calhoun said.

"If you don't line the boat up perfectly with the bridge, the current will start pulling one side of the boat and you'll hit the bridge abutment."

The sightseeing line still uses just the eight boats it started out with in 1945, boxy former Coast Guard cutters or landing craft from World War II. The boats, which travel at about 12 knots, can be difficult to maneuver through a narrow channel even in calm waters, Mr. Calhoun said.

Off the Flight Path

Q. *I thought that there was some rule that jets were not supposed to fly directly over Manhattan. But then I see them from time to time, sometimes at seemingly low altitudes. So is my memory wrong?*

A. Despite a lot of big, tall obstacles (like the Empire State Building, which was hit by a fog-blind B-25 in 1945), there hasn't ever been a ban on planes flying over Manhattan, says Mike Sammartino, the air traffic system manager with the Federal Aviation Administration.

The reason Manhattanites see so few jets overhead has to do with the alignment of La Guardia's runways, where most of the big planes that do pass over Manhattan are headed. (About 2 percent of flights landing at Kennedy use an approach that takes them over the World Trade Center, said Mr. Sammartino.)

La Guardia has two runways: Runway 13–31, which runs at approximately the same east-west orientation as 125th Street, and Runway 4–22, which runs perpendicular to 13–31. The approach for 13–31 calls for aligning the plane with the runway about 6 miles from the strip. Approaching from the south, that means passing over the Statue of Liberty, flying up the Hudson, banking right, and flying across Manhattan just above the northern end of Central Park.

In general, flights that land on 4–22 fly either over Brooklyn or toward the Manhattan side of the East River, then swing over the Bronx to approach the runway from the north.

The west side of Manhattan also sees a lot of private planes at lower altitudes; these use a flight corridor along the Hudson River that lends itself to aerial sightseeing.

Brooklyn's Shrub

Q. *I recently stumbled across the fact that the forsythia is the official botanic emblem of Brooklyn. How did it come to be that it's not a tree?*

A. True, forsythia is a shrub, not a tree. And one might expect Brooklyn's borough-sanctioned arbor to be the ailanthus of *A Tree Grows in . . .* fame. But files from the Brooklyn Botanic Garden tell a different story.

In 1940, Florence Abraham Blum, the wife of the president of the Abraham & Straus department store and a member of the garden's ladies auxiliary, led an effort to beautify the borough. She persuaded the borough president, John Cashmore, to anoint the forsythia as Brooklyn's official bloom. Borough residents were urged to plant the shrub in their front yards from the Heights to Coney Island to inspire brotherhood, unity, and understanding.

Mrs. Blum also began a Forsythia Day (still celebrated each April) and crowned a Forsythia Queen. The Hotel Granada, which opened in 1946 at Ashland Place and Lafayette Avenue in Fort Greene, named its dining room the Forsythia Room.

Starting in 1954, the garden bestowed a Forsythia Award for civic leadership, in honor of Mrs. Blum, who died in 1959. The award is still given annually to someone selected by borough officials and Botanic Garden members.

Awaiting "the Big One"

Q. *I understand there is a fault line that runs under New York City. Where does it run? When was the last earthquake? Are there any predictions about the next one—and are New York skyscrapers designed to withstand such a thing? I've heard reports that a large earthquake (over 5 on the Richter scale) is overdue for New York City. Is this true?*

A. Everyone knows New York City has more than its share of faults. At least two run across upper Manhattan, one along 125th Street and another near Dyckman Street in Inwood.

The last big earthquake in the city was on August 10, 1884. Equivalent to 5.5 on the Richter scale and centered under New York Harbor, it toppled hundreds of chimneys in the city and woke up chickens in western Pennsylvania. John Armbruster, a seismologist at Columbia University's Lamont-Doherty Geological Observatory in Palisades, New York, said the next "big one" might not be far away.

"A magnitude 5 hits the New York area about every hundred years," he said. "This is the longest period known without a magnitude 5 in New York."

And what might a magnitude 5, apparently ten years overdue, do when it comes?

Mr. Armbruster said the major skyscrapers in New York, including the older ones like the Chrysler Building and the Empire State Building, have been built to withstand that kind of shock. Some other buildings however, especially those built before the age of modern construction techniques, like brownstones, might not fare as well. Unlike Los Angeles, New York City has no building regulations specifically meant to prevent earthquake damage.

Where's Queens, N.Y.?

Q. *Why is it that you can mail a letter to Bronx, N.Y.; Brooklyn, N.Y.; and Staten Island, N.Y., but when it comes to Queens, Queens, N.Y., won't do? It has to be Flushing, Forest Hills, Jackson Heights, etc. Why does the Post Office discriminate?*

A. What you've got there is a convention that pre-dates 1898, when Brooklyn, Queens, and Staten Island were incorporated into New York City (the Bronx followed in 1914).

Queens had been a number of independent communities, and it kept that legacy in the form of four different postmasters. In comparison, the other boroughs have one each. The Brooklyn postmaster deals with Brooklyn, and so forth, except that the postmaster for Manhattan is called the New York postmaster. So the third line of the address, said Tom Gaynor, a postal spokesman, refers to the postmaster in charge.

Back to Queens: There is a postmaster for Long Island City, and all the ZIP codes under that jurisdiction begin with 111. The others are Flushing, 113; Jamaica, 114; and Far Rockaway, 116. So, for example, as far as the Post Office is concerned, Forest Hills is Flushing.

But nowadays, Mr. Gaynor said, the only thing that really matters is the ZIP code: you can leave off the city and state and a letter will still arrive.

More than Just a Road

Q. *Why are so many streets in Queens called boulevards?*

A. James Driscoll of the Queens Historical Society offered this explanation:

Until 1898, when Queens was incorporated into New York City, it was a county of towns and villages, some going back to the mid-1600s. Each developed its own roads. There were also roads linking various communities and roads linking the county to neighboring counties.

Beginning in 1911, the Queens Topographical Bureau started imposing the system known as the Philadelphia Grid. Streets running east–west were called avenues, roads, or drives; those running north–south, streets, places, and lanes.

The longer roads between communities and counties, which had no single orientation, were named boulevards.

By comparison, most of the development of Manhattan came after a grid system was imposed (that happened in 1811), precluding the need for that many categories of streets.

Traffic's Unjammer

Q. *Were all the avenues in Manhattan at one time designated for two-way traffic? If so, when did they switch to one-way and did they all change on the same date?*

A. With the goal of easing delays on streets ever more crowded with automobiles, most of the avenues were switched from two-way to one-way in a series of decisions that started in 1949 and culminated in the 1960s under the authority of Henry A. Barnes, an innovative, controversial traffic commissioner appointed by Mayor Robert F. Wagner and kept on by Mayor John V. Lindsay.

He considered ordering his workers not to paint the traditional green stripe down Fifth Avenue for the St. Patrick's Day parade, and turned down a proposed purple stripe for the Columbus Day parade. "Our men have more important things to do than paint polka-dot stripes up Fifth Avenue every time there is a parade," he said.

In the pre–politically correct year of 1962 he commented, "When a woman driver puts out her hand, you never know whether she is feeling to see if the window is open, drying her nail polish, or making a turn."

On the practical side, he promoted the use of seat belts, computerized traffic patterns, built municipal parking garages, and instituted widespread use of parking meters. He fought on behalf of mass transit against the master builder Robert Moses. And he instituted a regular pause at intersections when all traffic lights were red, allowing pedestrians to cross the street every which way. Largely abandoned now, it was called the Barnes Dance.

Two Companies on Call

Q. *I noticed that some Fire Department companies are referred to as "ladder" companies while others are "engine" companies. What's the difference?*

A. It's not as simple as who carries the hose (engine companies) and who carries the ladder (well, ladder companies, of course).

Ladder and engine companies have separate responsibilities in fighting fires. Ladder companies are charged with finding fires inside buildings and evacuating and rescuing those who are trapped there. They climb up to the roof, check the rear and basement areas, and go through doors to find the flames. Engine companies have the job of actually putting the fires out. Engine and ladder companies respond to every call, and all New York City firefighters are qualified to work on both.

The Broad Trail

Q. *Why is it that Broadway runs diagonally across the rest of the parallel avenues? Was it designed this way, and if so, what was the thinking behind the design?*

A. The thinking probably was something along the lines of: "How do I get from this part of the woods to the other part of the woods?"

Broadway is one of the oldest thoroughfares in Manhattan. It traces its roots to an Indian trail running from about the Battery to the area just south of City Hall. After Dutch settlers established a village (the first settlement consisted of four huts) at the southern tip of Manhattan in 1611, they carved a wider path, known in Dutch as Heere Wegh, or "the broad way," northward to about Park Row, along the same route as the existing thoroughfare.

After the British took over the Dutch settlement in 1664, the conquerors began calling the street Broadway, according to David W. Dunlap, real estate reporter for *The New York Times* and author of *On Broadway: A Journey Uptown over Time* (Rizzoli, 1990).

Broadway, at this point, was still a straight shot north, running roughly parallel to present-day avenues. But in 1703, Bloomingdale Road opened; it was a country highway running diagonally, southeast to northwest, from about Sixteenth Street to the settlements on the northern end of the island.

As the city grew during the eighteenth century, Broadway ran into and subsumed Bloomingdale Road and began to run on its crooked path north. The route of the street has remained the same ever since, resisting even the rigid layout of the Commissioners' Plan of 1811 that enforced a grid pattern on the rest of the island.

What Takeout Comes In

Q. *I've long admired the simple-yet-elegant cardboard cartons Chinese restaurants use to deliver take-out orders. Do they come from China?*

A. Many come from Hazleton, Pennsylvania (pop. 24,730), about 100 miles west of New York City. The cartons of folded cardboard, coated on the inside, with the wire handles—veritable icons of economy, ingenuity, and simplicity—can hold everything from mu shu pork to wonton soup, retaining the dish's heat while releasing steam. The Fold-Pak corporation, based in Newark, New York, is the nation's largest manufacturer of cardboard food pails for the restaurant and take-out food industry, and in its Hazleton plant it produces the majority of the containers used by New York's Chinese restaurants.

Robert E. Mullally, senior vice president of sales at Fold-Pak, estimates that his company ships about 100 million of the cartons each year to

New York City, where distributors in Brooklyn and Manhattan's Chinatown sell them to restaurants.

Fold-Pak cartons are available in plain white, or with a festive red pagoda design—for some reason less popular in New York than elsewhere, Mr. Mullally said.

The company, originally named Bloomer Brothers, began manufacturing the containers shortly after 1900, when they were used as oyster pails, Mr. Mullally said. The company, he said, became the Riegel Paper Corporation in the 1960s, then the Fold-Pak Corporation in 1977.

More than 90 percent of Fold-Pak's cartons shipped to New York are ultimately used by Chinese restaurants, Mr. Mullally said. The biodegradable cartons come in five sizes, holding from 8 to 64 ounces.

Mr. Mullally had no idea who makes the chopsticks.

A Cup of Inspiration

Q. *What inspired the Greek design on so many take-out coffee cups?*

A. You're not talking about just any cup. That's the legendary Anthora, perhaps the most successful cup in history.

Thirty years ago, the Sherri Cup Company of Kensington, Connecticut, had just started and was trying to break into New York, the caffeine capital of the East Coast. "New York City was the theater we were playing," said Frank Fonteyn, marketing manager for the company.

The design team came up with Anthora, a cup aimed at Greek-Americans who ran many diners and delis in the city: Greek lettering, Greek bordering, Greek vase, and the colors of the Greek flag—blue and white.

Apparently, it worked. In 1994, the company sold 500 million Anthoras, by far its most popular design. The cup's New York appeal, however, may be limiting. "We don't sell any in Boston," Mr. Fonteyn said.

Stadiums' First Innings

Q. *Now that there's a chance the Yankees will be on their way to the West Side of Manhattan, I wondered how Yankee Stadium came to be in the Bronx. And what about Shea Stadium?*

A. Long before George Steinbrenner, the Yankees sought greener diamonds. In their early days as the High-landers, they played in Hilltop Park on Broadway between 165th and 168th Streets. They moved in 1913 to the Polo Grounds, at 155th Street and Eighth Avenue, as tenants of the hated baseball Giants. Shortly after, the Yankees announced they were moving to Westchester Avenue at Clason Point Road in the Bronx.

By 1919, they said they were moving to Long Island City, Queens, and a year later they considered three other sites. As Colonel Jacob Ruppert, the team's co-owner, poured in money from the family breweries, the Yankees pressed their quest for a home of their own.

At long last, in 1921 they bought the 11.6-acre tract at 161st Street and River Avenue in the Bronx. The location was prime: it was close to subway and elevated train lines, and the land was largely undeveloped so there could be no complaints of disorderly conduct. And, to Colonel Ruppert's pleasure, it was in full view of the Polo Grounds across the river.

Shea Stadium was masterminded by New York's master builder, Robert Moses, who since the 1920s had harbored plans for a grand park and sports facility at Flushing Meadows in Queens. Sure, Brooklynites were aching for a stadium of their own, having lost the Dodgers to Los Angeles in 1957. But ultimately, says David Oats, president of the Flushing Meadows Park Association, it was Moses's decision to dovetail the building of the stadium with the 1964–1965 New York World's Fair that drove it home. The Mets played their first game there on April 17, 1964.

Sluggers at Home

Q. *Where did Babe Ruth live when he played for the Yankees? What about Joe DiMaggio, Lou Gehrig, and Mickey Mantle?*

A. The Babe was a devotee of the Upper West Side, living for many years at the Ansonia on Broadway and Seventy-third Street, and then successively at 345 West Eighty-eighth Street; 173 Riverside Drive, at Eighty-ninth Street; and 110 Riverside Drive, at Eighty-third Street. Gehrig preferred the quieter life in New Rochelle and later at 5204 Delafield Avenue in Riverdale. And though DiMaggio spent most of the season living in various hotels—and living it up at the Copacabana on East Sixtieth Street—he maintained a home in his native San Francisco.

Mantle lived early on at the Concourse Plaza Hotel in the Bronx, a couple of blocks from Yankee Stadium, before moving into an apartment over the Stage Deli at 834 Seventh

Avenue, with teammates Hank Bauer and Johnny Hopp, in the early 1950s. Later he lived in the St. Moritz Hotel on Central Park South, down the block from Harry's Bar, in which he admittedly spent a lot of time. In 1988, Mantle bought the location from Harry Helmsley (renaming it Mickey Mantle's Restaurant). Says John Lowy, the restaurant's co-owner, Mantle joked—tragically, as it turned out, considering that alcohol contributed to his death—that the bar his friends referred to as "Mickey's place" finally was.

Pedestrian Plastic

Q. *I recently watched as a road crew repainted a crosswalk at Ninety-second Street and Madison Avenue. Within minutes, cars were driving over the lines—yet not a drop of paint was smeared, splashed, or smudged. Do they use some kind of special paint?*

A. Actually, it's not paint. It's melted white plastic. The reflective thermal plastic has to be heated to about 500 degrees before it is applied by machine to the street, where it dries in about five minutes, city transportation officials say. If the temperature outside drops below 45 degrees, the plastic—it is also used to mark traffic lanes—cannot be applied, and paint is used. The busiest crosswalks, like those at Thirty-fourth Street and Herald Square or along Fifty-seventh Street in midtown, are worn away in less than a year. The department applies about 3 million feet of plastic pedestrian crosswalk a year, about half of it for school crossings.

The Islamic Angle

Q. *The Islamic Cultural Center at Ninety-sixth Street and Third Avenue sits at a peculiar angle on its site, its axis turned diagonally away from the Manhattan street grid. Is there some religious significance to this?*

A. Yes. The opulent building, like every mosque around the world, is oriented toward the *qiblah,* the direction of the ancient Kaaba shrine within the Grand Mosque in Mecca, said Jerrilynn D. Dodds, a professor of architectural history at the School of Architecture at City College. The Islamic Cultural Center, New York's first building designed as a mosque, is a cool, modernist island designed by Skidmore, Owings & Merrill, who made the orientation toward Mecca explicit by rotating the building 29 degrees off the street grid. Paid for in part by a consortium of Islamic governments, it was built for $17 million. Most of the mosques serving the city's six hundred thousand Muslims, in contrast, are financed by neighborhood residents and tend to lack architectural expression. All but a few mosques in New York are converted apartments, shops, garages, or assembly halls, and, lacking domes or minarets, most are indistinguishable from surrounding buildings. But, Professor Dodds said, the prayer hall within is completely oriented toward the *qiblah,* and has at its head a niche called a *mihrab,* which represents the presence of the Prophet. "These rooms often have carpets set on the diagonal, which reorient you toward Mecca," said Professor Dodds, who has visited most of the city's seventy mosques. "In very poor mosques, sometimes they just put marking tape or duct tape down on the floor."

Though New York's mosques are faithfully oriented toward the *qiblah*, they don't face Mecca in the conventional sense, Professor Dodds said. Instead, they are oriented north, toward the great circle route to Mecca, a curved path used by aviators that is the shortest distance between two points on the globe.

The Helpful Icy Blast

Q. *I often see a kind of over-grown scuba tank, labeled "Liquid Nitrogen" and marked "NYNEX," on street curbs. (For instance, there was one the other day at Broadway and Forty-first Street.) Sometimes the tanks have tubing running out of them, taped to the asphalt, and leading down under the sidewalk via manholes. What's going on here?*

A. Dry cleaning with chemistry!

But before you get images of NYNEX workers freezing their fingers off while washing with supercold liquids, here are the facts. NYNEX has many, many 3-inch cables running under the streets; each cable contains 3,600 pairs of copper wires (and each pair carries a conversation).

Steam, created by subways and heating vents, sometimes gets inside these cables and causes crossed connections and corrosion of the copper wires, said Bob Varettoni, a spokesman for NYNEX.

The tanks are actually more like glorified thermoses, keeping the nitrogen very, very cold. Nitrogen boils (that is, starts turning to gas) at about minus 320 degrees Fahrenheit. So when the nitrogen is pumped out of the tank into the tubing you see, it becomes a gas. The gas is compressed and then blown into the three-inch cables, sopping up moisture without otherwise affecting the copper wires, before escaping through a venting hole to dissipate in the air, like steam.

Sidewalk Gumshoe

Q. *What are those black flattened globs all over the sidewalks? I always thought they were dirty chewing gum. But not that many people chew gum. Is it tar? Congealed gunk?*

A. Go back to your starting proposition. Eddie Menendez, who works for the Times Square Business Improvement District and who last week was using a 2,000-pounds-per-square-inch steam hose to remove those globs is certain:

"That's years and years of chewing gum." He directed the hose at one sidewalk slab dotted with black spots, watching as they slowly disintegrated. "When you see color," he said, as one turned green, "that means it's new."

Prospect Park Secrets

Q. *I heard that there was a Quaker cemetery in Prospect Park. I also heard, oddly enough, that Montgomery Clift is buried there. Is either of these things true?*

A. Both are true. Before there was a park on the site, there was Friends' Cemetery, built in 1846. When the park was designed in the 1860s, a deal was struck to keep the southern two fifths of the lot, which runs along the west side of West Drive, said Jonathan Kuhn, director of art and antiquities for the Parks Department.

Today it is still run by the Quakers, and while it is not open to the public, the Urban Park Rangers give tours now and then.

"An occasional burial may still happen there," said Mr. Kuhn. "One would assume that there is still room at the inn."

While Clift's somewhat dissolute life may seem incongruous with his burial place (Marilyn Monroe is said to have once called him "the only person I know who is in worse shape than I am"), he was indeed laid to rest there in 1966.

Click, Click

Q. *What are those constantly clicking boxes attached to crosswalk lights?*

A. Inside those gray boxes, on posts at nearly every intersection in the city, are mechanisms that program traffic lights and crosswalk signs. They click because they have clocks inside.

The boxes are computerized in every borough except Manhattan to change lights according to the time of day. This way, a light turns green more quickly at two A.M., say, than during rush hour.

Manhattan signals will soon be computerized as well. This is important for more than the regulation of lights. If signals don't come back on after a blackout, workers will no longer have to go to each light and reprogram it individually.

Marble Hill's Exile

Q. *Why is there a small piece of Manhattan in the Bronx? Did it defect? What area code does it take? And which borough president do residents vote for?*

A. Marble Hill was originally attached to the northern part of Manhattan, but was severed in 1895 when the city deepened and straightened the waterway that connected the Hudson River to a creek known as Spuyten Duyvil (Dutch for "in spite of the Devil," thought to be a reference to the trouble it took to cross it). The creation of the United States Ship Canal made Marble Hill an island.

Around 1914, the creek was filled in and the area became physically a part of the Bronx, but it remained politically part of Manhattan.

All of its services come from the Bronx, and it takes a 718 area code, but residents vote for the Manhattan borough president.

Q. *Why is Rikers Island part of Bronx County when in fact it is only connected to Queens, by a bridge?*

A. The Bronx got the prison, which sits on its own

island, when original county lines were drawn up, and the only access was via ferry from the Bronx. In 1961, the Francis Bouno Bridge was built, connecting Rikers Island to Queens. The logic for putting the bridge there was simple: Queens is closer. But the prison remains under the Bronx's jurisdiction.

Park Markers

Q. *What are those numbers attached to the lampposts in Central Park? Do they signify something that strollers should know about?*

A. Every lamppost in Central Park has a little metal plate attached to its base that shows a four-digit number. The first two digits indicate the nearest cross street, so if the plate says 6325, Sixty-third Street is nearby.

The purpose is twofold: The markers enable maintenance workers to identify which lights need repair; and, as Skip Garrett, a spokesman for the Department of Parks and Recreation, said, "If you get lost in the park, you will know where the nearest cross street is."

Sexist Art?

Q. *What is the story behind that statue at Queens Borough Hall on Queens Boulevard that depicts a huge warrior stepping on two women?*

A. The 57-ton marble statue, *Civic Virtue*, created in 1914 by the Brooklyn-born Beaux Arts sculptor Frederick MacMonnies, has been a magnet of controversy almost

since the day it was erected outside its first home, City
Hall, in Manhattan.

The statue depicts a young man with a sword over his
shoulder stomping on two defeated women representing
vice and corruption. When the statue was unveiled in
March 1922, women had won suffrage only two years
before and many were not amused. Some booed and
hissed at the unveiling, to the embarrassment of Mayor
John F. Hylan.

How the statue ended up in Queens depends on
which story you believe. One is that Queens Borough
President George Upton Harvey persuaded the Board of
Estimate to pay for its transport in 1940. In another,
Mayor Fiorello H. La Guardia hated it so much he ban-
ished it to Queens.

The work draws criticism from women's groups to
this day.

9 A New York Gazetteer

Size

Total area in square miles: 321.8

By Borough

Bronx: 44.0
Brooklyn: 81.8
Manhattan: 23.7
Queens: 112.1
Staten Island: 60.2

Source: The Green Book, the Official Directory of the City of New York.

Population

New York City population (1990 census): 7,322,564

By Borough (1990)

Bronx: 1,203,789
Brooklyn: 2,300,664
Manhattan: 1,487,536
Queens: 1,951,598
Staten Island: 378,977

By Race (1990)

White: 4,473,839
Black: 2,291,807
Hispanic: 1,783,478
Other: 556,918

By Sex (1990)

Male: 3,437,667
Female: 3,884,897

Estimated visitors to New York City in 1998: 32,500,000

Sources: United States Census Bureau; *The Green Book, the Official Directory of the City of New York;* Office of Vital Statistics and Epidemiology; New York Convention and Visitors Bureau.

Vital Signs

Live births, 1996: 126,901
Marriages, 1996: 79,361
Deaths, 1996: 66,784
Infant mortality, 1996: 992

Most Popular Baby Names, 1996

Male, by rank: Michael, Christopher, Anthony, Kevin, Daniel, Joseph, Matthew, Justin, Jonathan, David
Female, by rank: Ashley, Jessica, Samantha, Stephanie, Nicole, Amanda, Jennifer, Michelle, Emily

Most Popular Baby Names, 1898

Male: John, William, Charles, George, Joseph, Edward, James, Louis, Francis, Samuel
Female: Mary, Catherine, Margaret, Annie, Rose, Marie, Esther, Sarah, Francis, Ida

Chief Causes of Death (1996)

Cause of Death	Male	Female
Heart disease	36.7%	45.8%
Malignant neoplasms	21.2	22.5
AIDS	10.7	4.1
Pneumonia and influenza	3.6	4.5
Cerebrovascular disease	2.6	3.7
Homicide	2.5	0.5
Chronic obstructive pulmonary disease	2.4	2.5
Accidents	2.3	1.4
Drug dependence or overdose	2.2	0.6
Diabetes mellitus	2.0	2.6
All other causes	13.7	11.6

Source: Office of Vital Statistics and Epidemiology.

Structures

Miles of streets: 6,400

Miles of waterfront: 578

Number of parks and playgrounds: 1,543

Total acreage of parks and playgrounds: 27,118

Acreage of Central Park: 843

Miles of tunnels: 161

Number of bridges: 2,027

Number of bridges over water: 76

Number of bridges over troubled water: 1

Sources: The Green Book, the Official Directory of the City of New York; New York Convention and Visitors Bureau; Parks Department; Simon and Garfunkel.

Travel

Passengers passing through at Newark, JFK, and La
    Guardia airports in 1997: 83,900,000
Domestic passengers: 59,700,000
International passengers: 24,200,000
Flights at all three airports in 1997: 1,200,000

Source: New York Convention and Visitors Bureau.

By Bus, Train, Boat, or Taxi

Number of City buses: 3,700
Number of bus stops: 14,000
Average weekday bus riders, 1995: 1,500,000
Yearly bus riders, 1995: 445,000,000
Miles of bus routes: 1,671
Number of subway cars: 5,917
Number of subway stations: 468
Average weekday subway riders, 1995: 3,500,000
Yearly subway riders, 1995: 1,080,000,000
Miles of subway track: 714
Miles of track used by passenger lines: 230
Daily passengers aboard the Staten Island Ferry: 59,000
Number of licensed taxis: 11,787
Cabbie nationalities: 85
Languages cabbies speak: 60

Sources: New York Convention and Visitors Bureau; Metropolitan Transit Authority.

Climate

Mean daily temperature in January: 31.5 degrees Fahrenheit

Mean daily temperature in February: 33.4 degrees

Mean daily temperature in March: 42.4 degrees

Mean daily temperature in April: 52.5 degrees

Mean daily temperature in May: 62.7 degrees

Mean daily temperature in June: 71.6 degrees

Mean daily temperature in July: 76.8 degrees

Mean daily temperature in August: 75.5 degrees

Mean daily temperature in September: 68.2 degrees

Mean daily temperature in October: 57.5 degrees

Mean daily temperature in November: 47.6 degrees

Mean daily temperature in December: 36.6 degrees

Hottest day on record: 106 degrees Fahrenheit, July 9, 1936

Coldest day on record: -15 degrees, February 9, 1934

Warmest month on average: 80.9 degrees, July 1955

Coldest month on average: 19.9 degrees, February 1934

Warmest years on average: 57.2 degrees, 1990 and 1991

Coldest year on average: 49.3 degrees, 1888

Average annual precipitation: 47.25 inches

Average annual snowfall: 28.2 inches

Greatest rainfall in twenty-four-hour period: 11.17 inches, October 8–9, 1903

Greatest snowfall in twenty-four-hour period: 26.4 inches, December 26–27, 1947

Wettest month: 16.85 inches, September 1882

Driest month: 0.02 inch, June 1949

Wettest year: 80.56 inches, 1983

Driest year: 26.09 inches, 1965

Longest consecutive streak of precipitation: 17 days, May 6–22, 1943

Longest dry spell: 36 days, October 9–November 13, 1924

Strongest wind recorded at Central Park: 70 miles per hour, September 12, 1960

Strongest wind recorded at the Battery: 113 miles per hour, October 14, 1954

Source: Penn State Department of Meteorology.

Sunrises and Sunsets

January

	RISE	SET		RISE	SET
1	7:20	16:38	17	7:17	16:55
2	7:20	16:39	18	7:17	16:56
3	7:20	16:40	19	7:16	16:57
4	7:20	16:41	20	7:16	16:58
5	7:20	16:42	21	7:15	16:59
6	7:20	16:43	22	7:15	17:00
7	7:20	16:44	23	7:14	17:02
8	7:20	16:45	24	7:13	17:03
9	7:20	16:46	25	7:13	17:04
10	7:20	16:47	26	7:12	17:05
11	7:20	16:48	27	7:11	17:06
12	7:19	16:49	28	7:10	17:08
13	7:19	16:50	29	7:09	17:09
14	7:19	16:51	30	7:08	17:10
15	7:18	16:52	31	7:08	17:11
16	7:18	16:53			

February

	RISE	SET		RISE	SET
1	7:07	17:13	16	6:49	17:31
2	7:06	17:14	17	6:48	17:32
3	7:05	17:15	18	6:47	17:33
4	7:04	17:16	19	6:45	17:35
5	7:03	17:18	20	6:44	17:36
6	7:01	17:19	21	6:43	17:37
7	7:00	17:20	22	6:41	17:38
8	6:59	17:21	23	6:40	17:39
9	6:58	17:22	24	6:38	17:41
10	6:57	17:24	25	6:37	17:42
11	6:56	17:25	26	6:35	17:43
12	6:55	17:26	27	6:34	17:44
13	6:53	17:27	28	6:32	17:45
14	6:52	17:29	29	6:31	17:46
15	6:51	17:30			

March

	RISE	SET		RISE	SET
1	6:29	17:47	13	6:10	18:01
2	6:28	17:49	14	6:09	18:02
3	6:26	17:50	15	6:07	18:03
4	6:25	17:51	16	6:05	18:04
5	6:23	17:52	17	6:04	18:05
6	6:21	17:53	18	6:02	18:06
7	6:20	17:54	19	6:00	18:07
8	6:18	17:55	20	5:59	18:08
9	6:17	17:56	21	5:57	18:09
10	6:15	17:57	22	5:55	18:10
11	6:13	17:59	23	5:54	18:12
12	6:12	18:00	24	5:52	18:13

	RISE	SET			RISE	SET
25	5:50	18:14		29	5:44	18:18
26	5:49	18:15		30	5:42	18:19
27	5:47	18:16		31	5:40	18:20
28	5:45	18:17				

April

Note: Daylight saving time begins on the first Sunday of April; change shown here is approximate.

	RISE	SET			RISE	SET
1	5:39	18:21		15	6:16	19:36
2	5:37	18:22		16	6:15	19:37
3	5:36	18:23		17	6:13	19:38
4	5:34	18:24		18	6:12	19:39
5	5:32	18:25		19	6:10	19:40
6	5:31	18:26		20	6:09	19:41
	EDT	**EDT**		21	6:08	19:42
7	6:29	19:27		22	6:06	19:43
8	6:27	19:28		23	6:05	19:44
9	6:26	19:29		24	6:03	19:45
10	6:24	19:30		25	6:02	19:46
11	6:23	19:31		26	6:00	19:47
12	6:21	19:33		27	5:59	19:48
13	6:20	19:34		28	5:58	19:49
14	6:18	19:35		29	5:56	19:50
				30	5:55	19:51

May

	RISE	SET			RISE	SET
1	5:54	19:52		4	5:50	19:56
2	5:53	19:54		5	5:49	19:57
3	5:51	19:55		6	5:48	19:58

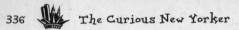

	RISE	SET		RISE	SET
7	5:47	19:59	20	5:34	20:11
8	5:45	20:00	21	5:33	20:12
9	5:44	20:01	22	5:32	20:13
10	5:43	20:02	23	5:32	20:14
11	5:42	20:03	24	5:31	20:15
12	5:41	20:04	25	5:30	20:16
13	5:40	20:05	26	5:30	20:17
14	5:39	20:06	27	5:29	20:17
15	5:38	20:07	28	5:28	20:18
16	5:37	20:08	29	5:28	20:19
17	5:36	20:09	30	5:27	20:20
18	5:36	20:09	31	5:27	20:21
19	5:35	20:10			

June

	RISE	SET		RISE	SET
1	5:26	20:21	16	5:24	20:29
2	5:26	20:22	17	5:24	20:30
3	5:26	20:23	18	5:24	20:30
4	5:25	20:23	19	5:24	20:30
5	5:25	20:24	20	5:24	20:31
6	5:25	20:25	21	5:25	20:31
7	5:24	20:25	22	5:25	20:31
8	5:24	20:26	23	5:25	20:31
9	5:24	20:26	24	5:25	20:31
10	5:24	20:27	25	5:26	20:31
11	5:24	20:27	26	5:26	20:31
12	5:24	20:28	27	5:26	20:31
13	5:24	20:28	28	5:27	20:31
14	5:24	20:29	29	5:27	20:31
15	5:24	20:29	30	5:28	20:31

July

	RISE	SET			RISE	SET
1	5:28	20:31		17	5:39	20:24
2	5:29	20:31		18	5:40	20:24
3	5:29	20:31		19	5:41	20:23
4	5:30	20:30		20	5:42	20:22
5	5:30	20:30		21	5:42	20:21
6	5:31	20:30		22	5:43	20:21
7	5:32	20:30		23	5:44	20:20
8	5:32	20:29		24	5:45	20:19
9	5:33	20:29		25	5:46	20:18
10	5:34	20:28		26	5:47	20:17
11	5:34	20:28		27	5:48	20:16
12	5:35	20:27		28	5:49	20:15
13	5:36	20:27		29	5:50	20:14
14	5:37	20:26		30	5:51	20:13
15	5:37	20:26		31	5:52	20:12
16	5:38	20:25				

August

	RISE	SET			RISE	SET
1	5:52	20:12		11	6:02	20:00
2	5:53	20:11		12	6:03	19:58
3	5:54	20:10		13	6:04	19:57
4	5:55	20:08		14	6:05	19:56
5	5:56	20:07		15	6:05	19:54
6	5:57	20:06		16	6:06	19:53
7	5:58	20:05		17	6:07	19:52
8	5:59	20:04		18	6:08	19:50
9	6:00	20:02		19	6:09	19:49
10	6:01	20:01		20	6:10	19:47

	RISE	SET		RISE	SET
21	6:11	19:46	27	6:17	19:37
22	6:12	19:44	28	6:18	19:35
23	6:13	19:43	29	6:19	19:34
24	6:14	19:41	30	6:20	19:32
25	6:15	19:40	31	6:21	19:30
26	6:16	19:38			

September

	RISE	SET		RISE	SET
1	6:22	19:29	16	6:37	19:04
2	6:23	19:27	17	6:38	19:02
3	6:24	19:25	18	6:39	19:00
4	6:25	19:24	19	6:40	18:59
5	6:26	19:22	20	6:41	18:57
6	6:27	19:21	21	6:42	18:55
7	6:28	19:19	22	6:43	18:54
8	6:29	19:17	23	6:44	18:52
9	6:30	19:16	24	6:45	18:50
10	6:31	19:14	25	6:46	18:49
11	6:32	19:12	26	6:47	18:47
12	6:33	19:11	27	6:48	18:45
13	6:34	19:09	28	6:49	18:44
14	6:35	19:07	29	6:50	18:42
15	6:36	19:05	30	6:51	18:40

October

Note: Daylight saving time ends on the last Sunday of October; change shown here is approximate.

	RISE	SET		RISE	SET
1	6:52	18:38	2	6:53	18:37

	RISE	SET		RISE	SET
3	6:54	18:35	18	7:10	18:12
4	6:55	18:34	19	7:11	18:10
5	6:56	18:32	20	7:12	18:09
6	6:57	18:30	21	7:13	18:07
7	6:58	18:29	22	7:14	18:06
8	6:59	18:27	23	7:15	18:04
9	7:00	18:25	24	7:17	18:03
10	7:01	18:24	25	7:18	18:02
11	7:02	18:22	26	7:19	18:00
12	7:03	18:21	27	7:20	17:59
13	7:04	18:19	28	7:21	17:58
14	7:06	18:18	**EST**EST**		
15	7:07	18:16	29	6:22	16:56
16	7:08	18:15	30	6:23	16:55
17	7:09	18:13	31	6:25	16:54

November

	RISE	SET		RISE	SET
1	6:26	16:52	13	6:40	16:40
2	6:27	16:51	14	6:41	16:39
3	6:28	16:50	15	6:42	16:38
4	6:29	16:49	16	6:44	16:37
5	6:31	16:48	17	6:45	16:36
6	6:32	16:47	18	6:46	16:36
7	6:33	16:46	19	6:47	16:35
8	6:34	16:45	20	6:48	16:34
9	6:35	16:44	21	6:49	16:34
10	6:36	16:43	22	6:50	16:33
11	6:38	16:42	23	6:52	16:32
12	6:39	16:41	24	6:53	16:32

	RISE	SET		RISE	SET
25	6:54	16:31	28	6:57	16:30
26	6:55	16:31	29	6:58	16:30
27	6:56	16:30	30	6:59	16:29

December

	RISE	SET		RISE	SET
1	7:00	16:29	17	7:14	16:30
2	7:01	16:29	18	7:15	16:30
3	7:02	16:28	19	7:15	16:30
4	7:03	16:28	20	7:16	16:31
5	7:04	16:28	21	7:16	16:31
6	7:05	16:28	22	7:17	16:32
7	7:06	16:28	23	7:17	16:32
8	7:07	16:28	24	7:18	16:33
9	7:08	16:28	25	7:18	16:33
10	7:09	16:28	26	7:19	16:34
11	7:10	16:28	27	7:19	16:35
12	7:10	16:28	28	7:19	16:35
13	7:11	16:28	29	7:20	16:36
14	7:12	16:29	30	7:20	16:37
15	7:13	16:29	31	7:20	16:38
16	7:13	16:29			

Source: Penn State University.

Address Hunter, Manhattan

Hunting for an address on an avenue in Manhattan without knowing the cross street does not have to be difficult. Drop the last figure, divide by 2, and add or subtract as indicated below. The answer is the nearest numbered cross street. This key does not apply to Broadway below

Eighth Street because of the many streets with names instead of numbers.

Avenues A, B, C, D: add 3
1st and 2nd Avenues: add 3
3rd Avenue: add 10
4th Avenue: add 8
5th Avenue:
    Up to 200, add 13
    201 to 400, add 16
    401 to 600, add 18
    601 to 775, add 20
    776 to 1286, drop last figure and subtract 18
    1287 to 1500, add 45
    1501 to 2000, add 24
Avenue of the Americas: subtract 12
7th Avenue:
    up to 110th St., add 12
    above 110th St., add 20
8th Avenue: add 10
9th Avenue: add 13
10th Avenue: add 14
11th Avenue: add 15
Amsterdam Avenue: add 60
Audubon Avenue: add 165
Broadway:
    754 to 858, subtract 29
    858 to 958, subtract 25
    above 100, subtract 30
Central Park West: divide street number by 10 and add 60

Columbus Avenue: add 60

Convent Avenue: add 127

Edgecombe Avenue: add 134

Fort Washington Avenue: add 158

Lenox Avenue: add 110

Lexington Avenue: add 22

Madison Avenue: add 26

Manhattan Avenue: add 100

Park Avenue: add 35

Pleasant Avenue: add 101

Riverside Drive

>   up to 567, divide house number by 10 and add 72

>   568 to 933, divide house number by 10 and add 77

St. Nicholas Avenue: add 110

Wadsworth Avenue: add 173

West End Avenue: add 60

York Avenue: add 4

Police Precincts and Their Neighborhoods

Addresses and phone numbers of police precincts, and the neighborhoods they cover.

Manhattan

Pct: 1
Address: 16 Erickson Place
Phone: 212-334-0611
Neighborhoods: Little Italy, Chinatown, TriBeCa, and
   Lower Manhattan

Pct: 5
Address: 19 Elizabeth Street
Phone: 212-334-0711
Neighborhoods: Lower East Side, Chinatown, and Little
    Italy

Pct: 6
Address: 233 West Tenth Street
Phone: 212-741-4811
Neighborhood: Greenwich Village

Pct: 7
Address: 19½ Pitt Street
Phone: 212-477-7311
Neighborhoods: Lower East Side and FDR Drive

Pct: 9
Address: 321 East Fifth Street
Phone: 212-477-7811
Neighborhoods: Lower East Side and East Village

Pct: 10
Address: 230 West Twentieth Street
Phone: 212-741-8211
Neighborhoods: Chelsea and Lincoln Tunnel

Pct: Midtown South
Address: 357 West Thirty-fifth Street
Phone: 212-239-9811
Neighborhoods: Chelsea, Clinton, and Midtown

Pct: 17
Address: 167 East Fifty-first Street
Phone: 212-826-3211

Neighborhoods: Turtle Bay, Tudor City, Murray Hill, Gramercy Park, Peter Cooper Village, and Stuyvesant Town

Pct: Midtown North
Address: 306 West Fifty-fourth Street
Phone: 212-767-8400
Neighborhood: Midtown above Forty-fifth Street

Pct: 19
Address: 153 East Sixty-seventh Street
Phone: 212-452-0600
Neighborhood: Upper East Side, Yorkville, Lenox Hill, and Roosevelt Island

Pct: 20
Address: 120 West Eighty-second Street
Phone: 212-580-6411
Neighborhoods: Lincoln Square and Columbus Avenue South

Pct: Central Park
Address: Eighty-sixth Street and Transverse Road
Phone: 212-570-4820
Neighborhood: Central Park

Pct: 23
Address: 162 East 102nd Street
Phone: 212-860-6411
Neighborhood: East Harlem

Pct: 24
Address: 151 West 100th Street
Phone: 212-678-1811

Neighborhoods: Upper West Side and Manhattan Valley

Pct: 25
Address: 120 East 119th Street
Phone: 212-860-6511
Neighborhood: East Harlem above 115th Street

Pct: 26
Address: 520 West 126th Street
Phone: 212-678-1611
Neighborhoods: West Harlem, Morningside Heights,
    Hamilton Heights, and Manhattanville

Pct: 28
Address: 2271–89 Eighth Avenue
Phone: 212-678-1611
Neighborhood: Central Harlem

Pct: 30
Address: 451 West 151st Street
Phone: 212-690-8811
Neighborhood: Central Harlem

Pct: 32
Address: 250 West 135th Street
Phone: 212-690-6311
Neighborhood: Central Harlem

Pct: 33
Address: 2120 Amsterdam Avenue
Phone: 212-927-3272
Neighborhoods: Washington Heights and Inwood

Pct: 34
Address: 4295 Broadway

Phone: 212-927-9711
Neighborhoods: Washington Heights and Inwood

The Bronx

Pct: 40
Address: 257 Alexander Avenue
Phone: 718-402-2270
Neighborhoods: Mott Haven, Port Morris, and Melrose

Pct: 41
Address: 1035 Longwood Avenue
Phone: 718-542-4774
Neighborhoods: Hunts Point, Longwood, and
    Morrisania

Pct: 45
Address: 2877 Barkley Avenue
Phone: 718-822-5411
Neighborhoods: Co-op City, City Island, Throgs Neck,
    Country Club, Zerega, Westchester Square, Hart
    Foland, and Pelham Bay Park

Pct: 46
Address: 2120 Ryer Avenue
Phone: 718-220-5211
Neighborhoods: Fordham, University Heights, Morris
    Heights, and Mount Hope

Pct: 47
Address: 4111 Laconia Avenue
Phone: 718-920-1211

Neighborhoods: Edenwald, Wakefield, Williamsbridge, Woodlawn, Norwood, and Baychester

Pct: 48
Address: 450 Cross Bronx Expressway
Phone: 718-299-3900
Neighborhoods: Belmont, Bathgate, West Farms, and East Tremont

Pct: 49
Address: 2121 Eastchester Road
Phone: 718-918-2000
Neighborhoods: Morris Park, Pelham Parkway, Allerton Avenue, Bronxdale, Laconia, and Van Nest

Pct: 50
Address: 3450 Kingsbridge Avenue
Phone: 718-543-5700
Neighborhoods: Riverdale, Spuyten Duyvil, Van Cortlandt Park, Kingsbridge Heights, and Marble Hill

Pct: 52
Address: 3016 Webster Avenue
Phone: 718-220-5811
Neighborhoods: Norwood, University Heights, and Jerome Park

Brooklyn

Pct: 60
Address: 2951 West Eighth Street
Phone: 718-946-3311
Neighborhoods: Coney Island and Brighton Beach

Pct: 61
Address: 2575 Coney Island Avenue
Phone: 718-627-6611
Neighborhoods: Sheepshead Bay and Manhattan Beach

Pct: 62
Address: 1925 Bath Avenue
Phone: 718-236-2611
Neighborhoods: Bath Beach, Gravesend, and Bensonhurst

Pct: 63
Address: 8144 Brooklyn Avenue
Phone: 718-258-4411
Neighborhoods: Bergen Beach and Mill Basin

Pct: 66
Address: 5822 Sixteenth Avenue
Phone: 718-851-5611
Neighborhood: Borough Park

Pct: 67
Address: 2820 Snyder Avenue
Phone: 718-287-3211
Neighborhoods: East Flatbush

Pct: 68
Address: 333 Sixty-fifth Street
Phone: 718-439-4211
Neighborhood: Bay Ridge

Pct: 69
Address: 9720 Foster Avenue
Phone: 718-257-6211
Neighborhoods: Flatlands and Canarsie

Pct: 70
Address: 154 Lawrence Avenue
Phone: 718-851-5511
Neighborhoods: Flatbush and Midwood

Pct: 71
Address: 421 Empire Boulevard
Phone: 718-735-0511
Neighborhood: Crown Heights

Pct: 72
Address: 830 Fourth Avenue
Phone: 718-965-6311
Neighborhoods: Sunset Park and Windsor Terrace

Pct: 73
Address: 1470 East New York Avenue
Phone: 718-495-5411
Neighborhood: Brownsville

Pct: 75
Address: 1000 Sutter Avenue
Phone: 718-827-3511
Neighborhoods: East New York and Cypress Hills

Pct: 76
Address: 191 Union Street
Phone: 718-834-3211
Neighborhoods: Red Hook and Carroll Gardens

Pct: 77
Address: 127 Utica Avenue
Phone: 718-735-0611
Neighborhood: Crown Heights

Pct: 78
Address: 65 Sixth Street
Phone: 718-636-6411
Neighborhood: Park Slope

Pct: 79
Address: 263 Tompkins Avenue
Phone: 718-635-6611
Neighborhood: Bedford-Stuyvesant

Pct: 81
Address: 30 Ralph Avenue
Phone: 718-574-0411
Neighborhood: Bedford-Stuyvesant

Pct: 83
Address: 480 Knickerbocker Avenue
Phone: 718-574-1605
Neighborhood: Bushwick

Pct: 84
Address: 301 Gold Street
Phone: 718-875-6811
Neighborhoods: Brooklyn Heights, Vinegar Hill, and
    Boerum Hill

Pct: 88
Address: 298 Classon Avenue
Phone: 718-636-6511
Neighborhood: Clinton Hill

Pct: 90
Address: 211 Union Avenue
Phone: 718-963-5311

Neighborhoods: Flushing Avenue and Williamsburg

Pct: 94
Address: 100 Meserole Avenue
Phone: 718-383-3879
Neighborhoods: Greenpoint and Williamsburg

Queens

Pct: 100
Address: 92-24 Rockaway Beach Boulevard
Phone: 718-318-4200
Neighborhoods: Breezy Point, Belle Harbor, Rockaway
    Park, and Rockaway

Pct: 101
Address: 16-12 Mott Avenue
Phone: 718-868-3400
Neighborhood: Far Rockaway

Pct: 102
Address: 87-34 118th Street
Phone: 718-805-3200
Neighborhoods: Richmond Hill, Woodhaven, Ozone Park,
    and Kew Gardens

Pct: 103
Address: 168-02 Ninety-first Avenue
Phone: 718-657-8181
Neighborhoods: Jamaica, South Jamaica, and Hollis

Pct: 104
Address: 64-02 Catalpa Avenue
Phone: 718-386-3004

Neighborhoods: Ridgewood, Glendale, Middle Village, Maspeth, and Liberty Park

Pct: 105
Address: 92-08 222nd Street
Phone: 718-776-9090
Neighborhoods: Queens Village, Glen Oaks, New Hyde Park, Bellerose, Cambria Heights, Laurelton, Rosedale, and Floral Park

Pct: 106
Address: 103-51 101st Street
Phone: 718-845-2211
Neighborhoods: Howard Beach, South Ozone Park, Richmond Hill, Tudor Village, and Lindenwood

Pct: 107
Address: 71-01 Parsons Boulevard
Phone: 718-969-5100
Neighborhoods: Fresh Meadows, Cunningham Heights, Hilltop Village, Pomonak Houses, Jamaica Estates, Holliswood, Flushing South, Utopia, Kew Gardens Hills, and Briarwood

Pct: 108
Address: 5-47 Fiftieth Avenue, between Fifth Street and Vernon Boulevard
Phone: 718-784-5411
Neighborhoods: Long Island City, Woodside, and Sunnyside

Pct: 109
Address: 37-05 Union Street
Phone: 718-321-2250

Neighborhoods: Flushing, Bay Terrace, College Point, Whitestone, Malba, Beechhurst, Queensboro Hill, and Willets Point

Pct: 110
Address: 94-41 Forty-third Avenue
Phone: 718-476-9311
Neighborhoods: Elmhurst, Corona, Roosevelt Avenue, Lefrak City, Queens Center Mall, Flushing Meadows, and Corona Park

Pct: 111
Address: 45-06 215th Street, corner of Northern Boulevard
Phone: 718-279-5200
Neighborhoods: Bayside, Douglaston, Little Neck, Auburndale, East Flushing, Oakland Gardens, and Hollis Hills

Pct: 112
Address: 68-40 Austin Street
Phone: 718-520-9311
Neighborhoods: Forest Hills and Rego Park

Pct: 113
Address: 167-02 Baisley Boulevard
Phone: 718-712-7733
Neighborhoods: St. Albans, Springfield Gardens, South Ozone Park, Baisley Park, Rochdale Village, and South Jamaica

Pct: 114
Address: 34-16 Astoria Boulevard
Phone: 718-626-9311

Neighborhoods: Astoria, Old Astoria, Long Island City, Queensbridge, Ditmars, Ravenswood, Steinway, Garden Bay, and Woodside

Pct: 115
Address: 92-15 Northern Boulevard
Phone: 718-533-2002
Neighborhoods: East Elmhurst, North Corona, and Jackson Heights

Staten Island

Pct: 120
Address: 78 Richmond Terrace, St. George
Phone: 718-876-8500
Neighborhoods: Arlington, Clifton, Elm Park, Graniteville, Livingston, Port Richmond, Randall Manor, Stapleton, Sunnyside, New Brighton, West Brighton, and Westerleigh

Pct: 122
Address: 2320 Hylan Blvd., New Dorp
Phone: 718-667-2211
Neighborhoods: Arrochar, Bulls Head, Dongan Hills, Grasmere, Oakwood, Ocean Breeze, Todt Hill, New Springville, and Midland Beach

Pct: 123
Address: 116 Main Street,
Phone: 718-948-9311
Neighborhoods: Annadale, Bay Terrace, Arden Heights, Great Kills, Richmond Valley, Tottenville, Prince's Bay, Rossville, and Woodrow

Source: New York City Police Department.

Community Boards

Manhattan

District 1:
Phone: 212-442-5050
Neighborhoods: Battery Park, Civic Center, Financial District, South Street Seaport, and TriBeCa
Meetings on third Tuesday of the month

District 2:
Phone: 212-979-2272
Neighborhoods: Greenwich Village, Little Italy, NoHo, SoHo, and West Village
Meetings on third Thursday of the month

District 3:
Phone: 212-533-5300
Neighborhoods: Chinatown, East Village, and Lower East Side
Meetings on third Tuesday of the month

District 4:
Phone: 212-736-4536
Neighborhoods: Chelsea and Clinton
Meetings on first Wednesday of the month

District 5:
Phone: 212-465-0907
Neighborhoods: Central Park South, Central Business District, Theater District, Gramercy Park, Little India, and Rockefeller Center
Meetings on second Thursday of the month

District 6:
Phone: 212-679-0907
Neighborhoods: Murray Hill, Turtle Bay, Stuyvesant
    Square, Peter Cooper Village, Beekman, and Sutton
Meetings on second Wednesday of the month

District 7:
Phone: 212-362-4008
Neighborhood: Upper West Side
Meetings on first Tuesday of the month

District 8:
Phone: 212-427-4840
Neighborhoods: Upper East Side and Roosevelt Island
Meetings on third Wednesday of the month

District 9:
Phone: 212-864-6200
Neighborhoods: Morningside Heights, Manhattanville,
    and Hamilton Heights
Meetings on third Thursday of the month

District 10:
Phone: 212-749-3105
Neighborhood: Central Harlem
Meetings on first Wednesday of the month

District 11:
Phone: 212-831-8929
Neighborhood: East Harlem
Meetings on third Tuesday of the month

District 12:
Phone: 212-568-8500
Neighborhoods: Washington Heights and Inwood
Meetings on fourth Tuesday of the month

Brooklyn

District 1:
Phone: 718-389-0009
Neighborhoods: Greenpoint and Williamsburg
Meetings on second Wednesday of the month

District 2:
Phone: 718-596-5410
Neighborhoods: Fort Greene, Downtown Brooklyn, Brooklyn Heights, and Clinton Hill
Meetings on second Wednesday of the month

District 3:
Phone: 718-622-6601
Neighborhood: Bedford-Stuyvesant
Meetings on first Monday of the month

District 4:
Phone: 718-628-8400
Neighborhood: Bushwick
Meetings on third Wednesday of the month

District 5:
Phone: 718-498-5711
Neighborhood: East New York
Meetings on every fourth Wednesday

District 6:
Phone: 718-643-3027
Neighborhood: Park Slope, Carrol Gardens, Cobble Hill, and Red Hook
Meetings on second Wednesday of the month

District 7:
Phone: 718-854-0003
Neighborhoods: Sunset Park and Windsor Terrace
Meetings on third Wednesday of the month

District 8:
Phone: 718-467-5574
Neighborhoods: Crown Heights and Prospect Heights
Meetings on second Thursday of the month

District 9:
Phone: 718-778-9279
Neighborhoods: Crown Heights, Prospect–Lefferts Gardens, and Wingate
Meetings on fourth Tuesday of the month

District 10:
Phone: 718-745-6827
Neighborhoods: Bay Ridge, Dyker Heights, and Fort Hamilton
Meetings on third Monday of the month

District 11:
Phone: 718-266-8800
Neighborhoods: Bensonhurst, Bath Beach, and Gravesend
Meetings on second Thursday of the month

District 12:
Phone: 718-851-0800
Neighborhoods: Borough Park, Midwood, Day Hill, and Kensington
Meetings on fourth Tuesday of the month

District 13:
Phone: 718-266-3001
Neighborhoods: Coney Island, Brighton Beach, and Gravesend
Meetings on fourth Wednesday of the month

District 14:
Phone: 718-859-6357
Neighborhoods: Flatbush and Midwood
Meetings on second Monday of the month

District 15:
Phone: 718-332-3008
Neighborhoods: Manhattan Beach, Sheepshead Bay, and Gravesend
Meetings on last Tuesday of the month

District 16:
Phone: 718-385-0323
Neighborhoods: Brownsville and Ocean Hill
Meetings on third Tuesday of the month

District 17:
Phone: 718-467-3536
Neighborhood: East Flatbush
Meetings on third Wednesday of the month

District 18:
Phone: 718-241-0422
Neighborhoods: Canarsie, Mill Basin, Marine Park, Bergen Beach, Flatlands, Georgetown, and Fraiser
Meetings on third Wednesday of the month

Queens

District 1:
Phone: 718-786-3335
Neighborhoods: Long Island City and Astoria
Meetings on third Tuesday of the month

District 2:
Phone: 718-596-5410
Neighborhoods: Long Island City, Sunnyside, and Wood-
side
Meetings on first Thursday of the month

District 3:
Phone: 718-458-2707
Neighborhoods: Jackson Heights, East Elmhurst, and
North Corona
Meetings on third Thursday of the month

District 4:
Phone: 718-760-3141
Neighborhoods: Corona, Corona Heights, and Elmhurst
Meetings on first Tuesday of the month

District 5:
Phone: 718-366-1834
Neighborhoods: Ridgewood, Maspeth, Glendale, Meadow
Village, and South Elmhurst
Meetings on second Wednesday of the month

District 6:
Phone: 718-263-9250
Neighborhoods: Forest Hills and Rego Park
Meetings on fourth Wednesday of the month

District 7:
Phone: 718-359-2800
Neighborhoods: Flushing, Whitestone, Malba, Beechherst, College Point, Bay Terrace
Meetings on second Monday of the month

District 8:
Phone: 718-591-6000
Neighborhoods: Kew Gardens Hills, Utopia, Fresh Meadows, Hill Crest, Briar Wood, Jamaica Hills, Jamaica Estates, Holliswood, and South Flushing

District 9:
Phone: 718-286-2686
Neighborhoods: Richmond Hill, Ozone Park, Woodhaven, and Kew Gardens
Meetings on second Tuesday of the month

District 10:
Phone: 718-843-4488
Neighborhoods: Howard Beach, Ozone Park, South Ozone Park, and Richmond Hill
Meetings on first Thursday of the month

District 11:
Phone: 718-225-1054
Neighborhoods: Auburndale, Bayside, Douglaston, Hollis Hills, Little Neck, and Oakland Gardens
Meetings on first Monday of the month

District 12:
Phone: 718-658-3308
Neighborhoods: Jamaica South, Jamaica Hollis, St. Albans,

South Ozone Park, Addisleigh Park, and Springfield
  Gardens North
Meetings on third Wednesday of the month

District 13:
Phone: 718-464-9700
Neighborhoods: New Hyde Park, Floral Park, Glen Oaks,
  Queens Village, Cambria Heights, Floralton, Spring-
  field Gardens, Rosedale, and Bellerose
Meetings on fourth Monday of the month

District 14:
Phone: 718-471-7300
Neighborhoods: Rockaways, Breezy Point, Broad Channel,
  Rocksbury, Seaside, Hammels, Edgemere, Arverne,
  and Wave Crest
Meetings on second Monday of the month

The Bronx

District 1:
Phone: 718-585-7117
Neighborhoods: Port Morris, Melrose, and Mott Haven
Meetings on last Thursday of the month

District 2:
Phone: 718-328-9125
Neighborhoods: Hunts Point and Longwood
Meetings on last Wednesday of the month

District 3:
Phone: 718-378-8054
Neighborhood: Morrisania
Meetings on second Tuesday of the month

District 4:
Phone: 718-299-0800
Neighborhoods: East and West Concourse, Mount Eden, High Bridge, and Concourse Village
Meetings on fourth Tuesday of the month

District 5:
Phone: 718-364-2030
Neighborhoods: Mount Hope, Morris Heights, and Fordham Heights
Meetings on fourth Wednesday of the month

District 6:
Phone: 718-579-6990
Neighborhoods: Bathgate, Belmont, Bronx Park South, Crotona Park North, East Tremont, and West Farms

District 7:
Phone: 718-933-5650
Neighborhoods: University Heights, Norwood, Fordham, Bedford, and Bedford Park
Meetings on third Tuesday of the month

District 8:
Phone: 718-884-3959
Neighborhoods: Kingsbridge, Marble Hill, North Riverdale, Spuyten Duyvil, Fieldston
Meetings on second Tuesday of the month

District 9:
Phone: 718-823-3034
Neighborhoods: Bronx River, Castle Hill, Clason Point,

Harding Park, Parkchester, Bruckner, Soundview, and
Unionport
Meetings on last Thursday of the month

District 10:
Phone: 718-892-1161
Neighborhoods: City Island, Throgs Neck, Pelham Bay,
Country Club, and Co-op City
Meetings on third Thursday of the month

District 11:
Phone: 718-892-6262
Neighborhoods: Allerton, Eastchester, Pelham Parkway,
and Morris Park
Meetings on third Thursday of the month

District 12:
Phone: 718-881-4455
Neighborhoods: Wakefield, Woodlawn, Williamsbridge,
Baychester, and Eastchester
Meetings on fourth Thursday of the month

Index